MCSE Exam
SQL Server™ 7
Administration

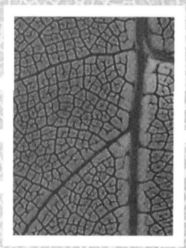

Rick Sawtell
Lance Mortensen
Joseph L. Jorden

San Francisco • Paris • Düsseldorf • Soest • London

Associate Publisher: Guy Hart-Davis
Contracts and Licensing Manager: Kristine O'Callaghan
Acquisitions & Developmental Editor: Neil Edde
Editor: Ronn Jost
Project Editor: Raquel Baker
Technical Editor: Scott Warmbrand
Book Designer: Bill Gibson
Graphic Illustrator: Tony Jonick
Electronic Publishing Specialist: Adrian Woolhouse
Project Team Leader: Shannon Murphy
Proofreaders: Davina Baum, Catherine Morris, and Laurie Stewart
Indexer: Marilyn Smith
Cover Designer: Archer Design
Cover Photographer: FPG International

SYBEX, Network Press, and the Network Press logo are registered trademarks of SYBEX Inc.

Exam Notes is a trademark of SYBEX Inc.

Screen reproductions produced with Collage Complete.
Collage Complete is a trademark of Inner Media Inc.

Microsoft, the Microsoft Internet Explorer logo, Windows, Windows NT, and the Windows logo are either registered trademarks or trademarks of Microsoft Corporation in the United States and/ or other countries.

SYBEX is an independent entity from Microsoft Corporation, and not affiliated with Microsoft Corporation in any manner. This publication may be used in assisting students to prepare for a Microsoft Certified Professional Exam. Neither Microsoft Corporation, its designated review company, nor SYBEX warrants that use of this publication will ensure passing the relevant exam. Microsoft is either a registered trademark or trademark of Microsoft Corporation in the United States and/or other countries.

TRADEMARKS: SYBEX has attempted throughout this book to distinguish proprietary trademarks from descriptive terms by following the capitalization style used by the manufacturer.

The author and publisher have made their best efforts to prepare this book, and the content is based upon final release software whenever possible. Portions of the manuscript may be based upon pre-release versions supplied by software manufacturer(s). The author and the publisher make no representation or warranties of any kind with regard to the completeness or accuracy of the contents herein and accept no liability of any kind including but not limited to performance, merchantability, fitness for any particular purpose, or any losses or damages of any kind caused or alleged to be caused directly or indirectly from this book.

Library of Congress Card Number: 99-62867
ISBN: 0-7821-2477-1

Manufactured in the United States of America

10 9 8 7 6 5 4 3 2

To my wife, Rachelle; my mother, Mary; and my father, Jerry. Thanks for sacrificing so much so that I could follow my dreams.

—Joseph L. Jorden

Dedicated to the countless administrators who will install or upgrade to SQL 7.

—Lance Mortensen

To all the MCSE students and their families for all the time, energy, and expense spent in pursuit of the MCSE. I hope you will agree that it was worth it.

—Rick Sawtell

Acknowledgments

I have to start by thanking all the authors of the *MCSE: SQL Server 7 Administration Study Guide* because it was their hard work that formed the basis of this book. I also need to thank Ronn Jost and Raquel Baker for making the book pretty, and my tech editor for making sure I told the truth about SQL. Thanks to the production folks: Shannon Murphy, Adrian Woolhouse, Davina Baum, Laurie Stewart, and Catherine Morris. Special thanks to Lance Mortensen for introducing me to Sybex, and Neil Edde for letting me write. I also need to thank Paul Afshar, Shiva Jahan, and Quinn Guiteras at Unitek for getting me started teaching.

I can't get away without thanking some personal friends and family: Bob and Jeanette Haskett and my entire immediate family, who have supported me through my trials, and Archie Thompson for getting so excited about my first book. Most important, though (at least to me), thanks to my beloved wife, Rachelle, for understanding all the late nights I spent pounding on the keyboard.

—Joseph L. Jorden

Thanks to Joe and Rick for working on the book with me, and the entire team at Sybex for another fine job. Thanks also to my family for putting up with my schedule. Bryce, Jessany, Devin, and Logan— you kids mean the world to me.

—Lance Mortensen

Thanks to the entire Sybex team and to everyone who participated on this project.

—Rick Sawtell

Table of Contents

Introduction

If you've purchased this book, you are probably chasing one of the Microsoft professional certifications: MCP, MCSE, MCSE+I, MCDBA, or MCT. All of these are great goals, and they are also great career builders. If you glance through any newspaper, you'll find employment opportunities for people with these certifications—these ads are there because finding qualified employees is a challenge in today's market. The certification means you know something about the product, but more importantly, it means you have the ability, determination, and focus to learn—the greatest skill any employee can have!

You've probably also heard all the rumors about how hard the Microsoft tests are—believe us, the rumors are true! Microsoft has designed a series of exams that truly test your knowledge of their products. Each test not only covers the materials presented in a particular class, it also covers the prerequisite knowledge for that course. This means two things for you—the first test can be a real hurdle, and each test *should* get easier since you've studied the basics over and over.

This book has been developed in alliance with the Microsoft Corporation to give you the knowledge and skills you need to prepare for one of the key exams of the MCSE certification program: 70-028, System Administration for Microsoft SQL Server 7.0. This book provides a solid introduction to Microsoft networking technologies and will help you on your way to MCSE certification.

Is This Book for You?

The MCSE Exam Notes books were designed to be succinct, portable exam review guides that can be used either in conjunction with a more complete study program (book, CBT courseware, classroom/ lab environment) or as an exam review for those who don't feel the need for more extensive test preparation. It isn't our goal to "give the answers away," but rather to identify those topics on which you can expect to be tested and provide sufficient coverage of these topics.

Perhaps you've been working with Microsoft networking technologies for years now. The thought of paying lots of money for a specialized MCSE exam preparation course probably doesn't sound too appealing. What can they teach you that you don't already know, right? Be careful, though. Many experienced network administrators have walked confidently into test centers only to walk sheepishly out of them after failing an MCSE exam. As they discovered, there's the Microsoft of the real world and the Microsoft of the MCSE exams. It's our goal with these Exam Notes books to show you where the two converge and where they diverge. After you've finished reading through this book, you should have a clear idea of how your understanding of the technologies involved matches up with the expectations of the MCSE test makers in Redmond.

Or perhaps you're relatively new to the world of Microsoft networking, drawn to it by the promise of challenging work and higher salaries. You've just waded through an 800-page MCSE study guide or taken a class at a local training center. There's lots of information to keep track of, isn't there? Well, by organizing the Exam Notes books according to the Microsoft exam objectives, and by breaking up the information into concise manageable pieces, we've created what we think is the handiest exam review guide available. Throw it in your briefcase and carry it to work with you. As you read through the book, you'll be able to identify quickly those areas you know best and those that require more in-depth review.

NOTE   The goal of the Exam Notes series is to help MCSE candidates familiarize themselves with the subjects on which they can expect to be tested in the MCSE exams. For complete, in-depth coverage of the technologies and topics involved, we recommend the MCSE Study Guide series from Sybex.

How Is This Book Organized?

As mentioned above, this book is organized according to the official exam objectives list prepared by Microsoft for the 70-028 exam. The chapters coincide with the broad objectives groupings, such as Planning, Installation and Configuration, Configuring and Managing Security, Managing and Maintaining Data, Monitoring and Optimization, and Troubleshooting. These groupings are also reflected in the organization of the MCSE exams themselves.

Within each chapter, the individual exam objectives are addressed in turn. And in turn, the objectives sections are further divided according to the type of information presented.

Critical Information

This section presents the greatest level of detail on information that is relevant to the objective. This is the place to start if you're unfamiliar with or uncertain about the technical issues related to the objective.

Necessary Procedures

Here you'll find instructions for procedures that require a lab computer to be completed. From installing operating systems to modifying configuration defaults, the information in these sections addresses the hands-on requirements for the MCSE exams.

NOTE Not every objective has procedures associated with it. For such objectives, the "Necessary Procedures" section has been left out.

Exam Essentials

In this section, we've put together a concise list of the most crucial topics of subject areas that you'll need to comprehend fully prior to taking the MCSE exam. This section can help you identify those topics that might require more study on your part.

Key Terms and Concepts

Here we've compiled a mini-glossary of the most important terms and concepts related to the specific objective. You'll understand what all those technical words mean within the context of the related subject matter.

Sample Questions

For each objective, we've included a selection of questions similar to those you'll encounter on the actual MCSE exam. Answers and explanations are provided so that you can gain some insight into the test-taking process.

SEE ALSO   For a more comprehensive collection of exam review questions, check out the MCSE Test Success series, also published by Sybex.

How Do You Become an MCSE?

Attaining Microsoft Certified Systems Engineer (MCSE) status is a challenge. The exams cover a wide range of topics and require dedicated study and expertise. This is, however, why the MCSE certificate is so valuable. If achieving the MCSE were too easy, the market would be quickly flooded by MCSEs, and the certification would become meaningless. Microsoft, keenly aware of this fact, has taken steps to ensure that the certification means its holder is truly knowledgeable and skilled.

To become an MCSE, you must pass four core requirements and two electives. Most people select the following exam combination for the MCSE core requirements for the most current track:

Client Requirement
70-073: Implementing and Supporting Windows NT Workstation 4.0

or

70-064: Implementing and Supporting Microsoft Windows 95

Networking Requirement
70-058: Networking Essentials

Windows NT Server 4.0 Requirement
70-067: Implementing and Supporting Windows NT Server 4.0

Windows NT Server 4.0 in the Enterprise Requirement
70-068: Implementing and Supporting Windows NT Server 4.0 in the Enterprise

Electives
Some of the more popular electives include the following:

70-059: Internetworking Microsoft TCP/IP on Microsoft Windows NT 4.0

70-087: Implementing and Supporting Microsoft Internet Information Server 4.0

70-081: Implementing and Supporting Microsoft Exchange Server 5.5

70-026: System Administration for Microsoft SQL Server 6.5

70-027: Implementing a Database Design on Microsoft SQL Server 6.5

70-028: System Administration for Microsoft SQL Server 7.0

70-088: Implementing and Supporting Microsoft Proxy Server 2.0

70-079: Implementing and Supporting Microsoft Internet Explorer 4.0 by Using the Internet Explorer Administration Kit

---

TIP This book is part of a series of MCSE Exam Notes books, published by Network Press (SYBEX), that covers four core requirements and your choice of several electives—the entire MCSE track!

Where Do You Take the Exams?

You may take the exams at any one of more than 800 Sylvan Prometric Authorized Testing Centers around the world or through Virtual University Enterprises (VUE).

For the location of a Sylvan testing center near you, call (800) 755-EXAM (755-3926). Outside the United States and Canada, contact your local Sylvan Prometric Registration Center. You can also register for an exam with Sylvan Prometric via the Internet. The Sylvan site can be reached through the Microsoft Training and Certification Web site or at http://www.slspro.com/msreg/microsoft.asp.

To register for an exam through VUE, call (888) 837-8616 (North America only) or visit their Web site at http://www.vue.com/ms/.

NOTE   At the time of this writing, the exams are $100 each.

When you schedule the exam, you'll be provided with instructions regarding appointment and cancellation procedures, and information about ID requirements and the testing center location.

What the Administering Microsoft SQL Server 7.0 Exam Measures

Microsoft wants to be sure that the DBAs who pass these tests know their stuff; to that end, you will see questions on a number of topics. You will be tested on your ability to plan before you implement SQL so that your users don't end up frustrated when you have to reinstall. Then, once you have a plan in place, you will be tested on your knowledge of how to install the product (manually and automatically). Since you don't want your users just romping through your data doing what they please, your knowledge of security management will also be tested.

As an administrator, it will be your duty to manage and maintain databases—creating them, sizing them, etc.—so you will be tested on your knowledge of data maintenance as well. Since a slow server is about as useful as an underwater fire extinguisher, you will also need to know how to optimize the system to run at its fullest potential. However, none of this hard work will serve any purpose if the machine crashes, so you need to know how to troubleshoot both for the exam and for the real world.

The test questions will require a great deal of flexibility on your part; some of them require you to think in terms of a global WAN, while other questions ask for details on how to optimize the CPU of a single server. During the test, think big, but be ready to switch gears at a moment's notice.

How Microsoft Develops the Exam Questions

Microsoft's exam development process consists of eight mandatory phases. The process takes an average of seven months and contains more than 150 specific steps. The phases of Microsoft Certified Professional exam development are listed here.

Phase 1: Job Analysis

Phase 1 is an analysis of all the tasks that make up the specific job function based on tasks performed by people who are currently performing the job function. This phase also identifies the knowledge, skills, and abilities that relate specifically to the certification for that performance area.

Phase 2: Objective Domain Definition

The results of the job analysis provide the framework used to develop exam objectives. The development of objectives involves translating the job function tasks into a comprehensive set of more specific and measurable knowledge, skills, and abilities. The resulting list of objectives, or the *objective domain,* is the basis for the development of both the certification exams and the training materials.

NOTE   The outline of all Exam Notes books is based upon the official exam objectives lists published by Microsoft. Objectives are subject to change without notification. We advise that you check the Microsoft Training & Certification Web site (www.microsoft.com\ train_cert\) for the most current objectives list.

Phase 3: Blueprint Survey

The final objective domain is transformed into a blueprint survey in which contributors—technology professionals who are performing the applicable job function—are asked to rate each objective. Based on the contributors' input, the objectives are prioritized and weighted. The actual exam items are written according to the prioritized objectives. The blueprint survey phase helps determine which objectives to measure, as well as the appropriate number and types of items to include on the exam.

Phase 4: Item Development

A pool of items is developed to measure the blueprinted objective domain. The number and types of items to be written are based on the results of the blueprint survey. During this phase, items are reviewed and revised to ensure that they are as follows:

- Technically accurate

- Clear, unambiguous, and plausible

- Not biased toward any population, subgroup, or culture

- Not misleading or tricky

- Testing at the correct level of Bloom's Taxonomy

- Testing for useful knowledge, not obscure or trivial facts

Items that meet these criteria are included in the initial item pool.

Phase 5: Alpha Review and Item Revision

During this phase, a panel of technical and job function experts reviews each item for technical accuracy, then answers each item, reaching consensus on all technical issues. Once the items have been verified as technically accurate, they are edited to ensure that they are expressed in the clearest language possible.

Phase 6: Beta Exam

The reviewed and edited items are collected into a beta exam pool. During the beta exam, each participant has the opportunity to respond to all the items in this beta exam pool. Based on the responses of all beta participants, Microsoft performs a statistical analysis to verify the validity of the exam items and determine which items will be used in the certification exam. Once the analysis has been completed, the items are distributed into multiple parallel forms, or versions, of the final certification exam.

Phase 7: Item Selection and Cut-Score Setting

The results of the beta exam are analyzed to determine which items should be included in the certification exam based on many factors, including item difficulty and relevance. Generally, the desired items are answered correctly by 25 to 90 percent of the beta exam candidates. This helps ensure that the exam consists of a variety of difficulty levels, from somewhat easy to extremely difficult.

Also during this phase, a panel of job function experts determines the cut score (minimum passing score) for the exam. The cut score differs from exam to exam because it is based on an item-by-item determination of the percentage of candidates who would be expected to answer the item correctly. The experts determine the cut score in a group session to increase the reliability.

Phase 8: Live Exam

Once all the other phases are complete, the exam is ready. Microsoft Certified Professional exams are administered by Sylvan Prometric.

Tips for Taking Your Administering Microsoft SQL Server 7.0 Exam

Here are some general tips for taking your exam successfully:

- Arrive early at the exam center so that you can relax and review your study materials, particularly tables and lists of exam-related information.

- Read the questions carefully. Don't be tempted to jump to an early conclusion. Make sure you know *exactly* what the question is asking.

- Don't leave any unanswered questions. They count against you.

- When answering multiple-choice questions you're not sure about, use a process of elimination to get rid of the obviously incorrect choices first. This will improve your odds if you need to make an educated guess.

- Because the hard questions will eat up the most time, save them for last. You can move forward and backward through the exam.

- This test has many exhibits (pictures). It can be difficult, if not impossible, to view both the questions and the exhibit simulation on the 14- and 15-inch screens usually found at the testing centers. Call around to each center and see if they have 17-inch monitors available. If they don't, perhaps you can arrange to bring in your own. Failing this, some people have found it useful to quickly draw the diagram on the scratch paper provided by the testing center and use the monitor to view just the question.

- Many participants run out of time before they are able to complete the test. If you are unsure of the answer to a question, you may want to choose one of the answers, mark the question, and go on—an unanswered question does not help you. Once your time is up, you cannot go on to another question. However, you can remain on the question you are on indefinitely when the time runs out. Therefore, when you are almost out of time, go to a question you feel you can figure out—given enough time—and work until you feel you have it (or the night security guard boots you out!).

- You are allowed to use the Windows calculator during your test. However, it may be better to memorize a table of the subnet addresses and write it down on the scratch paper supplied by the testing center before you start the test.

Once you have completed an exam, you will be given immediate, online notification of your pass or fail status. You will also receive a printed Examination Score Report indicating your pass or fail status and your exam results by section. (The test administrator will give you the printed score report.) Test scores are automatically forwarded to Microsoft within five working days after you take the test. You do not need to send your score to Microsoft. If you pass the exam, you will receive confirmation from Microsoft, typically within two to four weeks.

Contact Information

To find out more about Microsoft Education and Certification materials and programs, to register with Sylvan Prometric, or to get other useful information, check the following resources. Outside the United States or Canada, contact your local Microsoft office or Sylvan Prometric testing center.

Microsoft Certified Professional Program— (800) 636-7544

Call the MCPP number for information about the Microsoft Certified Professional Program and exams, and to order the latest Microsoft Roadmap to Education and Certification.

Sylvan Prometric Testing Centers—(800) 755-EXAM

Contact Sylvan to register for a Microsoft Certified Professional exam at any of more than 800 Sylvan Prometric testing centers around the world.

Microsoft Certification Development Team—*http:// www.microsoft.com/Train_Cert/mcp/examinfo/ certsd.htm*

Contact the Microsoft Certification Development Team through their Web site to volunteer for participation in one or more exam development phases or report a problem with an exam. Address written correspondence to:

Certification Development Team
Microsoft Education and Certification
One Microsoft Way
Redmond, WA 98052

Microsoft TechNet Technical Information Network— (800) 344-2121

This is an excellent resource for support professionals and system administrators. Outside the United States and Canada, call your local Microsoft subsidiary for information.

How to Contact the Author

Joe Jorden can be reached at jljorden@ix.netcom.com.

How to Contact the Publisher

Sybex welcomes reader feedback on all of their titles. Visit the Sybex Web site at www.sybex.com for book updates and additional certification information. You'll also find online forms to submit comments or suggestions regarding this or any other Sybex book.

CHAPTER

1

Planning

Microsoft Exam Objectives Covered in This Chapter:

Develop a security strategy. *(pages 4 – 16)*
- Assess whether to use Microsoft Windows NT accounts or Microsoft SQL Server logins.
- Assess whether to leverage the Windows NT group structure.
- Plan the use and structure of SQL Server roles. Server roles include fixed server, fixed database, and user-defined database.
- Assess whether to map Windows NT groups directly into a database or to map them to a role.
- Assess which Windows NT accounts will be used to run SQL Server services.
- Plan an *n*-tier application security strategy, and decide whether to use application roles or other mid-tier security mechanisms such as Microsoft Transaction Server.
- Plan the security requirements for linked databases.

Develop a SQL Server capacity plan. *(pages 16 – 26)*
- Plan the physical placement of files, including data files and transaction log files.
- Plan the use of filegroups.
- Plan for growth over time.
- Plan the physical hardware system.
- Assess communication requirements.

Develop a data availability solution. *(pages 26 – 34)*
- Choose the appropriate backup and restore strategy. Strategies include full database backup; full database backup and transaction log backup; differential database backup with full database backup and transaction log backup; and database files backup and transaction log backup.
- Assess whether to use a standby server.
- Assess whether to use clustering.

Develop a migration plan. *(pages 35 – 38)*
- Plan an upgrade from a previous version of SQL Server.
- Plan the migration of data from other data sources.

Develop a replication strategy. *(pages 39 – 55)*

- Given a scenario, design the appropriate replication model. Replication models include single Publisher and multiple Subscribers; multiple Publishers and single Subscriber; multiple Publishers and multiple Subscribers; and remote Distributor.
- Choose the replication type. Replication types include snapshot, transactional, and merge.

Suppose that you are going to take a vacation overseas—how do you go about it? Do you just randomly throw things in your suitcase, run to the airport hoping to buy a ticket, and see if you can find a hotel when you land? That would not be much of a vacation; it would be a disaster. If you really are going to take an overseas trip, you would get your tickets in advance, have lodging arrangements, and learn about the weather so that you could take the right clothes. You would plan your trip so that it would not turn out to be a disaster.

You must do the same with SQL Server. You cannot just start installing SQL and then expect it to work right when you are done; the installation must be planned, or SQL Server will not work right when you are done. That is what will be discussed here—planning SQL Server installation.

You'll start by planning the security systems that you'll need to put in place to keep prying eyes out of sensitive material. Then, you'll read about capacity planning, so that all of your users can access your data efficiently and avoid running out of space.

After security and capacity have been discussed, you can develop a data availability plan, deciding what types of backups to use so that you can bring your data back online quickly in the event of a disaster. Then, just in case you are migrating from another database server, you will set up a migration plan. Finally, a replication plan will be hashed out, so that all of your users can access data locally if you have more than one server.

Most of the sections here are based on concepts; the mechanics of configuring all of these things will be discussed in the following chapters. Therefore, you will not see any "Necessary Procedures" sections in this chapter. That does not mean that this chapter is unimportant, though; in fact, this is the most important chapter in the book since most of the concepts you will need to know to pass the exam are discussed here and only touched on in later chapters. Pay very close attention, then, as planning is discussed in relation to SQL Server 7.

Develop a security strategy.

- Assess whether to use Microsoft Windows NT accounts or Microsoft SQL Server logins.

- Assess whether to leverage the Windows NT group structure.

- Plan the use and structure of SQL Server roles. Server roles include fixed server, fixed database, and user-defined database.

- Assess whether to map Windows NT groups directly into a database or to map them to a role.

- Assess which Windows NT accounts will be used to run SQL Server services.

- Plan an *n*-tier application security strategy, and decide whether to use application roles or other mid-tier security mechanisms such as Microsoft Transaction Server.

- Plan the security requirements for linked databases.

Hackers are running rampant today; people are using their knowledge of computer systems to access sensitive data, steal corporate secrets, or just be malicious. SQL Server is especially prone to such attacks since it is where many companies store their sensitive data. To keep hackers out, you must have a good security plan.

In this section, the components of a good security plan will be examined. First, you'll figure out whether to use Windows NT accounts or SQL Server logins to grant access to your users. If you go with Windows NT accounts, you should read about the benefits of leveraging the group structure in Windows NT.

After your users have access to the server, you need to know how to limit what they are capable of doing with the data on your server; that is why the various roles at your disposal will be discussed. Then, you'll figure out which Windows NT accounts the SQL Server services will run under. After that, the security requirements for *n*-tier applications and linked databases will be covered.

Since you don't want just anybody accessing your data, these security concepts are going to be very important to you in the real world. Anything that is this important in the real world is also very important on the exam, so watch closely as the secrets of security are uncovered.

Critical Information

The first thing you need to understand to put together a good security plan is the difference between the two authentication modes. Then, you can read about how to set up accounts that take advantage of those modes.

Assessing Whether to Use Windows NT Accounts or SQL Server Logins

The type of accounts you use depends a great deal on your authentication mode. An *authentication mode* is how SQL processes user names and passwords. There are two such modes in SQL 7: Windows NT Authentication mode and Mixed mode.

In Windows NT Authentication mode, a user can simply sit down at their computer, log on to the Windows NT domain, and gain access to SQL Server. Here's how it works:

1. The user logs on to a Windows NT domain; the user name and password are verified by NT.

2. The user then opens a trusted connection (see Figure 1.1) with SQL Server.

3. SQL will then try to match the user name or group membership to an entry in the syslogins table.

4. Since this is a trusted connection, SQL does not need to verify the user password; that is, SQL trusts NT to perform that function.

FIGURE 1.1: Trusted connection to SQL Server

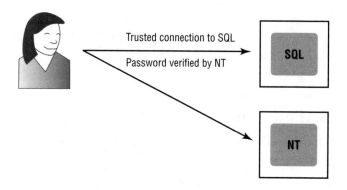

The main advantage to Windows NT Authentication mode is that users do not have to remember multiple user names and passwords. That will vastly increase security since there is less danger of users writing their passwords down and storing them in an unsafe place (such as a sticky note on their monitor). This mode also gives you tighter reign over security, since you can apply NT password policies that will do such things as expire passwords, require a minimum length for passwords, keep a history of passwords, and so on.

One of the disadvantages is that only users with a Windows NT network account (created in User Manager for Domains) can open a trusted connection to SQL Server. For example, that means that a Novell client running the IPX Net-Library cannot use Windows NT Authentication mode. If you have such clients, you will need to implement Mixed mode.

Mixed mode allows both NT Authentication and SQL Authentication. In SQL Authentication:

1. The user logs on to their network, NT or otherwise.

2. The user opens a nontrusted connection (see Figure 1.2) to SQL Server using a user name and password other than those used to gain network access.

3. SQL then matches the user name and password entered by the user to an entry in the syslogins table

FIGURE 1.2: Nontrusted connection to SQL Server

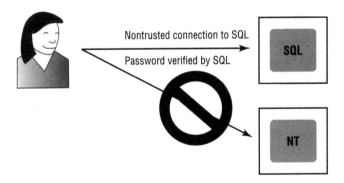

The primary advantage here is that anyone can gain access to SQL using Mixed mode, regardless of the network they log on to. This means that Mac users, Novell users, Banyan Vines users, and the like can gain access. You could also consider this to be a second layer of security, since hacking into the network in Mixed mode does not mean that someone has automatically hacked into SQL at the same time.

Ironically, multiple passwords can be a problem as well as an advantage. Consider that users will have one user name and password to log on to the network and a completely separate user name and password to gain access to SQL. When users have multiple sets of credentials, they tend to write them down and thus breach the security system you have worked so hard to set up.

Assessing Whether to Leverage the Windows NT Group Structure

While standard logins can be used by only one user, a Windows NT login can be mapped to one of the following:

- A single user

- A Windows NT group that an administrator has created

- A Windows NT built-in group (e.g., Administrators)

Before you create a Windows NT login, you must decide to which of these three you want to map it. Generally, you will want to map to a group that you have created. This will help you a great deal in later administration. For example, suppose you have an Accounting database to which all 50 of your accountants require access. You could create a separate login for each of them, which would require you to manage 50 SQL logins. On the other hand, if you create a Windows NT group for these 50 accountants and map your SQL login to this group, you will have only one SQL login to manage.

Planning to Use Server Roles and Map Groups

Once your users have access to SQL as a whole, they need to be limited in what they can do. That is what fixed server roles are used for. Some users may be allowed to do whatever they want, whereas other users may only be able to manage security. There are seven server roles to which you can assign users. The following list starts at the highest level and describes the administrative access granted:

Sysadmin: Members of the sysadmin role can do whatever they want in SQL Server. Be careful whom you assign to this role; people who are unfamiliar with SQL can accidentally create serious problems. This role is only for the database administrators (DBAs).

TIP Built-in\Administrators is automatically made a member of the sysadmin server role, giving SQL administrative rights to all of your NT administrators. Since not all of your NT administrators should have these rights, you may want to create a SQLAdmins group, add your SQL administrators to that group, and make the group a member of the sysadmins role. Afterward, you should remove Built-in\Administrators from the sysadmin role.

Serveradmin: These users can set serverwide configuration options, such as how much memory SQL can use or how much information to send over the network in a single frame. If you make your assistant DBAs members of this role, you can relieve yourself of some of the administrative burden.

Setupadmin: Members here can install replication and manage extended stored procedures (these are used to perform actions not native to SQL Server). Give this to the assistant DBAs as well.

Securityadmin: These users manage security issues such as creating and deleting logins, reading the audit logs, and granting users permission to create databases. This, too, is a good role for assistant DBAs.

Processadmin: SQL is capable of *multitasking*; that is, it can do more than one thing at a time by executing multiple processes. For instance, SQL might spawn one process for writing to cache and another for reading from cache. A member of the processadmin group can end (called *kill* in SQL) a process. This is another good role for assistant DBAs and developers. Developers especially need to kill processes that may have been triggered by an improperly designed query or stored procedure.

Dbcreator: These users can create and make changes to databases. This may be a good role for assistant DBAs as well as developers (who should be warned against creating unnecessary databases and wasting server space).

Diskadmin: These users manage files on disk. They do things such as mirroring databases and adding backup devices. Assistant DBAs should be members of this role.

TIP If you do not want users to have any administrative authority, do not assign them to a server role. This will limit them to being just normal users.

Once your users have access to a database through a database user account, you must limit what they can do in that individual database by assigning them to a database role. Fixed database roles have permissions already applied; that is, all you have to do is add users to these roles and the users inherit the associated permissions. (That is different from custom database roles, as you will see later.) There are several fixed database roles in SQL Server that you can use to grant permissions:

Db_owner: Members of this role can do everything the members of the other roles can do as well as some administrative functions.

Db_accessadmin: These users have the authority to say who gets access to the database by adding or removing users.

Db_datareader: Members here can read data from any table in the database.

Db_datawriter: These users can add, change, and delete data from all the tables in the database.

Db_ddladmin: Data Definition Language administrators can issue all DDL commands; this allows them to create, modify, or change database objects without viewing the data inside.

Db_securityadmin: Members here can add and remove users from database roles, and manage statement and object permissions.

Db_backupoperator: These users can back up the database.

Db_denydatareader: Members cannot read the data in the database, but they can make schema changes.

Db_denydatawriter: These users cannot make changes to the data in the database, but they are allowed to read the data.

Public: The purpose of this group is to grant users a default set of permissions in the database. All database users automatically join this group and cannot be removed.

There will, of course, be times when the fixed database roles do not meet your security needs. You might have several users who need Select, Update, and Execute permissions in your database and nothing more. Because none of the fixed database roles will give you that set of permissions, you can create a custom database role. When you create this new role, you will assign permissions to it and then assign users to the role; then, the users will inherit whatever permissions you assign to the role. That is different from the fixed database roles, where you did not need to assign permissions, but just added users.

NOTE You can make your custom database roles members of other database roles. This is referred to as nesting roles.

Suppose that your human resources department uses a custom program to access their database, and you don't want them using any other program for fear of damaging the data. You can set this level of security by using an *application role*. With this special role, your users will not be able to access data using just their SQL login and database account; they will have to use the proper application.

Once you've created an application role, the user logs on to SQL, is authenticated, and opens the approved application. The application executes the `sp_setapprole` stored procedure to enable the application role. Once the application role is enabled, SQL no longer sees users as themselves; it sees users as the application and grants them application role permissions.

You may have noticed, though, that these roles are just a way of grouping users together to grant similar permissions; Windows NT groups serve the same purpose. Which is better, having Windows NT groups directly in the database or mapping users to roles? Here's a quick rule of thumb: If you have a use for the group other than SQL database access (and permission to do so), you should create a Windows NT group and map it to the database role. If you have no other reason to group these users together besides SQL database access, you are probably better off creating separate accounts and adding them to the role individually.

Choosing Accounts to Run the SQL Server Services

As a security precaution, the SQL services log on with one of two types of user accounts. The first is a local system account, which allows SQL to start but not access any network resources. The second type is a domain user account; this is just like any other user account with extra rights (specifically *log on as a service* and *act as part of the operating system*). If you intend to perform replication, use multi-server jobs, or have SQL send e-mail, you must have the services log on with the domain user account (called a *service account* when used by a service).

When you create a service account for SQL Server, you can create a single account for all SQL Server services to use, or you can create separate accounts for the individual services.

While the service account assigned to the SQLAgent needs administrative rights (on both Windows NT and SQL Server), the account assigned to the other SQL Server services doesn't. You may want to create and assign separate accounts to limit the rights of the accounts assigned to the MSSQLServer service and also to help in auditing security issues. No matter how you do it, though, any service account you create needs rights to the \MSSQL7 folder and user rights on the domain.

Configuring *N*-Tier Security and Linked Databases

When your resources are spread across multiple SQL Servers, your users may need access to resources on multiple, or *n* number of, servers. This is especially true of something called a *distributed query* (see Figure 1.3), which returns result sets from databases on multiple servers.

Although you might wonder why you would want to perform distributed queries when you could just replicate the data between servers, there are practical reasons for doing the former. Don't forget that because SQL Server is designed to store terabytes of data, some of your databases may grow to several hundred megabytes in size—and you really don't want to replicate several hundred megabytes under normal circumstances.

FIGURE 1.3: Distributed query

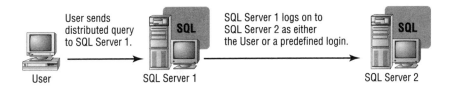

The first step is to inform SQL that it will be talking to other database servers by running the `sp_addlinkedserver` stored procedure. The procedure to link to a server named AccountingSQL looks something as follows:

```
sp_addlinkedserver @server='AccountingSQL',
@provider='SQL Server'.
```

Your users can then run distributed queries by simply specifying two different servers in the query. The query `select * from SQLServer .pubs.dbo.authors, AccountingSQL.pubs.dbo.employees` would access data from both the SQL Server (the server the user is logged in to, or the sending server) and the AccountingSQL server (the remote server) in the same result set.

The security issue here is that the sending server must log in to the remote server on behalf of the user to gain access to those data. SQL can use one of two methods to send this security information: security account delegation or linked-server login mapping. If your users have logged in using Windows NT Authentication, and all of the servers in the query are capable of understanding Windows NT domain security, you can use account delegation. Here's how it works:

1. If the servers are in different domains, you must make certain that the appropriate Windows NT trust relationships are in place. The remote server's domain must trust the sending server's domain.

2. Add a Windows NT login to the sending server for the user to log in with.

3. Add the same account to the remote server.

4. Create a user account for the login in the remote server's database and assign permissions.

5. When the user executes the distributed query, SQL will send the user's Windows NT security credentials to the remote server, allowing access.

If you have users who access SQL with standard logins, or if some of the servers do not participate in Windows NT domain security, you will need to add a linked login. Here's how to do it:

1. On the remote server, create a standard login and assign the necessary permissions.

2. On the sending server, map a local login to the remote login using the `sp_addlinkedsrvlogin` stored procedure. To map all local logins to the remote login RemUser, type **sp_addlinkedsrvlogin @rmtsrvname='AccountingSQL', @useself=FALSE, @locallogin=NULL, @rmtuser='RemUser', @rmtpassword='password'**.

3. When a user executes a distributed query, the sending server will log in to the AccountingSQL (remote) server as RemUser with a password of *password*.

Exam Essentials

A great deal of the exam is going to be based on your understanding of the concepts behind SQL, especially the security concepts. Since you need a secure network, Microsoft will test quite a bit on all of the concepts in this section, but here are a few special points to watch for.

Know your accounts.   You need to know the difference between SQL Server logins and Windows NT accounts. SQL Server login passwords are verified by SQL Server, whereas Windows NT account passwords are verified by Windows NT Server.

Know your roles.   It is not necessary to memorize the capabilities of each role, but you should have a general familiarity with each of them.

Know how to configure linked servers.   Remember that there are two ways to do this: account delegation, where you can use the Windows NT user account to access data, and SQL authentication, where you need to create a SQL login on the linked server with which to gain access.

Key Terms and Concepts

Linked server: This is a remote server (SQL Server or otherwise) that is configured to participate in a distributed query.

N-tier: This is an application that is configured to use multiple, or *n* amount of, servers.

Role: Roles are used to assign permissions to groups of users rather than individually.

Service account: This is a domain user account that is used by a service to log on.

Sample Questions

1. You have several Macintosh users on your network that require access to your SQL Server. Which type of account should they be assigned?

   A. Windows NT account

   B. SQL Server login

   Answer: B. Macintosh users require a SQL Server login since they do not log on to Windows NT networks.

2. Some of your users log in to SQL with SQL Server logins, and the rest use Windows NT accounts. For all of them to use the distributed queries you have created, what stored procedure should you run?

A. `sp_addlinkedlogin`

B. `sp_addsrvlogin`

C. `sp_addlinkedsrvlogin`

D. `sp_addlinkedsrv`

Answer: C. The others are misspelled.

Develop a SQL Server capacity plan.

- Plan the physical placement of files, including data files and transaction log files.
- Plan the use of filegroups.
- Plan for growth over time.
- Plan the physical hardware system.
- Assess communication requirements.

Imagine that one of the sales people in your company asks you why they are unable to add that huge new customer to the sales database, and the only answer you can give is, "We ran out of disk space; we'll have a new disk in tomorrow." This would reflect very poorly on you and your future with the company, so you need to make sure it doesn't happen. The way to avoid this is by creating a capacity plan—figuring out how big your databases are going to be and allocating resources accordingly.

In this section, where your data and transaction log files should be placed for maximum performance and space will be discussed. You'll also read about using filegroups for managing your data, especially

VLDBs (very large databases). You then get to engage in the fine art of prognostication (foretelling the future)—you'll plan for growth over time. Finally, the physical hardware that you need for all of this, and the communication links that are needed to maintain it all, will be discussed.

If you don't want to have to tell your boss that no one can work because the databases are full, you need to read this section carefully. Even though this information is not heavily tested, it will make your life much easier.

Critical Information

To know where to put your database files, you need to understand a little bit about them. When you create a database, you are allocating hard-disk space for one of three file types: database files, secondary database files, and transaction log files. Database files, which store data and system tables, have a default extension of .MDF. The transaction log is stored in one or more files, with a default .LDF extension. If you create a database that spans multiple database files, the additional database files have a default filename extension of .NDF. With that understanding, it is easier to answer the question of placement.

Physical Placement of Files

No one can actually tell you where to place your files; that is hardware dependent. Here, though, you will get some advice and some things to consider about where the files should go. The most important things to consider are disk space (present and future), speed, reliability, and fault tolerance. A RAID (Redundant Array of Inexpensive Disks) array takes all of this into consideration. There are four types you should consider.

RAID 0

RAID 0 uses disk striping; that is, it writes data across multiple hard-disk partitions in what is called a *stripe set*. This can greatly improve speed because multiple hard disks are working at the same time.

RAID 0 can be implemented through the use of Windows NT software or on third-party hardware. While RAID 0 gives you the best speed, it does not provide any fault tolerance. If one of the hard disks in the stripe set is damaged, you lose all of your data.

RAID 1

RAID 1 uses disk mirroring. Disk mirroring actually writes your information to disk twice—once to the primary file and once to the mirror. This gives you excellent fault tolerance, but it is fairly slow, because you must write to disk twice. Windows NT includes the ability to mirror your hard disks. RAID 1 requires only a single hard-disk controller.

RAID 5

RAID 5—striping with parity—writes data to the hard disk in stripe sets. Parity checksums will be written across all disks in the stripe set. This gives you excellent fault tolerance as well as excellent speed with a reasonable amount of overhead. The parity checksums can be used to re-create information lost if a single disk in the stripe set fails. If more than one disk in the stripe set fails, however, you will lose all your data. Although Windows NT supports RAID 5 in a software implementation, a hardware implementation is faster and more reliable—it is suggested that you use it if you can afford it.

RAID 10

RAID 10 (sometimes referred to as RAID 1+0) is the "big daddy." This level of RAID should be used in mission-critical systems that require 24 hours a day, 7 days a week uptime and the fastest possible access. RAID 10 implements striping with parity as in RAID 5 and then mirrors the stripe sets. You still have excellent speed and excellent fault tolerance, but you also have the added expense of using more than twice the disk space of RAID 1. Then again, RAID 10 is for a situation in which you can afford no SQL Server downtime.

Some other issues that you should keep in mind when planning your database file placement are as follows:

- All data and log files that a particular SQL Server manages must reside on that SQL Server machine. They cannot be over the network.

- Only one database is allowed per data file, but a single database can span multiple data files.

- Transaction logs must reside on their own file, but they can span multiple log files.

- Database files fill up their available space by striping across all data files in the filegroup. In this manner, you can eliminate hot spots and reduce contention in high volume OLTP (Online Transaction Processing) environments.

- Transaction log files do not use striping, but fill each log file to capacity before continuing to the next log file.

- For communication, backup devices can be created across a network. Databases must be on the local machine.

NOTE   It is strongly suggested that you place your transaction logs on separate physical hard drives. In this manner, you can recover your data up to the second in the event of a media failure. If you are using RAID 5 (striping with parity), this is not an issue.

Space Requirements and Growth

Another very important factor to consider in planning your data storage and placement requirements is growth. However, to plan for growth, you must understand how SQL stores data. There are two main types of storage structures in SQL Server 7: extents and data pages.

Extents and Pages

At the most fundamental level, everything in SQL Server is stored on an 8KB page, which is the smallest unit of I/O in SQL. The page is the one common denominator for all objects in SQL Server. There are many different types of pages, but every page has some factors in common. Pages are always 8KB in size and always have a header, leaving about 8092 bytes of usable space on every page.

There are five primary types of pages in SQL Server:

Data pages: Data pages hold the actual database records. Although 8092 bytes are free for use on a data page, records are limited in length to no more than 8000 bytes. This is because records cannot cross rows, and approximately 52 bytes are used for transaction log overhead in the transaction log entries. Transaction logs are held on standard data pages.

Index pages: Index pages store the index keys and levels making up the entire index tree. Unlike data pages, there is no limit to the total number of entries that can be made on an index page.

Text/image pages: Text and image pages hold the actual data associated with text, ntext, and image data types. When a text field is saved, the record will contain a 16-byte pointer to a linked list of text pages that hold the actual text data. Only the 16-byte pointer inside the record is counted against the 8000-byte record-size limit.

Statistics pages: Every index has a statistics page that tracks the distribution of values in that index. The statistics page is used by the query optimizer in choosing the most appropriate index for any given query request.

Pages are combined into *extents,* which are blocks of eight pages totaling 64KB in size. Because the extent is the basic unit of allocation for tables and indexes, and all objects are saved in a table of some kind, all objects are stored in extents. When an object needs more space, SQL allocates it another extent. This is done because it is much faster to allocate a lump of pages all together rather than each one separately, and it keeps the database from being horribly fragmented.

Estimating Required Space for Tables

Now that you understand how space is allocated, you can ask yourself the age-old question, How large should the databases be? If they are too large, you will waste space, yet if they are too small, you will be constantly expanding them. To find a balance, you must be able to accurately estimate the required space. To estimate that space, you need to do as follows:

1. Calculate the space used by a single row of the table.

2. Calculate the number of rows that will fit on one page.

3. Estimate the number of rows the table will hold.

4. Calculate the total number of pages that will be required to hold these rows.

To calculate the space used by a single row in a table, you need to add the storage requirements for each field in the table plus an additional 2 bytes per row of overhead. This will give you the total space that is occupied by a single row. For example, if a table in a database has three fields defined as Char(10), Int, and Money, the storage space required for each row could be calculated as follows:

- Char(10)=10 bytes

- Int=4 bytes

- Money=8 bytes

- Overhead=2 bytes

- Total=24 bytes

WARNING A row is limited to 2 bytes of overhead only when no variable-length data types (varchar and varbinary) have been used and no columns allow nulls. If variable-length columns are used or nulls are allowed, additional overhead must be added. The amount will depend on the data type and number of columns.

Once you know how much space is taken by each row in your table, you will be able to calculate the number of rows that can be contained on a single 8KB page; well, actually about 8092 bytes are free for storing data because of the header on each page. The total number of rows per page can be calculated as $8092 \div row\ size$. The resulting value will be rounded to the nearest whole number because a row cannot span pages. In the example above, each row requires 24 bytes of space to store. You can calculate the rows per page as follows:

$8092 \div 24 = 337$

In addition, the number of rows that can fit on one page may also depend on a fill factor that is used for the clustered index. *Fill factor* is a way of keeping the page from becoming 100 percent full when a clustered index is created. For example, if a clustered index is built on your table with a fill factor of 75 percent, this means that the data would be reorganized so that the data pages would be only 75 percent full. This means that instead of 8092 bytes free on each page, you could use only 6069 bytes.

Now that you know how to calculate the number of rows on a single page, you need to estimate the total number of rows that will be in your table. To do that, you have to know your data to estimate how many rows your table will eventually hold. When you make this estimate, try to consider as well as possible how large you expect your table to grow. If you do not allow for this growth in your estimates, the database will need to be expanded.

Once you have estimated the number of rows in your table, you can calculate the number of pages your table will take up by using the following equation:

number of rows in table÷number of rows per page

Here, the result will be rounded up to the nearest whole number.

In the example above, you saw that 337 rows would fit in a single page of the table. If you expect this table to eventually hold 1,000,000 records, the calculation would be as follows:

- 1,000,000÷337=2967.4

- Round the value to 2968 pages

Now, you can extend your calculation to determine the number of extents that must be allocated to this table to hold these data. Since all space is allocated in extents, you again need to round up to the nearest integer when calculating extents. Remember that there are eight 8KB pages per extent. Our calculation would be as follows:

2968÷8=371

Since a megabyte can store 16 extents, this table would take about 23.2MB of space to store. Now you are ready to estimate your index space.

Estimating Index Storage Requirements

Indexes in SQL Server are stored in a B-Tree format; that is, you can think of an index as a large tree. You can also think of an index as a table with a pyramid on top of it. The ultimate concept here is that for every index, there is a single entry point: the root of the tree or the apex of the pyramid.

When estimating storage requirements, the base of this pyramid can be thought of as a table. You go through the same process in estimating the "leaf" level of an index as you would in estimating the storage requirements of a table. Although the process is very similar, there are a couple of issues that are important to consider:

- You are adding the data types of the index keys, not the data rows.

- Clustered indexes use the data page as the leaf level. There is no need to add additional storage requirements for a clustered-index leaf level.

The toughest part of estimating the size of an index is estimating the size and number of levels you will have in your index. While there is a fairly long and complex series of calculations to determine this exactly, you will usually find it sufficient to add an additional 35 percent of the leaf-level space estimated for the other levels of the index.

Working with Filegroups

Filegroups are used for explicitly placing database objects onto a particular set of database files. For example, you can separate tables and their nonclustered indexes onto separate filegroups. This can improve performance because modifications to the table can be written to both the table and the index at the same time. This can be especially useful if you are not using striping with parity (RAID 5).

Another advantage of filegroups is the ability to back up only a single filegroup at a time. This can be extremely useful for a VLDB because the sheer size of the database could make the backup an extremely time-consuming process. Another advantage is the ability to mark the filegroup and all data on the files that are part of it as either READ-ONLY or READWRITE.

There are really only two disadvantages to using filegroups. The first is the administration that is involved in keeping track of the files in the filegroup and the database objects that are placed in them. The other disadvantage is that if you are working with a smaller database and have RAID 5 implemented, you may not be improving performance.

The two basic filegroups in SQL Server 7 are the primary, or default, filegroup that is created with every database and the user-defined filegroups that are created for a particular database. The primary filegroup will always contain the primary data file and any other files that are not specifically created on a user-defined filegroup. You can create additional filegroups using the ALTER DATABASE command or the Enterprise Manager.

Filegroups have several rules that you should follow when you are working with them:

- The first (or primary) data file must reside on the primary filegroup.

- All system files must be placed on the primary filegroup.

- A file cannot be a member of more than one filegroup at a time.

- Filegroups can be allocated indexes, tables, text, ntext, and image data.

- New data pages are not automatically allocated to user-defined filegroups if the primary filegroup runs out of space.

Exam Essentials

You need to be able to figure out how big your databases are going to be so that you can decide how many resources to allocate. When you take the test, you should remember the following points especially.

Know how to calculate the amount of space a table will take.
This is a simple mathematical process: First, calculate the amount of
data in a row. Next, 8092 divided by the row size will tell you the
number of rows in a page. Then, you need to estimate the total number
of rows your table will hold, after which you calculate the number of
pages your table will take as follows: *number of rows in*
table÷number of rows per page.

Know what filegroups are for. Filegroups are designed for two
purposes: First, for optimizing system performance by placing tables
on one filegroup and indexes on another; second, for optimizing
space usage since you can place large tables on separate filegroups
rather than all together.

Key Terms and Concepts

Extent: A group of eight pages, this is the smallest unit that SQL
will allocate for a table or index.

Filegroup: Filegroups are used for separating database objects
into separate files; for example, a table could be on the primary
filegroup while its index could be on a different physical disk in a
different filegroup.

Page: The smallest unit of allocation in SQL Server; a single page
is 8KB.

Sample Questions

1. What is the smallest unit of allocation in SQL, and how large is it?

A. Page; 2KB

B. Page; 8KB

C. Extent; 8KB

D. Extent; 64KB

Answer: B. The page is the smallest unit of allocation; the extent
(at 64KB or eight pages) is the largest.

2. You have a table with a record size of 100. Approximately how large will that table be with 100,000 records?

A. 100MB

B. 11MB

C. 10MB

D. 1MB

Answer: C. Using the mathematical formulae presented in this section, you should come up with about 10MB.

Develop a data availability solution.

- Choose the appropriate backup and restore strategy. Strategies include full database backup; full database backup and transaction log backup; differential database backup with full database backup and transaction log backup; and database files backup and transaction log backup.

- Assess whether to use a standby server.

- Assess whether to use clustering.

Most systems administrators don't realize the full extent of the damage that can come from a downed system. Think about this example: You have 20 sales people that cannot do any work without the SQL Server running, so when it goes down, they don't work and you lose money. How much money, though? You probably pay an average of $25 per hour for sales people, which means that you are losing $500 an hour in labor—this is the extent of some administrators' calculations, but there is more.

What happens to all those sales that could have been made while the system was down? What about the long-standing customers who tried to place an order, but went to your competition because they couldn't? All told, you could be losing several thousand dollars an hour if a critical system goes down for any length of time. That is why you need to become one with the concepts presented here.

In this section, you will read about how to prepare for a database system crash. You will look at how to effectively combine full, differential, filegroup, and transaction log backups to minimize downtime when a crash occurs. The value of a standby server and clustering so that your users don't even know when one of the systems goes down will also be discussed.

All of this information is going to prove extremely valuable both in your own networks and on the test that you are preparing for, so pay close attention.

Critical Information

As a database administrator, you need to be prepared for anything, from hardware failures to malicious updates. You need to be able to bring your data back to a consistent state, which requires a good backup strategy. To devise this strategy, you will need to answer a few questions, such as:

- What type of backup will you use?
- How often will the backups occur?
- Will backups be on hard disk or tape?
- Who will be responsible for the backups?
- How will the backups be verified?
- What are the policies for backing up nonlogged operations?
- Does a standby server make sense for the installation?

SQL Backup Types

There are four types of backups that you can use to back up your data. Most often, you will use a combination of the following:

Full database backups: With full database backups, the entire database is backed up. Although they are the easiest to implement and restore from, full database backups may not be practical because of the amount of time required for very large databases.

Transaction log backups: Because the transaction log records all changes made to a database, backing up the log (after performing an occasional full database backup) allows you to re-create the database without having to do a full database backup every time.

Differential database backups: New with SQL 7, differential backups back up only data that have changed since the last full backup. These could be more efficient than transaction log backups for databases with existing data that change often. For example, if a person's bank account changes 10 times in one day, the transaction log backup would contain all 10 changes, while the differential backup would contain just the final amount.

Filegroup backups: Also new with SQL 7, filegroup backups allow you to back up different pieces of the database, based on the various files that make up the database. Usually, filegroup backups are done when the time required to perform a full database backup is prohibitive.

How Often Will the Backups Occur?

The frequency of your backups is directly proportional to the amount of data loss you can tolerate in the event of a system crash. For example, if you back up only once a week on Sunday, and then have a system crash on Friday, you would lose the entire week's work. Conversely, if you were to back up the transaction log every hour, the most data you will lose will be an hour's worth.

For your user databases, you may want to consider a combination of the four types of backups. If, for example, you have a database that does not change very much, perhaps containing archive data, you may just want to do a full backup once a week. If you have a database that changes throughout the day, though, you will want to use a different strategy.

For a database that changes regularly, you could perform a full backup once a week, then transaction log backups every day. That would give you recovery up to the day before the crash.

If you need more protection than that, you could perform a full backup once a week and transaction log backups every two hours. This would get you good recovery, but the restoration is slow because you must restore the full backup and then each transaction log backup in sequence.

For a faster restoration, you could do the full backup once a week, transaction log backups during the day, and differential backups at night throughout the week. With this final strategy, your restorations would be much faster because you need to restore only the full backup, the differential from the night before, and the transaction log backups up to the time of the crash.

If you are working with a very large database (VLDB), you may not be able to back up the entire database at one time. In that instance, you can back up certain files of the database by using a filegroup backup. First, you would perform a full database backup, then during the day perform regular transaction log backups and at night perform a filegroup backup, getting a different filegroup each night. With this strategy, you would then need to restore only the full backup, then the filegroup backup for the failed file and any transaction log backups that occurred since the filegroup backup of the restored filegroup.

For your system databases, consider the following suggestions:

Master database: Schedule it for weekly backups and perform a manual backup after major modifications to your databases, devices, or users.

MSDB database: Schedule it for weekly backups and perform a manual backup after major changes to tasks, events, operators, or alerts.

Tempdb database: Don't bother backing it up, because it is automatically cleared every time SQL Server is stopped and started.

Model database: You should make a baseline backup of this, and then manually back it up whenever it changes (which won't be very often).

Pubs and Northwind databases: Don't bother backing these up, because they are simply sample databases that give you live data to practice on.

To What Medium Will the Backups Be Made?

SQL Server can back up databases to tape or a dump device (a file). If a tape drive is used, it must be on the Windows NT HCL (hardware compatibility list) and installed in the computer running SQL Server.

TIP SQL Server 7 and Windows NT now use compatible file formats for tape backups. You can use the same tape drive and tape to perform both SQL Server and Windows NT backups (unlike in earlier versions of SQL Server).

Who Is Responsible for the Backups?

If there is only one DBA in your company, you have no problem deciding who gets to perform the backups, but if there is more than one, you must decide who does what. You need to have a plan in place to make sure that one of the administrators is performing the backups on a regular basis and that when that administrator goes on vacation, another can take over in their place.

How Will the Backups Be Verified?

More than likely, you have a fire extinguisher in your home or office—have you ever looked at the top of it? There is a gauge that tells you whether it is full. If you don't check that gauge on your extinguisher regularly, it may not work for you when you need it. The same is true of your backups—you must verify that they are good before you need to use them.

You could have SQL verify each backup for you, or you could play it safe and verify them yourself by restoring them to a separate computer.

Not only does this verify the integrity of your backups, it helps prepare you in case you have to bring up a spare server quickly.

What Are the Policies for Backing Up Nonlogged Operations?

While most transactions are logged by SQL Server in the transaction log, some are not. This means that if a database has to be restored, any and all of the nonlogged operations that happened since the last backup would be lost. You need to back up your databases immediately after you perform any of the following tasks:

- Fast bulk copies when Select Into/Bulk Copy is enabled

- `Select Into` commands when Select Into/Bulk Copy is enabled

TIP   Back up the database before starting a nonlogged operation, in case you need to restore the database to its previous state.

NT Clustering

You can obtain an additional component for Windows NT Server 4 called Cluster Server that allows you to have two separate computers using the same SCSI hard drive. Using this product, if one server fails for any reason, the backup system can take over all of the functions of the failed system, and the users won't even notice what happened. The only drawback to this solution is the expense—you need to purchase two computers instead of one, and you need to purchase the Cluster Server separately.

Standby Servers

A standby server is the budget version of clustering. It can easily be set up to receive periodic copies of the data from the primary server. If the primary server goes down, the standby server can be renamed as the primary server and rebooted; it will then look and act like the primary server. Making a standby server work correctly involves a few steps:

1. Create the primary server as usual.

2. Create the secondary server with a unique name.

3. Do periodic full backups of the databases on the primary server.

4. Restore the backup files to the standby server.

5. Do frequent backups of the transaction log on the primary server.

6. Restore the backups of the transaction log to the standby server using the Standby switch if you wish to make the standby database read-only, or with the No Recovery switch otherwise.

7. If you have the time to prepare to switch servers, perform a transaction log backup of the primary server and a restoration on the standby server, and take the primary server offline.

8. Set the databases on the standby server for real use by using the Recover switch.

9. Rename the standby server as the primary server and reboot the standby server.

10. Use the standby server normally until the primary server is ready to come back online; then, simply follow steps 1 through 9 again.

Exam Essentials

Backing up your files and having your data available at all times is extremely important to you in the real world and equally important on the exam. When you take the test, remember the following points.

Know the backup types. You should know the four backup types: full, transaction log, differential, and filegroup, and what they are used for.

Know how to use standby systems. You will need to know how to configure and use a standby server. This is not a complicated process, but you should understand it.

Key Terms and Concepts

Cluster server: This Microsoft product links two servers with a shared hard drive so that, in the event of a failure, one server can take over the functions of the failed system.

Differential backup: This backup records all changes since the last full backup of your database.

Filegroup backup: This backup will back up a single filegroup of a database rather than the whole thing. This is typically used to speed up backups for VLDBs.

Full backup: This backup will back up the entire database.

Transaction log backup: This backup will back up all transactions in the transaction log. It can be used to restore up to a certain point in time and is the only backup type that will clear the transaction log automatically.

Sample Questions

1. When using a standby server, what is the best way to keep the data on the secondary server up to date?

   A. After restoring a full backup to the secondary, perform regular differential backups on the primary and restore them to the secondary.

   B. After restoring a full backup to the secondary, perform regular differential backups on the primary and restore them to the secondary using the STANDBY option.

   C. After restoring a full backup to the secondary, perform regular transaction log backups on the primary and restore them to the secondary.

D. After restoring a full backup to the secondary, perform regular transaction log backups on the primary and restore them to the secondary using the STANDBY option.

Answer: D. You should perform regular transaction log backups on the primary and restore them to the secondary. The STANDBY option is used so that SQL will accept further restorations while still allowing users to access the data as read-only.

2. Your database crashes on Tuesday at 3:00 P.M. Using the following backup schedule, which backups would you have to restore to bring the database back up to date?

- Saturday at 1:00 A.M.; full backup

- Weekdays every two hours starting at 8:00 A.M.; transaction log backups

- Weekdays at 10:00 P.M.; differential backup

   A. Restore Saturday's full backup and all of the available transaction logs from Tuesday.

   B. Restore Saturday's full backup, all of the transaction log backups from Monday, then the Monday differential, and finally the transaction log backups from Tuesday.

   C. Restore Saturday's full backup, the differential from Monday, and the available transaction log backups from Tuesday.

   D. Restore the differential backup from Monday and the available transaction log backups from Tuesday.

Answer: C. If you use differential backups during the week, you need to restore only the full backup, then the differential, and then the transaction log backups that occurred after the differential backup.

Develop a migration plan.

- Plan an upgrade from a previous version of SQL Server.
- Plan the migration of data from other data sources.

You may be one of hundreds, if not thousands, of people who have SQL 6.5 server in place right now, but since you found out what SQL 7 is capable of, you've decided to install this latest version. Can you imagine the chaos if there were no upgrade path? You would need to manually rebuild all of your data—Microsoft would probably not sell many copies of SQL 7 that way. Fortunately, there is not only an upgrade path from older versions of SQL, but there is a migration path from other database applications as well. In this section, you will read about what you need to do to prepare for a successful upgrade or migration to SQL 7.

Critical Information

SQL Server 7 allows you to upgrade databases and entire servers from SQL Server 6 and 6.5 using the Upgrade Wizard, but it does not support upgrades directly from earlier versions (4.21). Since the upgrade process is irreversible, you will need to carefully consider the following questions before you can run the Wizard successfully.

TIP   Because upgrades—especially live, in-place upgrades—have the chance of failing, always do a full backup of your 6.5 server and databases first.

The first question to consider is whether you meet the following upgrade requirements:

- Service Pack 4 for Windows NT

- Internet Explorer 4.01 Service Pack 1

- 32MB of RAM

- 180MB of free hard-drive space (for full installation), plus free space equal to about 1.5 times the size of the databases being upgraded

- If upgrading SQL 6.5, Service Pack 3 (or higher) for SQL 6.5 is required

- If upgrading SQL 6, Service Pack 3 (or higher) for SQL 6 is required

- Named Pipes installed with the default pipe name `Pipe\SQL\Query`

WARNING   If you are upgrading servers involved in replication, you must upgrade the distribution server first, because SQL Server 7 has support for SQL Server 6.x replication tasks. The reverse is not necessarily true.

Once you meet the hardware and software requirements, you can move into the deeper questions.

One-Computer vs. Two-Computer Upgrades

One of the first questions to answer is whether to leave the old SQL Server in place and migrate the data to a new server, or upgrade the original 6.x server to SQL Server 7.

The main advantage of using a second box is that the original server is untouched during the upgrade and can quickly be brought back online if there is a problem with the upgrade. The major disadvantage here is that a second server at least as powerful as the original 6.x server must be purchased or leased.

Upgrading vs. Side-by-Side Installation

If you decide to go with the one-computer upgrade, you have one more decision to make. You can perform a live upgrade by installing SQL 7 in the same folder that 6.*x* occupied, or you can install 7 in a different folder.

The advantage of installing SQL 7 on top of 6.*x* is that the conversion is quick and painless, and all functions and settings of 6.*x* are carried into 7. The disadvantage is that if the upgrade fails for any reason (such as a power interruption), there is no 6.*x* server to go back to.

The advantage of installing 7 in a different folder than 6.*x* is that the SQL 7 installation can be thoroughly tested before converting your databases to the 7 format. Not only that, but you can preserve your old databases, which would allow you to switch between SQL 6.*x* and 7 by running a simple program (Switch to SQL 6.5/Switch to 7). The disadvantage of installing SQL 7 in a new folder is that it will take significantly more hard-drive space (because you have two copies of each database) and requires manually converting your databases and settings.

Migrating from Other Data Sources

The Upgrade Wizard will not handle an upgrade from any other vendor's database system. This means that if you are running Oracle, Sybase, or even Access, you will need to migrate the data using other tools provided by SQL. Those tools are discussed in detail in Chapter 4.

Exam Essentials

This section will not be heavily tested, but there is a good point to bear in mind as you take the exam.

Know the types of upgrades. You should know the advantages and disadvantages of side-by-side installation and whether to use one computer or two in upgrading.

Key Terms and Concepts

SQL Switch: This is a program that will allow you to switch between SQL 6.5 and 7 if you have installed them in separate directories.

Sample Questions

1. If you decide that you need to revert to SQL 6.5 from 7 after performing a live upgrade, what is the best way to do this?

    A. Run the Upgrade Wizard and instruct it to revert to SQL 6.5.

    B. Run the SQL Switch program.

    C. Uninstall SQL 7 and reinstall SQL 6.5, then restore all databases from backups.

    D. There is no way to revert after a live upgrade.

    Answer: C. While there is no way to downgrade a database after it has been upgraded, there is a way to revert to SQL 6.5—it is just time consuming.

2. True or false. The Upgrade Wizard is the best tool for upgrading from Access to SQL Server 7.

    A. True

    B. False

    Answer: B. The Upgrade Wizard will only upgrade SQL 6.*x* to SQL 7; other products must be migrated using the tools discussed in Chapter 4.

Develop a replication strategy.

- Given a scenario, design the appropriate replication model. Replication models include single Publisher and multiple Subscribers; multiple Publishers and single Subscriber; multiple Publishers and multiple Subscribers; and remote Distributor.

- Choose the replication type. Replication types include snapshot, transactional, and merge.

If you have a very popular database, perhaps a catalog database used by all your sales people, do you want them all to access the data from a single server? In a small organization, that may work fine, but if you have hundreds or thousands of users spread out across a wide area, that single server will become a bottleneck that will bring your server to its knees. With replication, you can make copies of the data on remote servers so that all of your users can access the data they need locally, without going over a WAN link to your server.

In this final section, the fine points of replication will be examined. The proper model to use for a given scenario as well as which replication type would be best will be discussed. The concepts you are about to read about will be tested heavily and will save you from endless support calls when you have too many users for one server, so pay close attention.

Critical Information

You use replication to put copies of the same data at different locations throughout the enterprise. The most common of the many reasons you might want to replicate your data include:

- Moving data closer to the user

- Reducing locking conflicts when multiple sites wish to work with the same data

- Allowing site autonomy so that each location can set up its own rules and procedures for working with its copy of the data

- Removing the impact of read-intensive operations such as report generation and ad-hoc query processing from the OLTP database

To describe and implement replication, SQL Server 7 uses a Publisher/Subscriber metaphor. Your server can play different roles as part of the replication scenario: It can be a Publisher, Subscriber, Distributor, or any combination of these. The data that are replicated are published in the form of an article, which is stored in a publication. These publications can be pushed to Subscribers, meaning that the subscription is initiated at the Publisher, or pulled, meaning that the subscription is initiated at the Subscriber.

NOTE One of the major differences between push and pull subscriptions is that with push subscriptions, the replication agent runs on the distribution server; with pull subscriptions, it runs on the Subscriber. There will be more discussion of the agents in Chapter 4.

Here is a list of key terms used as part of the Publisher/Subscriber metaphor:

Publisher: This is the source database where replication begins. The Publisher makes data available for replication.

Subscriber: The Subscriber is the destination database where replication ends and either receives a snapshot of all the published data or applies transactions that have been replicated to it.

Distributor: This is the intermediary between the Publisher and Subscriber. The Distributor receives published transactions or snapshots, and then stores and forwards these publications to the Subscribers.

Publication: The publication is the storage container for different articles. A Subscriber can subscribe to an individual article or an entire publication. If they subscribe to an individual article, they are actually subscribing to the whole publication, but just reading one article.

Article: An article is the data, transactions, or stored procedures that are stored within a publication. This is the actual information that is going to be replicated. Articles can be partitioned vertically, in which only a subset of columns is replicated; horizontally, in which a subset of records is replicated; or a combination of both.

Two-phase commit: Two-phase commit (sometimes referred to as *2PC*) is a form of replication in which modifications made to the Publishing database are made at the Subscription database at exactly the same time. This is handled through the use of distributed transactions. As with any transaction, either all statements commit successfully or all modifications are rolled back. To accomplish this task, two-phase commit uses the Microsoft Distributed Transaction Coordinator (MS-DTC), which implements a portion of the functionality of the Microsoft Transaction Server. In this chapter, the focus will be on replication as opposed to two-phase commits.

NOTE   A Publisher can publish data to one or more Distributors. A Subscriber can subscribe through one or more Distributors. A Distributor can have one or more Publishers and Subscribers.

Now that you have the lingo down, you are ready to look into the various replication models. There are four of them to consider here.

Single Publisher with Multiple Subscribers

As shown in Figure 1.4, both the Publishing database and the Distribution database are on the same SQL Server. This configuration is useful when modeling replication strategies for the following business scenarios:

- Asynchronous order processing during communication outages

- Distribution of price lists, customer lists, vendor lists, etc.

- Removal of MIS activities from the Online Transaction Processing (OLTP) environment

- Establishment of executive information systems

The main advantage of this model is the ability to move data to a separate SQL Server, thus allowing the publishing server to continue to handle online transaction-processing duties without having to absorb the impact of the ad-hoc queries generally found in MIS departments.

You can use any type of replication here—transactional, merge, or snapshot. If you do not have to update things such as text, ntext, and image data types, it is suggested that you use transactional replication here. MIS departments generally don't need to make changes to the subscribed data.

FIGURE 1.4: Single Publisher with multiple Subscribers

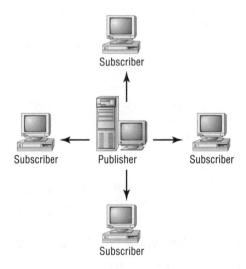

NOTE You can further reduce the impact of replication on your OLTP server by implementing pull subscriptions. This would force the distribution agent to run on each Subscriber rather than on the OLTP distribution server.

Multiple Publishers with a Single Subscriber

The model shown in Figure 1.5 is very useful in the following situations:

- Roll-up reporting
- Local warehouse inventory management
- Local customer order processing

FIGURE 1.5: Multiple Publishers with a single Subscriber

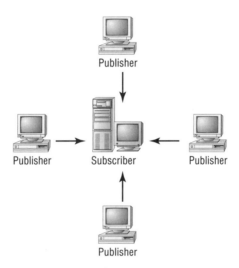

You need to keep several things in mind when you attempt to use this model. Because multiple Publishers are writing to a single table in the database, you must take some precautions to ensure that referential integrity is maintained. If your New York office sends an order with a key of 1000, and your Milwaukee office also sends an order with a key of 1000, you would have two records with the same primary key. You could get bad data in your database, because the primary key is designed to guarantee the uniqueness of each record. In this situation, only one of those records would post.

To make sure that this doesn't become a problem, implement a composite primary key, using the original order ID number along with a location-specific code. You could, for example, give the New York branch a location code of NY and the Milwaukee branch a location code of MW. This way, the new composite keys would be NY1000 and MW1000. There would be no more conflicting records, and both orders would be filled from the Denver offices.

This scenario is especially suited to transactional replication, because the data at the Denver site is really read-only. Snapshot replication wouldn't work here, because that would overwrite everyone else's data. You could use merge replication if the other locations needed to be able to see all the orders placed.

Multiple Publishers with Multiple Subscribers

This model is used when a single table needs to be maintained on multiple servers. Each server subscribes to the table and also publishes the table to other servers. This model can be particularly useful in the following business situations:

- Reservations systems

- Regional order-processing systems

- Multiple warehouse implementations

To illustrate this model, think of a regional order-processing system as shown in Figure 1.6. Suppose you place an order on Monday and want to check on that order on Tuesday. When you call up, you may be routed to any of several regional order-processing centers, which is just fine, because with this model, each of these centers should have a copy of your order.

It is probably best to use transactional replication for this scenario, using some type of region code (as described in the previous scenario). Each order-processing center should publish only its own data, but it should subscribe to data being published by the other Publishers. In addition, each location should update only the data it owns. This scenario is also a good candidate for transactional replication with an updating Subscriber. In this case, each center could update data owned by another center; however, this update would take place at both servers and therefore maintain transactional consistency.

FIGURE 1.6: Multiple Publishers with multiple Subscribers

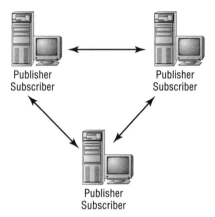

Using a Remote Distributor

In this model, you remove the impact of the distribution process from your OLTP server, which gives you the best possible speed on the OLTP server. This model is useful in situations where you need the optimal performance out of your OLTP server. As discussed earlier, a single distribution server can work with multiple Distributors and multiple Subscribers. Figure 1.7 shows a representation of this strategy.

This calls for transactional replication and minimizing the impact of replication on the Publishing database. By moving just transactions, rather than moving snapshots or attempting to merge data at the Publisher, you can gain the most speed and have the lowest impact on the Publisher.

Heterogeneous Replication

In addition to the replication scenarios just discussed, it is possible to replicate data to non-Microsoft SQL Server databases. This is known as *heterogeneous database replication.* Currently, SQL Server supports replication to MS Access, Oracle, and IBM databases that conform to the IBM DRDA (Distributed Relational Database Architecture)

F I G U R E 1.7: Central Publisher with a remote Distributor

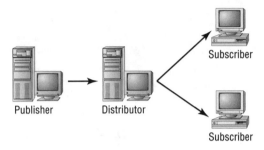

data protocol. To replicate to an ODBC data source, the Subscriber must meet the following ODBC driver requirements:

- It must run in 32-bit mode.
- It must be thread-safe.
- It must allow updates.
- It must support the T-SQL DDL (Data Definition Language).
- It must fully support the ODBC Level 1 Conformance standard.

When you publish to these ODBC Subscribers, you need to keep the following rules in mind:

- Only push subscriptions are supported.
- ODBC does not support batched statements.
- The ODBC DSN (Data Source Name) must conform to the SQL Server naming conventions.
- Snapshot data will be sent using bulk copy's character format.
- Data types will be mapped as closely as possible.

Internet Replication

You can even configure your SQL Server to publish to the Internet. If you do, you must make some additional configuration changes to your SQL Server 7 computer. For either a push or pull style of replication, the following items must be configured:

- TCP/IP must be installed on the computers where the merge agent and distribution agents are running.

- The publishing server and the distribution server should be on the same side of the firewall.

- The publishing server and the distribution server should have a direct network connection to each other (rather than a connection across the Internet). This is for both security and latency concerns.

Some additional configuration changes need to be made if you are going to allow pull subscriptions:

- Microsoft's IIS must be installed on the same server as your distribution server.

- Both the merge and distribution agents must be configured with the correct FTP address. This is done through the distribution agent or from a command prompt.

- The working folder must be available to your subscription servers.

- The FTP home folder on your IIS computer should be set to the distribution working folder. This is normally *ServerName*\C$\ MSSQL7\ReplData.

Distribution Types

Now that you have the models down, you are almost ready to choose a type; the two basic types are replication or distributed transactions. The main difference between the two types is in the timing. With distributed transactions, your data are 100 percent in synchronization, 100 percent of the time. When you use replication, there is some latency involved. It may be as little as a few seconds, or as long as several days or even weeks. Distributed transactions require that the replicated databases be connected at all times or they will fail, whereas replication is unaffected by this condition.

Before you choose a type, though, you should understand the factors that influence your decision. The three main items to consider are autonomy, latency, and transactional consistency:

Autonomy: This refers to how much independence you wish to give each Subscriber with regard to the replicated data. Will the replicated data be considered read-only? How long will the data at a Subscriber be valid? How often do you need to connect to the Distributor to download more data?

Latency: This refers to how often your data will be updated. Do they need to be in synchronization at all times? Is every minute enough? What if you are a salesperson on the road who dials in to the office once a day? Is this good enough?

Transactional consistency: Although there are several types of replication, the most common method is to move transactions from the Publisher through the Distributor and onto the Subscriber. Transactional consistency comes into play here. Do all the transactions that are stored need to be applied at the same time and in order? What happens if there is a delay in the processing?

Once you understand these factors, there are a few more questions to answer before you can choose a distribution type:

- What are you going to publish? Will it be all the data in a table, or will you partition information?

- Who has access to your publications? Are these Subscribers connected, or are they dial-up users?

- Will Subscribers be able to update your data, or is their information considered read-only?

- How often should you synchronize your Publishers and Subscribers?

- How fast is your network? Can Subscribers be connected at all times? How much traffic is there on your network?

When you factor in latency, autonomy, and consistency, you actually end up with six different distribution types:

- Distributed transactions

- Transactional replication
- Transactional replication with updating subscribers
- Snapshot replication
- Snapshot replication with updating subscribers
- Merge replication

Distributed transactions have the least amount of latency and autonomy, but they have the highest level of consistency. Merge replication has the highest amount of latency and autonomy, and a lower level of consistency.

Using Distributed Transactions

When you use distributed transactions or 2PC to replicate your data, you have almost no autonomy or latency, but you do have guaranteed transactional consistency. With 2PC, either all changes are made at exactly the same time or none of the changes are made. Remember that all the affected subscribers must be in contact with the Publisher at all times.

This type of distribution is most useful in situations where Subscribers must have real-time data, as in a reservations system.

For example, think of a cruise line that has only so many rooms of a particular type available. If someone in Dallas wants the Captain's Suite and someone in California also wants the Captain's Suite, the first one to book the room will get it. The other booking won't be allowed, because that location will immediately show up as already booked.

Using Transactional Replication

When you use this distribution method, transactions are gathered from the Publishers and stored in the Distribution database. Subscribers then receive these transactions and must work with the data as if they were read-only. This is because any changes made to their local copy of the data might not allow newly downloaded transactions to be applied properly, which would destroy the transactional consistency.

The advantages to this approach include the fact that transactions are relatively small items to move through the system (unlike snapshot replication, which will be looked at shortly). The main disadvantage of using transactional replication is that Subscribers must treat the data as read-only.

Use this distribution method when Subscribers can treat their data as read-only and need the updated information with a minimal amount of latency, such as in an order-processing/distribution system with several locations where orders are taken. Each of those order locations would be a Publisher, and the published orders could then be replicated to a Subscription database at your central warehouse. The central warehouse could then accept the orders, fill them, and ship them out.

Using Transactional Replication with Updating Subscribers

This will probably become the most popular form of replication in SQL Server 7. When you use transactional replication with updating Subscribers, you are gaining site autonomy, minimizing latency, and keeping transactional consistency. This (in most cases) would be considered the best possible solution.

When you implement transactional replication with updating Subscribers, you are essentially working with all the tenets of transactional replication. The major difference is that when you change the subscription data, 2PC changes the Publishing database as well. In this fashion, your local Subscriber is updated at exactly the same time as the Publisher. Other Subscribers will have your changes downloaded to them at their next synchronization.

This scenario can be useful for a reservations system that needs to be updated frequently, but does not need total synchronization. Let's use a library as an example here. You wish to reserve a book on SQL Server 7. You go to the computer, look up the book you wish to reserve, and find that one copy is currently available. When you try to reserve the book, however, you might find that your data aren't 100 percent up to date and the book has already been checked out. In this example, when you try to reserve your book, the Subscriber automatically runs a 2PC to the Publisher. At the Publisher, someone has already checked out that last copy, and therefore the update fails. At the next synchronization, your Subscriber will be updated with the news that the last copy has been checked out.

Using Snapshot Replication

When you use snapshot replication as your distribution method, you are actually moving an entire copy of the published items through the Distributor and on to the Subscribers. This type of replication allows for a high level of both site autonomy and transactional consistency because all records are going to be copied from the Publisher, and the local copy of the data will be overwritten at the next synchronization. Latency may be a bit higher because you probably will not move an entire snapshot every few minutes.

OLAP (Online Analytical Processing) servers are prime candidates for this type of replication. The data at each Subscriber are considered read-only and don't have to be 100 percent in synchronization all the time. This allows your MIS departments to run their reporting and ad-hoc queries on reasonably fresh data without affecting the OLTP server (which is doing all of the order-processing work).

Keep in mind that administrators and MIS ad-hoc queries generally don't modify the data. They are looking for historical information, such as how many widgets they sold, etc., so that data that are a few hours or even a few days old will generally not make a difference to the results returned by the queries.

Using Snapshot Replication with Updating Subscribers

The initial portion of this distribution style works just as in snapshot replication, with the added ability for the Subscriber to update the Publisher with new information. The updates use the 2PC protocol as described above.

This maintains a high level of site autonomy, a high level of transactional consistency, and a moderate level of latency. The data may be downloaded to the Subscriber only once a day, but any updates the Subscriber tries to make to data must first be approved by the Publisher.

This type of distribution is useful when you have read-only data that need to be updated infrequently. If your data need to be updated often, it is suggested that you use transactional replication with updating Subscribers.

Snapshot replication might be useful when auditing your database, downloading portions of the data, and double-checking that everything is being updated properly. The occasional mistake could then be quickly fixed and auditing could continue.

Using Merge Replication

Merge replication provides the highest amount of site autonomy, the highest latency, and the lowest level of transactional consistency. Merge replication allows each Subscriber to make changes to their local copy of the data. At some point, these changes are merged with those made by other Subscribers as well as changes made at the Publisher. Ultimately, all sites receive the updates from all other sites. This is known as *convergence*. That is, all changes from all sites converge and are redistributed so that all sites have the same changes.

Transactional consistency is nearly nonexistent here, because different sites may all be making changes to the same data, resulting in conflicts. SQL Server 7 will automatically choose a particular change over another change and then converge those data. To simplify: Sooner or later, all sites will have the same copy of the data, but those data may not necessarily be what you wanted.

For example, Subscriber A makes changes to record 100. Subscriber B also makes changes to record 100. While this doesn't sound too bad, suppose the changes that Subscriber A made to record 100 are due to changes that were made to record 50. If Subscriber B doesn't have the same data in record 50, Subscriber B will make a different decision. Obviously, this can be incredibly complex.

You might wonder why anyone would want to use merge replication. There are, however, many reasons to use it, and with some careful planning, you can make merge replication work to your advantage. There are triggers you can modify to determine which record is the correct record to use. The default rule when records are changed at multiple sites is to take the changes based on a site priority. Converge the results and then send them out. The exception to this general rule is when the main database is changed as well as all of the user databases. In this case, the user changes are applied first and then the main database changes.

For example, say you have a central server that you call Main and 20 salespeople who are using merge replication. If one of your salespeople modifies record 25 and you modify record 25 at the Main server, when the records are converged, the user changes will first be placed in the Main server, and then the Main server changes will overwrite them.

If you design your Publishers and Subscribers to minimize conflicts, merge replication can be very advantageous. Look at the highway patrol, for example. A patrol car might pull over a car and write up a ticket for speeding. At the end of the day, that piece of data is merged with data from other officers who have also written tickets. The data are then converged back to all of the different squad-car computers. It is unlikely that the same individual will be stopped by two different police officers on the same day. If it does happen, however, the situation can be remedied using either the default conflict-resolution triggers or custom triggers that the police departments can create themselves.

Exam Essentials

Replication will be tested on quite a bit since Microsoft wants to be sure that you are capable of administering both large and small networks. The following points will help you with the replication sections of the exam.

Know the Publisher/Subscriber metaphor. Publishers contain the original copy of the data where changes are made. Subscribers receive copies of the data from the Publishers. The data are disseminated through the Distributor.

Know the types of replication. While the types of replication can be used in different ways, there are basically three types: snapshot, transactional, and merge. You should be familiar with all three.

Know the models. You also need to be familiar with the various models; that is, who publishes, who subscribes, and who distributes.

Key Terms and Concepts

Article: The smallest unit in replication; this can be a full table or a subset of a table.

Distributor: All of the changes made on a published database are stored at the Distributor and then disseminated to all of the Subscribers.

Horizontal partitioning: This is publishing only a subset of records from a table.

Merge replication: With this type of replication, all servers publish and subscribe to the same article, and all users can make changes.

Publication: This is a group of articles. A publication cannot span databases.

Publisher: This contains the original copy of the data to be replicated.

Snapshot replication: This type of replication copies the entire database to its Subscribers.

Subscriber: This server receives a copy of the data from a Publisher.

Transactional replication: This type of replication copies transactions from the Publisher to the Subscriber as opposed to the full database.

Vertical partitioning: This is publishing only a subset of columns from a table.

Sample Questions

1. You work for a large company that has regional offices all over the U.S. and corporate headquarters in New York. You want to know the inventory status of each of the regional offices at the end of the day. Which is the best model to use?

   A. Single Publisher with multiple Subscribers

   B. Multiple Publishers with single Subscriber

   C. Multiple Publishers with multiple Subscribers

   Answer: B. The headquarters in New York should subscribe to the inventory databases that are published from each of the regional offices.

2. Which of the following types of replication makes a complete replicate of the published data on the Subscriber?

   A. Merge

   B. Transactional

   C. Copy

   D. Snapshot

   Answer: D. Snapshot is the only type that copies the full database every time. Incidentally, copy is not a type of replication.

CHAPTER

2

Installation and Configuration

Microsoft Exam Objectives Covered in This Chapter:

Install SQL Server 7. *(pages 59 – 73)*

- Choose the character set.
- Choose the Unicode collation.
- Choose the appropriate sort order.
- Install Net-Libraries and protocols.
- Install services.
- Install and configure a SQL Server client.
- Perform an unattended installation.
- Upgrade from a SQL Server 6.*x* database.

Configure SQL Server. *(pages 73 – 79)*

- Configure SQL Mail.
- Configure default American National Standards Institute (ANSI) settings.

Implement full-text searching. *(pages 80 – 85)*

N ow that you have a plan for implementing SQL Server, you're ready to start the installation process—but be careful. More often than not, we click the Next key every time we see it and accept the default settings for our software, which can prove hazardous to SQL Server. Many options in setup will need your attention if you want SQL Server to function properly when you're done; in fact, if you misconfigure some of these options, you will need to reinstall SQL Server to make corrections.

Just to be sure you don't fall into that trap, each and every screen in the setup program and the various options on those screens will be analyzed. Pay close attention to those options—since Microsoft wants to be sure that SQL Server DBAs are capable of installing the software that they will be administering, these options can affect your performance on the exam as well as the performance of your server.

Afterward, some important post-installation configuration options will be discussed. While there are not nearly as many options to configure here as there were with previous versions of SQL, you still need to pay attention to them. Specifically, you will configure SQL to e-mail and page someone when there is a problem by setting up SQL Mail. Then, you will learn how to configure the options that make SQL ANSI-compliant. Finally, you will read about a topic that not only proves useful in your networks, but that you also get pounded with on the test—the fine points of implementing full-text search.

▶ Install SQL Server 7.

- Choose the character set.
- Choose the Unicode collation.
- Choose the appropriate sort order.
- Install Net-Libraries and protocols.
- Install services.
- Install and configure a SQL Server client.
- Perform an unattended installation.
- Upgrade from a SQL Server 6.*x* database.

To use SQL, or any other product, you need to install it first. As with any other installation program, there are options to consider: Where will the files be stored, what options will be installed, etc. With SQL, these options become very important because if they are mis-configured, SQL may not function properly—it may just be slow, or it may not work the way you want it to at all. So, pay close attention to each screen, and each option on each screen—not only for the sake of your server, but for the sake of your exam score, since these options will be tested.

Critical Information

While the installation process is relatively painless, once your decisions are implemented, they can be difficult to change. Therefore, it is a good idea to carefully consider each of the options in the setup program, rather than just clicking the Next button. The first option you will need to know for the exam is the character set.

Choosing a Character Set

A *character set* defines how SQL sees the characters you type in. The first 128 characters in the set are defined by the first 7 bits of the byte used to store them—by using the 8th bit of that byte, you get 128 extended characters for a total of 256 characters in a set. The most important thing to remember here is that SQL supports only one character set at a time, and, once installed, that character set cannot be changed. To help overcome this limitation, SQL supports Unicode characters (as you will soon see).

It is crucial to pick a character set that will be recognized by the applications installed on the SQL Server. For instance, if an application wishes to store the character $1/2$, it will be able to do so only if certain character sets have been selected.

SQL Server supports the following character sets:

1252 (ISO 8859, ANSI): This is the default character set for SQL Server 6.*x* and 7, and should be chosen when you are using Windows clients exclusively.

850 (multilingual): This is the old default character set and is still in use in many databases, especially those upgraded from earlier versions of SQL Server. This would be a good choice for multinational companies.

437 (U.S. English): Although this is a popular character set because it contains support for graphic characters not normally supported by databases, its compatibility with other languages is limited.

Selecting Unicode Collation

SQL Server 7 supports Unicode character types. Unicode characters are represented by 2 bytes (rather than a single byte), allowing 65,536 possible characters for a given field instead of the 256 allowed by a code page. In plain English, this means that Unicode makes it possible to store characters from multiple languages on one computer. The Unicode sort order is used to sort those Unicode data so that they are organized and neat.

The sort order for Unicode data, the default Unicode collation, is case-insensitive, width-insensitive, and Kana (Japanese)-insensitive. Use the default selection unless you have been specifically instructed to change it. If you need to support multiple languages, but have to use the 850 or 437 character sets, you can choose the Unicode data type when you create your columns.

Choosing the Right Sort Order

The *sort order* determines how data are stored, compared, and returned during queries. The available sort-order selections will be determined by the character set chosen. The main sort orders include the following:

Dictionary sort order, case-insensitive: This is the default sort order and treats upper- and lowercase characters the same for comparison purposes. This can improve performance since SQL does not have to differentiate between upper- and lowercase characters when storing, retrieving, and indexing data.

Dictionary sort order, case-sensitive: This sort order retains and enforces all cases in the database when using SQL Server. This means that McDonald (with an uppercase D) and Mcdonald (with a lowercase d) are entirely different words in this sort order. Since SQL has to take the time to differentiate the characters, this sort order slows performance.

Binary sort order: The fastest and simplest sort order, binary sort order sorts everything by the binary representation of the data, not as a dictionary would sort characters.

TIP If you choose a case-sensitive sort order, all SQL passwords are case-sensitive. If you choose a case-insensitive sort order, passwords (and all other key words) are also case-insensitive.

Installing Network Libraries and Protocols

SQL Server doesn't automatically support every protocol that is installed on the computer—SQL has to be told that the protocols are there and how to use them. That is why you need to install Net-Libraries. SQL Server supports the following protocols and standards:

TCP/IP: Support for this industry-standard protocol is enabled by default using TCP port 1433. Since SQL relies on the operating system for TCP/IP configuration settings, such as address and subnet mask, connections to the SQL Server that do not function properly may be caused by TCP/IP configuration problems and not by SQL Server.

IPX/SPX: Support for this protocol, used by NetWare servers and clients, is not enabled by default. Installing IPX/SPX on the SQL Server allows NetWare clients to connect to the SQL Server even if they don't have a Microsoft client installed. If you enable support for IPX/SPX, you can also configure the name of the server that NetWare clients will see. Both NetWare and Microsoft clients should use the same server name to avoid confusion.

Named Pipes: Support for this networking standard is enabled by default. Named Pipes is a common method for connecting to a resource over a network. Note that Microsoft's NetBEUI, TCP/IP, and NWLINK (IPX/SPX) support the Named Pipes specification natively.

Multi-Protocol: Support for this standard is enabled by default. Multi-Protocol support allows clients to connect via two or more methods, allowing encryption across TCP/IP and IPX/SPX.

AppleTalk: Support for this protocol is not enabled by default. AppleTalk is used by Macintosh clients.

DecNet: Support for this protocol is not enabled by default. DecNet is used by some older Digital clients.

Installing the SQL Server Services

When you set up the full version of SQL, three separate services are installed: MSSQLSERVER, SQLAGENT, and MS-DTC. With the desktop version, you will not get MS-DTC. You can install a fourth service separately—MSSearch—which provides full-text indexes for SQL Server 7. Here is what these services do:

MSSQLSERVER: This is the actual database engine and is required for any computer you wish to be a SQL Server. To check whether the service has been installed, go to Control Panel ➤ Services and look for it by name.

SQLAGENT: SQLAGENT is a helper service designed to take care of the automation performed in SQL Server. Although this service is not technically required, you should not run without it. You can check on its installation by going to Control Panel ➤ Services.

MS-DTC: The MS-DTC (Database Transaction Coordinator) service is an optional service designed to take care of transactions that span multiple SQL Servers. When a transaction is performed across two or more servers, the MS-DTC service ensures that the transaction is performed on all servers; otherwise, the transaction is rolled back.

MSSearch: When you install full-text index support, you install the MSSearch service, which will allow you to perform English queries. It is basically the same service supported by Microsoft's Index Server engine.

Installing SQL Clients

When Microsoft speaks of a software client, they mean one of two things: ODBC or DB-Library and OLE-DB connections. Most of the applications you use to create custom front ends, such as Office 95/97 and IIS, install ODBC drivers for SQL Server. If client computers already have ODBC and SQL drivers installed, all you will need to do is configure the ODBC connections via the ODBC Data Sources applet of the Control Panel. Once inside the ODBC applet, you generally add one of two types of configurations:

- User DSN is usable only by the user who created it.

- System DSN is usable by any user and application contained on the computer.

When you install a SQL client (not ODBC), you can install just the client piece (which lets the client connect to SQL Server), or you can install the SQL Server management tools (Enterprise Manager, Query Analyzer, etc.). To install the Client Connectivity software and/or the management tools, choose a Custom installation and leave only the management tools selected.

Performing Unattended Installations

SQL Server can be installed without prompts by using various batch files and initialization files that are contained on the CD-ROM, as shown in Table 2.1.

T A B L E 2.1: Sample Batch and Initialization Files for SQL Server 7

Batch File	Initialization File	Action
Sql70cli.bat	Sql70cli.iss	Installs SQL Server administration tools
Sql70ins.bat	Sql70ins.iss	Installs a typical version of SQL Server
Sql70cst.bat	Sql70cst.iss	Performs a custom installation, which can be used to install all components
Sql70rem.bat		Uninstalls SQL Server

You can edit the sample initialization files to fit your site, or you can edit the initialization file that is created during an installation (stored as setup.iss in the \MSSQL7\install folder).

You can also run the SQL setup program as follows:

```
Setupsql.exe k=Rc
```

This will generate the script file in the \Windows or \Winnt folder. Choose Cancel when prompted to copy files, or a full installation will take place.

Upgrading from a SQL 6.x Database

Databases can be upgraded using the Upgrade Wizard. SQL Server 6 and 6.5 databases can be directly upgraded to SQL Server 7, while any SQL 4.21 databases must first be upgraded to SQL 6.x before you can upgrade them to SQL 7.

NOTE   SQL Server 7 cannot load backups made from earlier versions of SQL Server. It must be able to read the live database to create a converted copy of it.

When upgrading SQL Servers and databases, you may run into problems, such as when objects in the old databases cannot be created in the new database. This happens when:

- The object has been renamed with the sp_rename stored procedure.

- The accompanying text in syscomments is missing.

- Stored procedures have been created within other stored procedures.

- The owner of an object's login ID is not created at the new server.

- The older server was using integrated security, but the new server is using mixed security, and the NT groups have not been created at the new server.

Other issues that you may encounter when upgrading servers and databases include the following:

- The upgrade process will fail if @@Servername returns NULL.

- Stored procedures that reference or modify system tables will not be converted.

Servers involved with replication should be upgraded in a certain order: The distribution server must be upgraded first. Many SQL 7 replication functions will not be enabled until all involved servers are upgraded.

WARNING You may opt to have the Upgrade Wizard delete old SQL 6.*x* devices and databases. If you do, all devices and databases will be deleted whether or not they were upgraded. For this reason, if you have the Wizard delete old databases, you should upgrade all user databases at the same time.

Necessary Procedures

The most important procedure in this chapter is the actual setup of SQL Server. In this section, each screen in the setup program and the available options will be examined. There is no need to memorize each and every option on each and every screen, but you should have a general familiarity with the setup program. The most important thing is knowing what will happen if any of these options are mis-configured—for example, if the sort order is set improperly.

Installing SQL Server 7

To successfully install SQL Server 7, use the following steps:

1. In User Manager, create the account that will be used as the service account.

2. Run the setup program from the SQL Server 7 CD-ROM.

3. Install the prerequisites (Windows NT SP4 and IE 4.01 SP1 if not already installed) by choosing the appropriate operating system from the main setup screen. Reboot after installing all prerequisites and rerun the setup program.

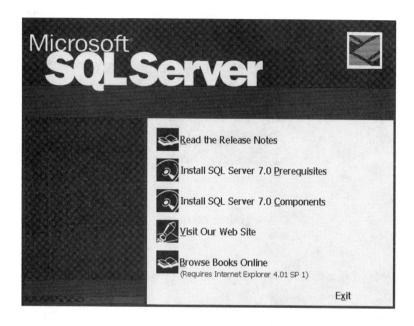

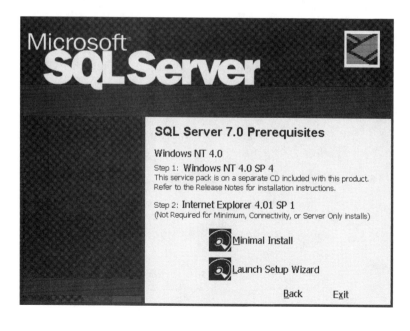

4. Select the appropriate version of SQL Server to install. Choose Desktop if on a workstation or Standard (full) if on a server. Choose Next.

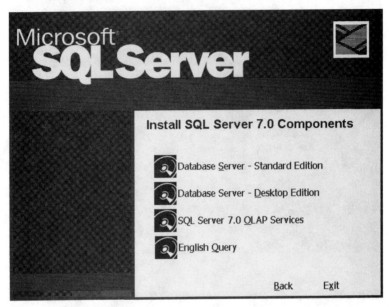

5. Select Local installation if you are running the setup program on the computer you wish to become the SQL Server; otherwise, choose Remote and supply the name of the remote server. Choose Next.

6. Select Next at the Introduction screen.

7. Select the appropriate license information, enter your CD key, and select OK.

8. Enter your name and company name, then select Next.

9. At the Upgrade Wizard prompt, inform SQL whether or not to perform an upgrade (you can upgrade later via the Upgrade Wizard). Select Next.

10. Select an installation type. Select Next to continue.

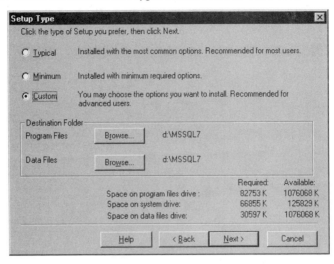

11. If you selected Custom, then select the Server Components, Management Tools, Client Connectivity, and Books Online checkboxes. Select Next to continue.

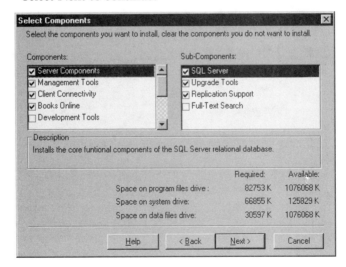

12. Select the Sort Order, Character Set, Unicode Support, and Installation folders (note that it may be best to leave the default settings). Select Next to continue.

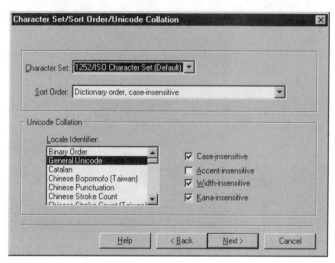

13. Select the network support to install. Note that Named Pipes, TCP/IP, and Multi-Protocol Net-Libraries are already selected. Select Next to continue.

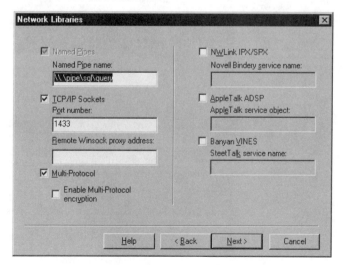

14. Select the service account created in step 1 for the SQL services to use. Select Next to continue.

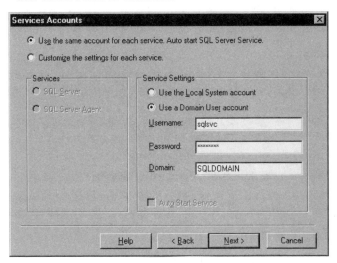

15. Click Next to go to the Licensing screen.

16. Enter your appropriate licensing information. Choose Continue, check the Agree box, and choose OK.

17. Review and adjust the installation settings as needed, then click Next to start the installation. The installation will take several minutes.

18. Choose OK when prompted that the installation has finished.

Exam Essentials

You probably noticed that there is a lot of information in this section. While it is all valuable, there are a few specific areas that you should be sure to understand before going into the exam. You need to know the implications of the wrong sort order and character sets, how to perform an unattended installation, and how to upgrade your databases.

Know the implications of using the wrong sort order or character set. If you want to change the sort order or character set after you have installed SQL, you will need to reinstall. This is because SQL will need to rebuild all of the databases including Master, Model, and MSDB.

Know the files for performing an unattended installation. You need to know the files required to perform an unattended installation and how to get them, either from the CD or from the setup program.

Know the issues involved in upgrading databases. It is a good idea to be familiar with the problems that can occur during an upgrade, since you will get hit with questions on them.

Key Terms and Concepts

Character set: This defines how SQL sees the characters stored in your databases.

Net-Library: Net-Libraries define how SQL will use the underlying network protocols.

Setup script: Setup scripts are used in unattended installations to supply configuration values.

Sort order: This defines whether SQL treats characters as case-sensitive, and whether they are sorted as binary values rather than character values.

Unicode: Like a character set, this defines how SQL sees your characters—the difference is that Unicode understands 65,536 characters as opposed to the character set's 256 characters.

Sample Questions

1. Your company is based in New York with branches in Singapore, Paris, and Taiwan. All of these branches will need access to data

stored on your server in their own language. How can you accomplish this?

A. You can't.

B. Choose a different sort order for each database.

C. Choose the desired character set when you create the database.

D. Choose the default Unicode character set, which allows different character sets in each database.

Answer: D. Unicode makes it possible to store data from more than one language, no matter what character set is used.

2. You want to create a file for use in future unattended installations. How can you accomplish this using the setup program?

A. `Setupsql.exe k=Rc`

B. `Setupsql.exe Rc=k`

C. `Setupsql.exe k=setup.iss`

D. `Setupsql.exe Rc=setup.iss`

Answer: A. Running the setup program with the `k=Rc` option will create a script file for future use.

Configure SQL Server.

- Configure SQL Mail.
- Configure default American National Standards Institute (ANSI) settings.

Thankfully, the terrors of SQL 6.5 have been vanquished. Gone are the days when you had to configure memory settings, user connections, and procedure cache just to get your system to function. These days, while you may need to configure some of those options, you are *required* to perform only some minor configurations.

One of the things you need to configure is SQL Mail so that SQL can send you an e-mail or a page if something goes wrong. You also need to be familiar with the ANSI settings—while they are not tested as much as SQL Mail, you need to be sure that SQL's ANSI compliance is set to your liking.

Critical Information

For the most part, SQL is self tuning. You may need to change memory settings or user connections, but it is not required. In fact, changing even the ANSI-setting defaults is not required (just highly recommended). One thing that does require your attention to work, however, is SQL Mail.

SQL Mail

Without SQL Mail, your server will be able to alert you of problems via only a net-send message that pops up on your computer screen—which is great, unless you are not in front of your screen. When you're not in front of your screen, you need an e-mail or a page, which is what SQL Mail is for. The main issues involved with SQL Mail are as follows:

- You must have a MAPI-compliant mail server (i.e., MS Exchange Server).

- You need to install Outlook on the SQL Server.

- If you want to be paged, you will need an alphanumeric pager that is capable of receiving pages via SMTP (Internet) mail.

ANSI Settings

SQL Server complies with the American National Standards Institute (ANSI) SQL-92 specifications. Because of this, you need to be aware of some options that will affect the ANSI-specific settings:

ANSI NULL default: This setting specifies whether new columns that are created have a default value of NULL. The default is NOT NULL.

ANSI NULL: When this is set to True, all comparisons with a NULL value will return a result of NULL (unknown). If it is set to False (the default), any non-Unicode comparisons against a NULL value will return True if the value is NULL (compare NULL to NULL) or False if the value is anything else (compare "Bob" to NULL).

ANSI warnings: If this is set to True, errors or warnings are issued when divide-by-zero errors occur or NULL values appear in aggregate functions. If this is set to False (the default), errors or warnings are not generated for these events.

Necessary Procedures

If you want to know when there is a problem, you will need to configure SQL Mail to send you e-mail or page you over the Internet. You will also need to understand how to configure the various ANSI options.

NOTE   These procedures are placed in the order in which they are listed in the Microsoft exam objectives list—it does not matter in which order you configure them in real life. If you want to set up ANSI first, then SQL Mail, feel free to do so.

Configuring SQL Mail

To get SQL Mail up and running, use the following steps:

1. Ensure the availability of a MAPI-compliant server, such as MS Exchange Server.

2. Create a mailbox for the SQL service account on the mail server.

3. Install Microsoft Outlook on the SQL Server.

4. Log on to Windows NT on the SQL Server using the SQL service account.

5. In the Control Panel, double-click the Mail and Fax (or just Mail on some systems) icon.

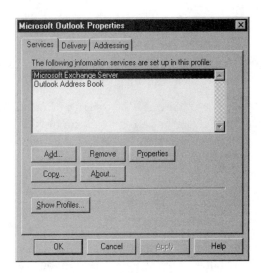

6. Click the Add button to create a mail profile.

7. Be certain that Exchange Server support is installed.

8. Write down the profile name when you have finished creating it.

9. Open Outlook to test the new profile—you may be asked to verify the Exchange Server and mailbox names at this point.

10. Log off Windows NT and log back on using your normal account.

11. Open Enterprise Manager, right-click your server, and select Properties.

12. On the Server Settings tab, click the Change button and type in the name of the profile you wrote down in step 8.

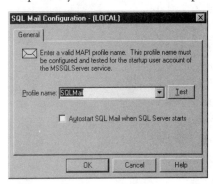

13. Click the Test button to verify connectivity, then click OK and OK again.

Configuring ANSI Settings

To configure the ANSI settings, use the following steps:

1. Set the properties of SQL Server by opening Enterprise Manager, highlighting the server, and choosing Tools ➤ Properties, or by right-clicking and choosing Properties.

2. Go to the Connections option screen by clicking the Connections tab.

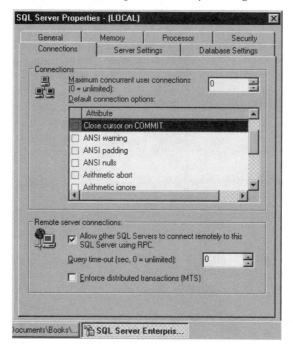

3. Set various options as desired. Choose OK to save your settings.

4. Set the desired database options by highlighting a database, right-clicking, and choosing Properties.

5. Go to the Options tab.

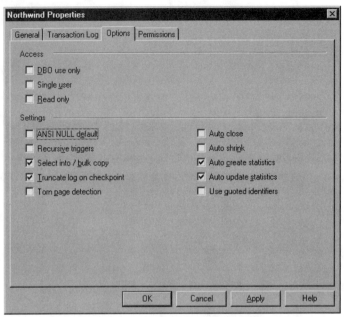

6. Set the various database options as desired. Choose OK to save your settings.

Exam Essentials

This was a brief section that covered a few important settings. While the entire section has very good points, here is a short summary of what you should take into the exam with you.

Know how to configure SQL Mail.   Specifically, you should know the steps to take to make SQL Mail work and what to do if there is a problem configuring it.

Know what the ANSI settings are.   You should familiarize yourself with the ANSI settings listed earlier and understand what they do.

Key Terms and Concepts

ANSI settings: These are settings in SQL that specifically affect ANSI SQL-92 compliance.

SQL Mail: SQL Mail is used to send e-mail and pager alerts to administrators when problems arise.

Sample Questions

1. When SQL is first installed, what configuration is required for SQL to make use of the available RAM?

   A. Changing the Memory setting on the Configuration tab in the Server Properties dialog box

   B. Running `sp_configure 'memory', `*`amount_of_ram`*

   C. Setting min and max server memory settings

   D. None—SQL does this dynamically

   Answer: D. While you can set the min and max memory settings, you aren't required to do so—SQL can assign itself memory dynamically. The first two options are valid in SQL 6.5, but not in 7.

2. True or false. To create a mail profile for the SQL service account, you must log on as the SQL service.

   A. True

   B. False

   Answer: A. You must log in as the SQL service account to create this profile.

Implement full-text searching.

It is probably safe to assume that when you store data in SQL, you would like to use them again later. That task becomes quite daunting if you can't find the data you are looking for, which is why Microsoft has developed the full-text search service. Full-text search is actually a modified Index Server engine that allows you to index and search entire character and text fields, as opposed to how searching functioned in earlier versions of SQL, which would search only the first 255 characters of a field.

While this new service will make it much easier for your users to find the data they are looking for, it makes SQL Server a little more challenging to administer. In turn, anything that makes SQL more challenging to administer will be tested—in this case, quite a bit. So, for the sake of your users' sanity and your certification, immerse yourself in the following information on full-text searching.

Critical Information

To make this service work, the first thing you need to do is install the MSSearch service, which is done by running a Custom setup and selecting the Full-Text Search option. When that is done, you can start creating catalogs and full-text indexes.

Each database has one (and only one) catalog, which is a collection of full-text indexes. A full-text index is a lot like a regular index, with a few small differences:

- While full-text indexes can be administered through the database, they are stored in the file system.

- Only one is allowed per table.

- They are not changed automatically with the addition of new data—they must be *repopulated* at scheduled intervals.

These catalogs and full-text indexes can be created through either stored procedures or Enterprise Manager. However, the easiest way is through the Full-Text Wizard (to be examined in the "Necessary Procedures" section). Before you jump in with both feet, consider a few caveats:

- Remember that while a catalog can contain multiple indexes, a full-text index cannot span catalogs.

- Tables containing a timestamp column can do incremental re-populations, while tables that do not contain a timestamp column will do full repopulations.

- Back up the catalog files occasionally. Catalog files, which contain the full-text indexes, are stored as separate files; by default, they are not backed up when the database is backed up.

- Periodically monitor the size of the catalogs by using Performance Monitor or by checking the size of the files using Explorer or My Computer.

Necessary Procedures

Full-text searching is not installed by default—you must add it. Once it is installed, there are no default settings to rely on—you must configure it to make it work. The procedure that follows will help you install, configure, and subsequently administer the full-text searching capability.

Implementing Full-Text Searching

To implement full-text searching on a database, you need to do as follows:

1. Make certain that the Full-Text Search engine is installed, which can be done by running a Custom setup with the setup program.

2. Start Enterprise Manager.

3. Highlight the database you want to modify and go to Tools ➤ Full-Text Indexing. This will start the Full-Text Indexing Wizard. Choose Next to proceed.

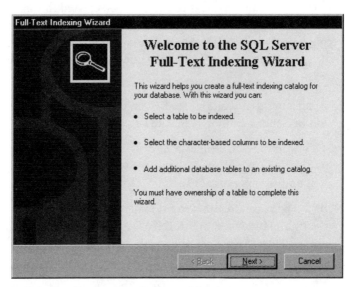

4. Select a database and choose Next.

5. Select an available table and choose Next.

6. Select the default index and choose Next.

7. Select the columns to be indexed.

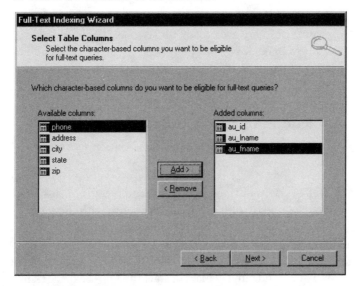

8. Create a new catalog (index) for the searches by entering a name for the new catalog. Note that if you have already created a catalog, you could have chosen to either use a previous catalog or create a new one. Choose Next when finished.

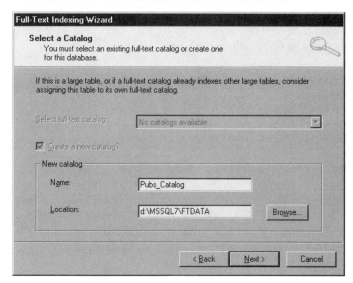

9. You can schedule the catalog for periodic updates by selecting the New Schedule button and entering a name and schedule.

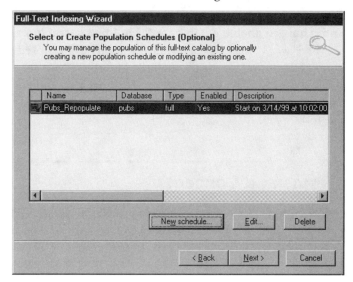

10. Choose OK and Next to save the schedule and go to the summary page.

11. Choose Finish to create the index. You should now see a note that the Wizard completed successfully. Note that the catalog will not be populated until it is updated manually or as scheduled.

12. Choose OK to close the screen.

13. To populate the index, go to the Pubs database, highlight the Full-Text Catalogs folder, right-click, and choose Repopulate All Catalogs.

Exam Essentials

Even though this was a short section, it is going to be tested quite a bit. You really need to understand the full-text search capability—specifically, you need to know what repopulating is and how to do it, and how to set up full-text search in the first place.

Know what repopulating is and when it happens. Full-text indexes are not automatically updated when the data in the underlying table change. You must either force or, preferably, schedule a repopulation to update the full-text index.

Know how to enable a database for full-text searching. There are three ways to do this: The first way is by using stored procedures. The second way is through the Enterprise Manager by right-clicking the Full-Text Catalogs icon. The final way, and possibly the easiest, is through the Full-Text Indexing Wizard accessed through the Tools menu.

Key Terms and Concepts

Full-text catalog: A catalog is a collection of full-text indexes; each database may have only one.

Full-text index: This is the entity that makes full-text searching possible. It stores references to words in text and character fields. These may be defined only in a base table, not in temporary tables or views.

Populate: To build a full-text index. The process of updating the full-text index is referred to as repopulating.

Sample Questions

1. You have just enabled the Accounting database for full-text searching and created a full-text index for the Employees table using the Full-Text Search Wizard. When will the full-text index be repopulated next?

   A. On demand—when you run the `sp_repopulate` stored procedure.

   B. Whenever the data in the Employees table are updated.

   C. At scheduled times.

   D. There is no need to repopulate.

   Answer: C. This will happen on schedule. You can force it to repopulate through either the Enterprise Manager or the `sp_fulltext_catalog` stored procedure.

2. True or false. To make the server easier to administer, you should create a single full-text catalog to contain all full-text indexes from all databases on your server.

   A. True

   B. False

   Answer: B. You cannot create a single, giant catalog. Each database must have its own catalog.

CHAPTER

3

Configuring and
Managing Security

Microsoft Exam Objectives Covered in This Chapter:

▶ **Assign SQL Server access through Windows NT accounts, SQL Server logins, and built-in administrator logins.** *(pages 89 – 96)*

▶ **Assign database access to Windows NT accounts, SQL Server logins, the guest user account, and the dbo user account.** *(pages 96 – 101)*

▶ **Create and assign SQL Server roles. Server roles include fixed server, fixed database, public, user-defined database, and application.** *(pages 101 – 110)*

▶ **Grant to database users and roles the appropriate permissions on database objects and statements.** *(pages 111 – 118)*

▶ **Audit server and database activity.** *(pages 118 – 123)*

In Chapter 1, planning was emphasized as an important part of the SQL Server implementation process—and one of the most important things to plan is security. Since you have a security plan, you already know what types of logins you want to use, what databases your users need access to, and what sort of things they will be allowed to do once inside. Now it is time to run down the mechanics of implementing this plan.

The first thing to be discussed is probably the most important: the authentication modes. In your networks, if you don't employ the proper authentication mode, some of your users may not be able to log in to SQL Server—you can be sure to expect some exam questions on what mode to use. After you have that topic down pat, the methods for creating both Windows NT and standard logins can be discussed so that your users can gain access to the server.

Just because your users have access to the server, though, does not mean they have access to any of the databases stored there. So, the methods for gaining access to a database through database user accounts need to be rehashed. While the mechanics of creating the accounts is a fairly simple process, you need to pay special attention to two user accounts: guest and dbo. In real-world situations, these two special user accounts will come in handy more often than you might expect, and because of that, they pop up on the exam more often than you might expect—so watch for them.

Once you have a firm grasp of database user accounts, grouping those accounts together for easier administration will be examined. This involves gaining a firm understanding of fixed server roles, fixed database roles, and custom roles. Once you understand the roles, granting, revoking, and denying permissions, both statement and object, for both roles and users, can be examined. Pay close attention here because these concepts are very important in the exam and in the real world—if you set permissions incorrectly, users that need access may not get it and vice versa.

Finally, no security system is complete without the capability to monitor the system, so Profiler will be discussed. A full discussion of Profiler will come in Chapter 5; here, you will find just enough information to audit database activity to make sure your security plan is working as expected.

Assign SQL Server access through Windows NT accounts, SQL Server logins, and built-in administrator logins.

If you own a business housed in your very own building, you do not want just anyone to be able to walk right in. Since you want only your employees to have access, you would give them keys to the front door. The same principle holds true with SQL Server—you need to give users a "key," called a *login* in SQL, so that they can gain access to the system as a whole.

Before logins can be discussed, though, authentication modes need to be examined, since the authentication mode you use will affect the type of logins you assign to your users. You will surely see these concepts on the exam, and not as simple questions either. Most likely, these questions will be presented as story questions that take you through a series of problems—for example, a user needs access, but can't log in—and the problems will all stem from the fact that the wrong login type was assigned or the wrong authentication mode was used, so make sure you understand these topics.

Critical Information

For the exam, you will need to know how to create the two types of logins (Windows NT and standard) and what the differences are between the two. You will need a firm grasp of the differences between authentication modes, which is how SQL processes user names and passwords. Finally, you will need to understand the role that the Windows NT Administrators group plays in SQL security.

Working with Windows NT Authentication

In Windows NT Authentication mode, a user can simply sit down at their computer, log on to the Windows NT domain, and gain access to SQL Server. This is referred to as a *trusted* connection because SQL trusts Windows NT to verify the user's password. SQL will need to verify only the user's login account, which it does by matching either the Windows NT user name or the group membership (an important exam concept) to an entry in the syslogins table in the Master database. This means that you could add 50 users to a local group in Windows NT (specifically in User Manager) and create a single Windows NT login for that group—all 50 users will have access using that one Windows NT login.

For the exam, it is important to know that only users with the Named Pipes, TCP/IP, or Multi-Protocol Net-Libraries can open a trusted connection to SQL Server. So, if you have clients that require other Net-Libraries (such as NetWare), you will need to implement Mixed mode.

Mixed Mode and Standard Logins

Mixed mode allows both NT authentication and SQL authentication. In SQL authentication, the user logs on to their network (Windows NT or otherwise), opens a nontrusted connection to SQL, and supplies a user name and password to gain access. In this method, SQL must verify both the user name and password by matching them with a record in the syslogins table. When Mixed mode is used, anyone can gain access to SQL, regardless of the Net-Library used.

Built-In Administrator Logins

SA login is the first of two administrative accounts that are created as soon as SQL is installed. Short for System Administrator, SA is a standard login with a blank default password that is capable of doing anything on the system. It is a very good idea to change this password immediately after installation. For the test, remember that SA is not for everyday use—it is for backward compatibility only.

The second administrative account is the built-in administrator Windows NT group-type login. This login grants administrative access to your Windows NT Administrators local group. For the test and real life, it is a good idea to create a local Windows NT group (perhaps SQLAdmins) with all of your SQL administrators, create a Windows NT login for the new group, and grant it administrative access by adding it to the sysadmins server role. Once that is done, you can delete the built-in administrators login account (or at least remove it from the sysadmins role).

Necessary Procedures

Since there is not a great deal of effort involved in creating login accounts, you will not see a great deal of it on the test—but it may be touched on, so you need to know how to do it through Enterprise Manager and via Transact-SQL (T-SQL). Here, you will find procedures for creating standard login accounts graphically and then with T-SQL. Then, the same sets of procedures for Windows NT accounts will be examined.

Creating Standard Logins

Creating a standard login via Enterprise Manager is a simple process; just follow these steps:

1. Open Enterprise Manager and expand your server by clicking the + sign next to the icon named after your server.

2. Expand the Security folder and click the Logins icon.

3. Choose Action ➤ New Login.

4. Type the name for your new user in the Name box.

5. In the Authentication section, select SQL Server Authentication.

6. In the Password text box, type **password**.

7. Under Defaults, select a default database—leaving this as Master will connect your users to the Master database.

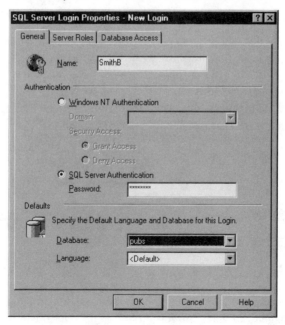

8. Click the OK button.

9. Retype the password in the Confirm New Password text box.

10. Click OK to create your new standard login.

To create a standard login using Transact-SQL, you will use the `sp_addlogin` stored procedure:

```
sp_addlogin 'username', 'password', 'default_database'
```

Creating Windows NT Logins in Enterprise Manager

Creating Windows NT logins in Enterprise Manager is not much different than creating standard logins. The biggest difference is that the Windows NT account must already have been created in User Manager for Domains—if it has not, the creation of the new login will fail. Follow these steps to create a Windows NT login:

1. Verify that the Windows NT account (user or group) you are using exists in User Manager—if it does not, create it.

2. In Enterprise Manager, expand your server and click Logins in the Security folder.

3. Choose Actions ➢ New Login.

4. In the Name box, type a valid Windows NT account name (user or group).

5. Select Windows NT Authentication and select your domain from the Domain drop-down list.

6. Under Defaults, select a default database.

7. Click OK to create the new login.

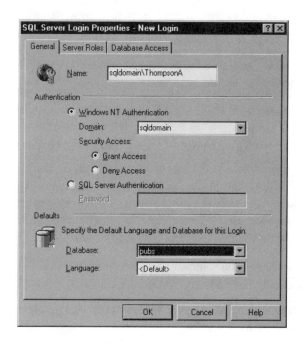

Creating Windows NT Logins Using T-SQL

To create a Windows NT login using T-SQL, you will use the `sp_grantlogin` stored procedure:

```
sp_grantlogin 'NTdomain\accountname'
```

Here, you will notice an immediate but subtle difference between creating standard and Windows NT logins with T-SQL—`sp_grant`login is for Windows NT logins, and `sp_add`login is for standard.

NOTE With `sp_grantlogin`, you cannot assign a password (since that is done in User Manager), nor can you assign a default database.

Exam Essentials

While you should remember all of the points in the previous section, there are some special points that you should take with you into the test center.

Know the procedures for creating logins.   You should understand the mechanics of creating both types of logins via T-SQL and Enterprise Manager. If you are using T-SQL, you should understand the caveats about using `sp_grantlogin` as opposed to `sp_addlogin` (you can't assign a default database with `sp_grantlogin`).

Know your Net-Libraries.   Only Named Pipes, TCP/IP Sockets, and Multi-Protocol are capable of performing Windows NT Authentication since they are the only protocols that can make trusted connections.

Know how to grant administrative access.   You don't want all of your Windows NT administrators to have administrative access to SQL, so you should know how to prevent that by removing the built-in administrators group in SQL and creating a new SQLAdmins group.

Key Terms and Concepts

Nontrusted connection: When a user connects over a nontrusted connection, SQL must validate the password.

SQL login: Also referred to as a standard login, a SQL login is an account used for gaining access to SQL Server where both the user name and password are verified by SQL.

Trusted connection: When a user connects to SQL over a trusted connection, SQL trusts Windows NT to validate the user's password.

Windows NT login: An account used for gaining access to SQL Server where only the user name is verified by SQL—the password is verified by Windows NT.

Sample Questions

1. You have a network comprised of Windows 95, Windows 98, and Macintosh clients. Which authentication mode should you use?

   A. Mixed

   B. Windows NT Authentication

   Answer: **A.** Your Macintosh users will require Mixed mode since they are incapable of making a trusted connection.

2. What is the default password for the SA account?

   A. Password

   B. Blank (no password)

   C. SA

   D. A random password that is displayed during the setup process

   Answer: **B.** There is no password assigned to the SA account initially. You will need to assign one right away.

Assign database access to Windows NT accounts, SQL Server logins, the guest user account, and the dbo user account.

Back to the building analogy—just because your users have a key to the building does not mean that they have access to the resources (such as file cabinets) inside. Similarly, in SQL, just because your users have a login account does not mean that they have access to the resources (such as databases) stored there.

For your users to be able to gain access to those resources, you need to create a database user account for them in each and every database to which they need access. In this section, you will read about not only how to create user accounts in the database, but also how to use the two accounts that already exist—dbo and guest. These two special accounts can prove useful if properly used, but very dangerous if improperly used—you can be sure to find these two accounts on the test.

Critical Information

For the test, it is important to know not only how to create the database user account, but also to know what it is used for. As mentioned, once you use a key to get in the front door of an office building, you don't automatically have access to all of the file cabinets in that office—you will need to be issued a separate key for each file cabinet.

In SQL, the key that gets you in the front door is a login, and the separate key for each file cabinet is a database user account. Once your user has a database account (and permissions applied to that account), they will be able to work with the data inside.

When you first look in the Users folder of one of your databases, you notice that two users already exist: dbo and guest. Members of the sysadmin fixed server role automatically become the dbo (database owner) user in every database on the system. In this way, they can perform all the necessary administrative functions in the databases, such as adding users and creating tables. *Guest user* is a catch-all term used for people who have a SQL login, but not a user account in the database. These users can log in to SQL as themselves and access any database where they do not have a user account. The guest account should be limited in function since anybody with a SQL login can use it.

NOTE Whenever a member of the sysadmin fixed server role creates an object (such as a table), it is not owned by that login—it is owned by the dbo. If MorrisL created a table, it would not be referred to as `MorrisL.table`, but instead as `dbo.table`.

Necessary Procedures

While there is not a great deal of effort involved in creating database user accounts, you need to know how to do it. The steps required to create a user account using Enterprise Manager will be discussed first, then the procedures for T-SQL will be examined.

Creating a Database User Account in Enterprise Manager

The process for creating a database user account in Enterprise Manager is as follows:

1. Open Enterprise Manager and expand your server.

2. Expand Databases by clicking on the + sign next to the icon.

3. Click the Database Users icon.

4. Choose Action ➤ New Database User.

5. In the Login Name box, select one of the available names; note that only logins that you have already created are available.

6. You can enter a name in the Login Name box. Then, SQL will see the user as whatever you type here instead of as their login name.

7. Click OK.

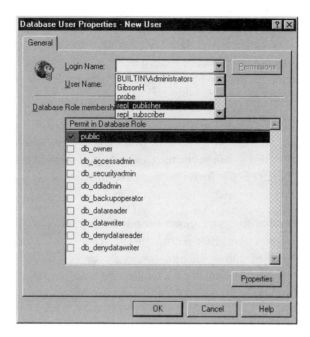

Creating a Database User Account with T-SQL

To create a database user account with T-SQL, you need to use the sp_grantdbaccess stored procedure. The syntax is as follows:

```
sp_grantdbaccess 'login', 'name_in_db'
```

For example, by executing sp_grantdbaccess 'Sales', 'SalesUsers', you would create a user account in your database called SalesUsers that would allow the Sales login to access your database.

Exam Essentials

Since users will not get access to a database without a user account, it is important for you to know how to create and work with user accounts. Here are a few points that you should pay special attention to before taking the exam.

Know what database user accounts are for and how to create them. You should know that logins are for gaining access to SQL Server as a whole, and database user accounts are for gaining access to a single database once logged in. You will also need to know the mechanics of creating these accounts through T-SQL and Enterprise Manager.

Remember what the dbo user is for. In SQL 6.5, it was necessary to alias database user accounts to the dbo user to avoid broken ownership chains. That is not the case in SQL 7—members of the sysadmins database are already considered the dbo in every database so that they can perform administration.

Know when to use a guest account. A guest account is very useful for systems that require public access, such as a kiosk at a library where hundreds of users need access each day. Rather than create a user account for each user, you would simply use the guest account and assign it very limited permissions.

Key Terms and Concepts

Database user account: A database user account is used for gaining access to a single database once a user is logged in.

dbo: This is a powerful user in each database to which members of the sysadmins fixed server role are mapped.

Guest user account: This is a user account in each database that is used to grant access to users who have a login, but no specific database user account.

Sample Questions

1. True or false. The best way to grant users access to a database is through the guest account.

A. True

B. False

Answer: B. Using the guest account may be fast, but it is not secure—use guest on a public access or similar system.

2. JohnsonK is a member of the sysadmins fixed server role. She creates a table in the Sales database called Customers. Who is the owner of the table?

A. JohnsonK

B. Sysadmins

C. Administrators

D. dbo

Answer: D. Whenever a member of the sysadmins group creates an object, it belongs to the dbo user.

Create and assign SQL Server roles. Server roles include fixed server, fixed database, public, user-defined database, and application.

If you own a business, what should your users be able to do once inside? The managers probably have permission to do whatever they want; the janitorial staff have permission to do next to nothing. In a similar fashion, you need to limit your users' administrative access in SQL Server, both to the server as a whole and in each database where they have access.

In this section, limiting administrative access to the server as a whole by assigning users to fixed server roles will be discussed. Then, limiting access in a specific database by assigning users to a database role that can be fixed or user defined will be examined. Finally, limiting access on an application-specific basis by using application roles will be discussed.

NOTE These roles will be tested on quite a bit, so you should be familiar with them. You should especially study application roles—not because they are heavily tested, but because they are a bit esoteric and difficult to grasp if you haven't used them before.

Critical Information

Fixed server roles are used to limit the amount of administrative access that a user has once logged in to SQL Server. Some users may be allowed to do whatever they want, whereas other users may be able only to manage security. For the test, you do not need to memorize each permission for each role, but you should have a general understanding of what each role is capable of—for example, sysadmins can do whatever they want, whereas processadmins can only kill a process.

Available Fixed Server Roles

Here is a list of the fixed server roles:

Sysadmin: Members of the sysadmin role can do whatever they want in SQL Server. Be careful whom you assign to this role—people who are unfamiliar with SQL can accidentally create serious problems. This role is only for the database administrators (DBAs).

Serveradmin: These users can set serverwide configuration options, such as how much memory SQL can use or how much information to send over the network in a single frame. If you make your assistant DBAs members of this role, you can relieve yourself of some of the administrative burden.

Setupadmin: Members here can install replication and manage extended stored procedures (used to perform actions not native to SQL Server). Give this to the assistant DBAs as well.

Securityadmin: These users manage security issues, such as creating and deleting logins, reading the audit logs, and granting users permission to create databases. This, too, is a good role for assistant DBAs.

Processadmin: SQL is capable of multitasking; that is, it can do more than one thing at a time by executing multiple processes. For instance, SQL might spawn one process for writing to cache and another for reading from cache. A member of the processadmin group can end (called *kill* in SQL) a process. This is another good role for assistant DBAs and developers. Developers especially need to kill processes that may have been triggered by an improperly designed query or stored procedure.

Dbcreator: These users can create and make changes to databases. This may be a good role for assistant DBAs as well as developers (who should be warned against creating unnecessary databases and wasting server space).

Diskadmin: These users manage files on disk. They do things such as mirroring databases and adding backup devices. Assistant DBAs should be members of this role.

Available Fixed Database Roles

Database roles are used to limit what users can do inside a single database. If, for example, you do not want a user to be able to modify data, but you do want them to read data, then add them to the db_datareader role. Here is a list of the default database roles:

Db_owner: Members of this role can do everything the members of the other roles can do as well as some administrative functions.

Db_accessadmin: These users have the authority to say who gets access to the database by adding or removing users.

Db_datareader: Members here can read data from any table in the database.

Db_datawriter: These users can add, change, and delete data from all the tables in the database.

Db_ddladmin: DDL (Data Definition Language) administrators can issue all DDL commands; this allows them to create, modify, drop, or change database objects without viewing the data inside.

Db_securityadmin: Members here can add and remove users from database roles, and manage statement and object permissions.

Db_backupoperator: These users can back up and restore the database.

Db_denydatareader: Members cannot read the data in the database, but they can make schema changes.

Db_denydatawriter: These users cannot make changes to the data in the database, but they are allowed to read the data.

Public: The purpose of this group is to grant users a default set of permissions in the database. For the test, it is important to note that all database users automatically join this group and cannot be removed.

There will, of course, be times when the fixed database roles do not meet your security needs. You might have several users who need select, update, and execute permissions in your database and nothing more. Because none of the fixed database roles will give you that set of permissions, you can create a custom database role, assign permissions to it, and then assign users to the role. That is different from the fixed database roles, where you did not need to assign permissions, but just added users.

If you have a custom application for accessing data, you may even want to restrict access to your database to that one application. You can accomplish this with an application role, which will force your users to employ the proper application for data access.

Once you've created an application role, the user logs on to SQL, is authenticated, and opens the approved application. The application executes the `sp_setapprole` stored procedure to enable the application role. Once the application role is enabled, SQL no longer sees users as themselves; it sees users as the application and grants them application-role permissions.

Necessary Procedures

For the test, one of the first things you need to know is how to add users to fixed server roles through Enterprise Manager or T-SQL. Once you have limited what the users can do at the server level, you need to restrict what they can do in each database by adding them to a database role. Finally, you will see the procedures for creating and activating an application role so that you can restrict which applications users are allowed to employ in manipulating data.

Adding Users to Fixed Server Roles in Enterprise Manager

The procedure for adding users to fixed server roles in Enterprise Manager is as follows:

1. Open Enterprise Manager and select Server Roles.

2. Double-click the fixed server role to which you want to add users.

3. Click Add, select the login you wish to add, and click OK.

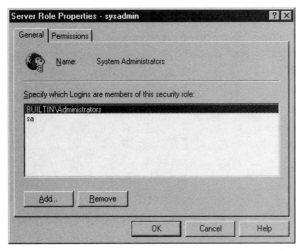

Adding Users to Fixed Server Roles Using T-SQL

To add a user to a fixed server role using T-SQL, you will use the
`sp_addsrvrolemember` stored procedure:

```
sp_addsrvrolemember 'login', 'server_role'
```

Adding Users to a Database Role in Enterprise Manager

The procedure for adding users to a database role in Enterprise Manager is as follows:

1. Open Enterprise Manager, expand your server and databases, then select the database with which you want to work.

2. Click Database Roles.

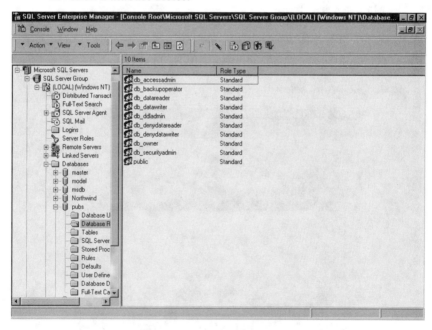

3. In the contents pane, double-click the role you want to modify.

4. Click the Add button.

5. Select a database user account and click OK.

Adding Users to a Database Role Using T-SQL

To accomplish this task using T-SQL, you need to use the sp_addrolemember stored procedure:

```
sp_addrolemember 'role_name' 'user_name'
```

If you create an application role, you will be able to force your users to access the database with only approved applications.

Creating an Application Role in Enterprise Manager

Here's how to create an application role with Enterprise Manager:

1. Open Enterprise Manager and select Database Roles in the database in which you want to create the role.

2. Choose Action ➤ New Database Role.

3. In the Name box, type the name of the new role.

4. Under Database Role Type, select Application Role.

5. Enter the password that will be used to activate the role in the Password box.

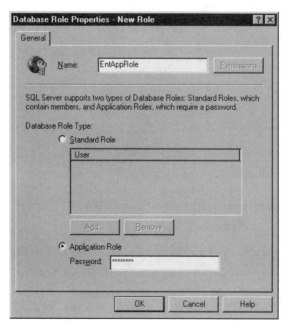

6. Click OK to get back to the Enterprise Manager.

7. To grant permissions to the new role, double-click it and click the Permissions button.

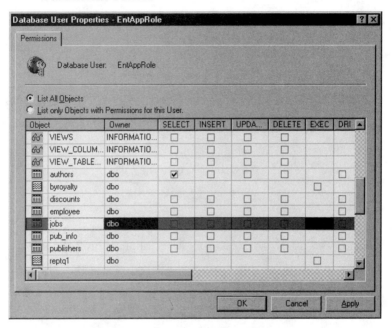

8. Click OK to get back to the previous dialog box, and click OK again to return to Enterprise Manager.

Creating an Application Role Using T-SQL

If you would rather use T-SQL to create an application role, you will need to use the `sp_addapprole` stored procedure:

```
sp_addapprole 'new_role_name', 'password'
```

Activating an Application Role

Once you've created the application role, you need to place some T-SQL code in your application to activate it. The stored procedure to use is `sp_setapprole`:

```
sp_setapprole 'rolename', 'password'
```

Exam Essentials

Limiting user access is a very important topic on the exam, so you should know how to use the fixed server, fixed database, and custom and application roles. A few points of special interest in this regard are listed here for you.

Know what the fixed server roles are capable of.   On the test, you may be asked what permissions a fixed server role will grant you. It is not necessary to memorize every permission, but you should have a general understanding of what each role is for.

Know the permissions granted by the fixed database roles. Again you don't need to memorize all of the permissions of every role, but it is a good idea to know what the roles are capable of.

Know when and how to use an application role.   You should know not only how to create an application role, but how to use it. Remember that you activate the application role by using the `sp_setapprole` stored procedure.

Key Terms and Concepts

Application role: This is used to apply permissions to a specific application so that only that application can be used to gain access to the data.

Fixed database role: This is used to apply permissions to a group of users in a specific database.

Fixed server role: This is used to apply server-level permissions to groups of users.

Public role: This is a role in each database of which every user is a member. Users cannot be removed from this role.

Sample Questions

1. You want to grant administrative rights on the server to some of your users. How should you do this?

    A. Add the users to the Windows NT Administrators local group.

    B. Add logins for each user separately and make each of them members of the sysadmins fixed server role.

    C. Add each of the users to a new Windows NT group called SQLAdmins, add a login for the new group, and make the new login a member of the sysadmins fixed server role.

    D. Create logins for each user and add each user to the db_owner database role in each database.

    Answer: C. Answer A would work, but it lowers security, and B would increase administrative load. Answer D would give administrative rights only in the databases, not at the server level.

2. You want to give a group of users the permission to read and update data, but not insert new data or delete existing records. In which database role(s) should you put them?

    A. Db_datareader and db_datawriter.

    B. Db_denydatawriter and db_datareader.

    C. Db_dataupdater.

    D. You should create a custom role.

    Answer: D. None of the other roles will give you the combination of rights you require—you must create a custom role and assign permissions.

Grant to database users and roles the appropriate permissions on database objects and statements.

Adding users to roles to grant them permissions is easy and saves time, but it doesn't work for every situation. It is very possible that a fixed database role will give a user too much or too little permission—in those instances, you will need to understand how to grant permissions and which permissions are available.

In this section, the available permissions, both statement and object, and how to apply them will be discussed. The three states of permissions and how these can affect your users will also be examined. You don't need to memorize each of these permissions for the test, but it is a good idea to have a general understanding of each of them and what they are for. It is especially important to understand the effects of the three states of permissions: grant, revoke, and deny. In your own SQL Servers, if you don't grant users the right permissions or if you grant permissions at the wrong level, your users may have too much or too little access.

TIP You will find this information in quite a few exam questions, so learn it well.

Critical Information

The first type of permissions you will need to understand is statement permissions, which have nothing to do with the actual data; they allow users to create the structure that holds the data. Do not grant these permissions haphazardly, however—it can lead to such problems as broken ownership chains (discussed later) and wasted server resources. It is best to restrict these permissions to DBAs, assistant DBAs, and developers. The statement permissions you have to work with are as follows:

- Create Database

- Create Table

- Create View

- Create Procedure

- Create Index

- Create Rule

- Create Default

- Backup Database

- Backup Log

NOTE   The Create Database permission can be granted only on the Master database.

Once the structure exists to hold the data, your users will require object permissions to start working with the data contained therein. Using object permissions, you can control who is allowed to read from, write to, or otherwise manipulate your data. Here is a list of object permissions and what they are used for:

Select: When granted, allows users to read data from the table or view. When granted at the column level, this will allow users to read from a single column.

Insert: Allows users to insert new rows into a table.

Update: Allows users to modify existing data in a table. When granted on a column, users will be able to modify data in that single column.

Delete: Allows users to remove rows from a table.

References: When two tables are linked with a foreign key, this allows the user to select data from the primary table without having Select permission on the referenced table.

Execute: This allows users to execute the stored procedure where the permission is applied.

It is also good to know that SQL understands the concept of owner-ship. When a user creates an object, they own that object and can do whatever they want with it. For example, if a user named JacksonR creates a table, she can assign permissions as she chooses, granting access only to those users she deems worthy. That is a good thing until you consider what is known as an *ownership chain*.

Suppose that GibsonH creates a table and grants permissions on that table to ThompsonA (see Figure 3.1). Then, ThompsonA creates a view based on that table and grants Select permission to SmithB. SmithB will not be able to select from the view because the ownership chain has been broken. SQL will check permissions on an underlying object (in this case, the table) only when the object owner changes. Therefore, if ThompsonA had created both the table and the view, there would be no problem since SQL would check only the permis-sions on the view. However, because the owner changed from accounting (which owned the view) to ThompsonA (who owned the table), SQL needed to check the permissions on both the view and the table.

The best way to avoid broken ownership chains is to make all the users who need to create objects members of either the db_owner or the db_ddladmin fixed database roles. Then, if they need to create objects, they can specify the owner as dbo (i.e., `create table dbo.`*`table_name`*`'`). This way, the dbo would own all objects in the database, and since the ownership would never change, SQL would never need to check any underlying permissions.

Finally, you should understand the three states of any permission: granted, revoked, or denied.

Grant: Granting allows users to use a specific permission. For instance, if you grant SmithB Select permission on a table, he can

FIGURE 3.1: Example of a broken ownership chain (broken between Table1 and View1)

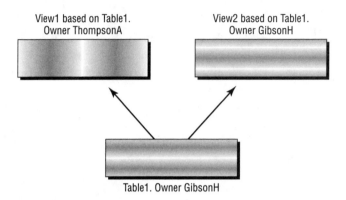

read the data within. A granted permission is signified by a black check mark on the Permissions tab.

Revoke: In this state, while users are not explicitly allowed to use a revoked permission, if they are a member of a role that is allowed, they will inherit the permission. That is, if you revoke the Select permission from SmithB, he cannot use it. If he is a member of a role that has been granted Select permission, SmithB can read the data just as if he had the Select permission. Revocation is signified by a blank check box on the Permissions tab.

Deny: If you deny a permission, the user does not get the permission—no matter what. If you deny SmithB Select permission on a table, then, even if he is a member of a role with Select permission, he cannot read the data. Denial is signified by a red X on the Permissions tab.

Necessary Procedures

Since not much effort is required in actually assigning the permissions, you will not see a great deal of this information on the test, if any at all. Still, you need to know how to do it, both through Enterprise Manager and T-SQL.

Assigning Permissions with Enterprise Manager

The procedures for assigning object and statement permissions through Enterprise Manager are exactly the same:

1. Open Enterprise Manager and expand your server, then expand Databases.

2. Right-click the database you want to modify and select Properties.

3. In the Properties dialog box, select the Permissions tab.

4. From the Permissions tab, you may grant, revoke, or deny any of the available permissions.

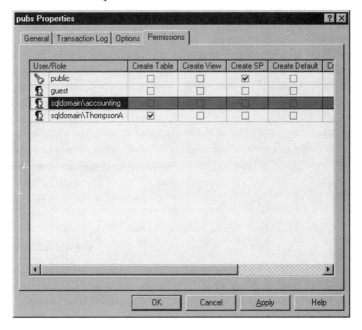

Assigning Permissions Using T-SQL

Assigning object and statement permissions is a little bit different when using T-SQL. In either case, you use the same three commands. Here are some examples for statement permissions:

Grant: GRANT *permission* to *user name*

Revoke: REVOKE *permission* from *user name*

Deny: DENY *permission* to *user name*

Here are some examples of the same three commands for assigning object permissions:

Grant: GRANT *permission* on *object* to *user name*

Revoke: REVOKE *permission* on *object* from *user name*

Deny: DENY *permission* on *object* to *user name*

Exam Essentials

You won't be asked too much about the permissions themselves (i.e., you won't see a question such as, What is Create Database for?); rather, you will be asked about how to use them and set them. Besides that general knowledge, here are some points to remember.

Know how to avoid broken ownership chains. The best way to avoid broken ownership chains is by assigning users that need to create objects to the db_owner or db_ddladmin database roles and having them create objects as dbo (i.e., create table dbo.*table_ name*).

Remember what the deny state is for. Deny takes precedence over grant and revoke. When a user is specifically denied permission, they cannot inherit it through membership in a role where the permission is granted.

Key Terms and Concepts

Broken ownership chain: When not all objects in a chain are owned by the same user and SQL must check permissions on underlying objects, the ownership chain is broken.

Object permissions: These are permissions that allow users to manipulate the data in a database.

Statement permissions: These are permissions that, when granted, allow users to create or modify objects in the database.

Sample Questions

1. GibsonH is a member of the accounting and finance groups. Accounting has Select permission on the Employees table in the Accounting database. The Select permission has been revoked from finance on the same table. Can GibsonH select from the Employees table?

   A. Yes

   B. No

   Answer: A. Since the permission was merely revoked from finance and not denied, GibsonH will be able to read from the Employees table since he inherits the Select permission from accounting.

2. Several of your users need to be able to create objects in your database. What is the best way to avoid broken ownership chains?

   A. Make all the users who need to create objects members of the db_owner fixed database role.

   B. Make all the users who need to create objects members of the db_ddladmin fixed database role.

   C. Make all the users who need to create objects members of the sysadmin fixed server role.

   D. Create a custom fixed server role with the proper object permissions and make those users members of this new role.

   Answer: B. While membership in any of these roles would have allowed users to create objects with dbo as the owner, the db_owner and sysadmin roles would grant too much administrative authority. Db_ddladmin is just the right amount of authority since it limits what the user can do.

3. SamuelsR owns a table and grants ChenJ Select permission. ChenJ creates a view and grants AdamsK Select permission. What are the results when AdamsK tries to select from the view?

   A. AdamsK can select from the table since she has permission to do so.

   B. AdamsK cannot read from the table since she has not been given permission on the underlying table.

Answer: B. This is a prime example of a broken ownership chain—since the owner changed from the view (ChenJ) to the table (SamuelsR), SQL had to verify permissions at each level.

Audit server and database activity.

Most people at one time or another have had to pass through a security checkpoint. At that checkpoint, a security guard sat watching monitors and searching packages. Why was this guard there? Because you can have the most advanced security system in the world, but without someone keeping watch, it will eventually fail. A thief would simply need to probe the system systematically for weak spots and, once they were found, take advantage of them to break in. With a guard watching, this becomes a great deal more difficult.

The same is true for SQL. You cannot simply put a security system in place and then leave it. You must keep watch to make certain no one is probing for weak spots and attempting to break in. This task of keeping watch has been delegated to Profiler, a tool that you will become friends with in the real world. Profiler is capable not only of monitoring security, but of tracking any event on the server—because of that power, you will find a number of questions on the exam that involve Profiler in some way. You should know when and how to use it.

Critical Information

Profiler is used to track and record activity on the SQL Server, which is done by performing a trace. A *trace* is a record of the data captured about events, which can be stored in a database table, in a trace log file that can be opened and read in Profiler, or in both. Traces can be one of two types: *shared*, viewable by anyone, or *private*, viewable only by the owner. Security traces should be private so that only you have access.

The actions that are monitored on the server are known as *events*, and those events are logically grouped together in *event classes*. Not all of these events have to do with security; in fact, most of them have to do with optimization and troubleshooting. Table 3.1 lists the classes and events that are important from a security standpoint.

T A B L E 3.1: Classes and Events

Event Class	Event
Misc	**Loginfailed:** This will tell you if someone has tried to log in unsuccessfully. If you notice someone repeatedly failing to log in, it means either the user forgot their password or someone is trying to hack in using the user's account.
	ServiceControl: This monitors SQL Server starts, stops, and pauses. If you note a stop or pause and you are the only administrator, it means there is a problem with the server itself—or someone has hacked in with an administrative account.
Objects	**Object:Deleted:** This will tell you if an object, such as a table, has been deleted. From a security standpoint, this is after the fact, since the damage may have already been done. By monitoring this, however, you should be able to catch the culprit if something is improperly deleted.

T A B L E 3.1: Classes and Events *(cont.)*

Event Class	Event
SQL Operators	**Delete:** This is logged just before a delete statement is executed. It does not stop delete statements from executing, it just records them. This event will be useful in catching a hacker if something is illicitly deleted.

Necessary Procedures

For the purpose of the exam, it is a good idea to know how to create a trace and add the appropriate events.

Creating a Trace and Adding the Appropriate Events

To create a trace and add the appropriate events, follow these steps:

1. Open Profiler in the SQL Server 7 program group.

2. Choose File ➣ New ➣ Trace.

3. Enter a name for your trace in the Trace Name box.

4. For Trace Type, select Private.

5. To run the trace against your own machine, select Local.

6. Click the checkbox next to Capture to File and click OK to select the default filename.

7. Click the checkbox next to Capture to Table and fill in the subsequent dialog box:

   - Server: Local
   - Database: *Database_name*
   - Owner: *Yourself*
   - Table: *Table_name*

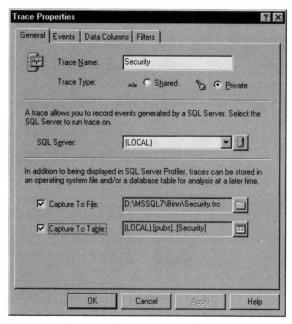

8. Click OK to return to the previous dialog box.

9. Select the Events tab.

10. Under Selected Events, remove any unneeded classes.

11. Under Available Events, select the events you want to monitor and click Add.

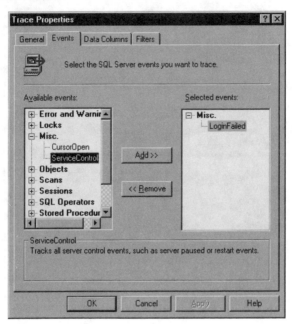

12. Click OK to start the trace.

Exam Essentials

The previous section won't get hit very hard on the test, if at all. Nevertheless, you need to know how to audit security for your own networks. When you go into the test, there is one important point to take with you.

Know what events to use in a security trace. Not all events are useful for monitoring security, so it is a good idea to remember which ones are useful.

Key Terms and Concepts

Event: This is an action occurring on the server, such as a select statement or a user login failure.

Trace: This is a group of events that are recorded in Profiler and stored in a file, a table, or both.

Sample Questions

1. You have suspicions that some of the temporary employees in your company are trying to gain access to sensitive company information stored in SQL databases. How can you confirm these suspicions?

   A. Monitor the security log in Event Viewer.

   B. Monitor the Login_activity event in Profiler.

   C. Monitor the Loginfailed counter in Performance Monitor.

   D. Monitor the Loginfailed event in Profiler.

   Answer: D. The Loginfailed event in Profiler will tell you who is trying, and failing, to log in to SQL. This information is not logged in Event Viewer. The items in answers B and C do not even exist.

2. True or false. By tracking the Delete event under the SQL Operators event class, you can actually stop users from deleting objects.

   A. True

   B. False

   Answer: B. While this event will tell you just before an object is deleted, it will not stop the delete statement from executing.

CHAPTER

4

Managing and Maintaining Data

Microsoft Exam Objectives Covered in This Chapter:

Create and manage databases. *(pages 128 – 147)*
- Create data files, filegroups, and transaction log files.
- Specify growth characteristics.

Load data by using various methods. Methods include the INSERT statement, the SELECT INTO statement, the bcp utility, Data Transformation Services (DTS), and the BULK INSERT statement. *(pages 148 – 173)*

Back up system databases and user databases by performing a full database backup, a transaction log backup, a differential database backup, and a filegroup backup. *(pages 174 – 188)*

Restore system databases and user databases from a full database backup, a transaction log backup, a differential database backup, and a filegroup backup. *(pages 188 – 200)*

Manage replication. *(pages 200 – 237)*
- Configure servers, including Distributor, Publisher, and Subscriber.
- Create publications.
- Set up and manage subscriptions.

Automate administrative tasks. *(pages 238 – 257)*
- Define jobs.
- Define alerts.
- Define operators.
- Set up SQLAgentMail for job notification and alerts.

Enable access to remote data. *(pages 258 – 261)*
- Set up linked servers.
- Set up security for linked databases.

I t is probably safe to say that you are installing and configuring SQL Server so that you can use it to store data, which means that you will need to create databases. In this chapter, how to create the data files used for storing data (and their associated transaction logs) and how to lump them all together in filegroups (watch the filegroup section for the exam) will be covered. Knowing how to create a database is not enough, though—you need more.

When you first create a database, it is empty, and since a blank database is useless, you need to know how to load it with data. The methods discussed here are INSERT, SELECT INTO, bcp, DTS, and BULK INSERT.

Once you have data loaded into your database, what if they get damaged or lost? Since you can't just let fate decide what happens to your data, the mechanics of backing up will be discussed. Then, if the unthinkable happens and your data do get corrupted or damaged in some way, the procedures for restoring them from those backups will be covered. The sections on backups and restorations will prove to be some of the most important information you will ever read on SQL Server for real life and exam purposes—please pay close attention.

Once you have created and populated your database, what if it turns out to be extremely popular? Having everyone in your organization access that database from your one, lone server could cause a massive bottleneck. Since bottlenecks slow system performance and should be avoided, how to replicate your databases to other servers in the organization so that your users can access a local copy will be discussed.

All of the tasks mentioned here are going to take some system resources, which could slow the system, so it is best to perform them off-hours. However, since you probably don't want to wait until everyone leaves to perform these duties, automating these (and other) routine tasks will be covered.

Finally, many companies today have multiple SQL Servers in their organization with different databases on each one. The caveat is that people need to access data from multiple servers in some of their queries. These queries are referred to as distributed queries—you will learn how to configure SQL Server to allow this process to happen.

Create and manage databases.

- Create data files, filegroups, and transaction log files.
- Specify growth characteristics.

The first step in making your database server useful is to create databases, which will be discussed here. However, what do you do when you find that your database is running out of space or it is using too much space? To fix those problems, expanding and shrinking databases as well as dropping databases when you no longer require them will be discussed.

Critical Information

As with almost everything in SQL, there are two ways to create databases: graphically in Enterprise Manager and via Transact-SQL (T-SQL). When you employ the graphic method of creating databases, Enterprise Manager actually performs the T-SQL statements in the background for you. Bearing that in mind, most of the discussion will involve creating a database with T-SQL.

Creating Data and Transaction Log Files

When you create a database, you must specify the logical name of the database, the physical filename where the database file will reside, and the size of the database file. Optional parameters include the maximum size to which the database is allowed to grow, as well as the growth characteristics. Also, while it is not required, you can also specify the logical and physical filenames of the transaction log with maximum size and growth characteristics. If you opt not to specify the transaction log parameters, SQL will create a transaction log for you in the same directory as the data file. The basic syntax of the CREATE DATABASE statement is as follows:

```
CREATE DATABASE db_name
```

```
[ON {[PRIMARY]
(NAME = logical name,
 FILENAME = 'physical filename',
 [SIZE = initial size,]
 [MAXSIZE = maxsize,]
 [FILEGROWTH = [filegrowth MB | %])} [...n]]
[LOG ON
{(NAME = logical name,
 FILENAME = 'physical filename',
 [SIZE = initial size],
 [MAXSIZE = maxsize],
 [FILEGROWTH = filegrowth MB | %])} [...n]]
 [FOR LOAD | FOR ATTACH]
```

The following list explains the uses of the listed parameters:

db_name: This is the name that you are going to give this database. It must follow the rules for SQL Server identifiers.

PRIMARY: This parameter, the name of the filegroup, defaults to PRIMARY. (Filegroups are an advanced topic that will be covered later in this chapter.) In short, filegroups allow you to place individual database objects in separate files. For example, you might place a large table on one filegroup and the table's index on another filegroup. In this manner, writes to the table do not interfere with writes to the index. These filegroups are used with the ALTER DATABASE statement, not the CREATE DATABASE statement.

logical name: This is the logical name of the database file, which you will use to reference this particular database file while in SQL Server.

'physical filename': Since the database file is stored on disk, you must provide a filename and complete path. Note that it is surrounded by single quotation marks.

initial size: This is the initial size of the database expressed in either kilobytes or megabytes. Keep in mind that this will allocate hard-disk space, just like any other file on disk.

maxsize: This is the maximum size to which the database can grow, specified in either kilobytes or megabytes. This is useful when you specify filegrowth options.

filegrowth: This option specifies the size of the increments by which a given database file should grow. It can be expressed in either kilobytes or megabytes, or as a percentage. If not specified, the default is 1MB.

FOR LOAD: This option marks the database for dbo (database owner) use only and is used for backward compatibility with SQL Server 6.5. This means that the database is not marked online, but is waiting for data to be loaded into it through a SELECT INTO/ BULK COPY operation or through the restoration of a backup.

FOR ATTACH: This option reattaches the files that make up a database. It essentially re-creates entries in the system tables regarding this database file.

The following listing is an example of how to create a database using the CREATE DATABASE statement. In this example, you will create a database that has data spanning two files and a transaction log. You will also set the autogrowth and maxsize parameters.

```
CREATE DATABASE Complex
ON PRIMARY
(NAME = Complex_Data1,
 FILENAME = 'C:\MSSQL7\Data\Complex_Data1.mdf',
 SIZE = 5MB,
 MAXSIZE = 10MB,
 FILEGROWTH = 1MB)
(NAME = Complex_Data2,
 FILENAME = 'C:\MSSQL7\Data\Complex_Data2.ndf',
 SIZE = 2MB,
 MAXSIZE = 10MB,
 FILEGROWTH = 2MB)
LOG ON
(NAME = Complex_Log1,
 FILENAME = 'D:\Logs\Complex_Log1.ldf',
 SIZE = 2MB,
```

```
MAXSIZE = 8MB,
FILEGROWTH = 1MB)
```

This creates a database with an initial size of 9MB—5MB for the first file, 2MB for the second file, and 2MB for the log. The database has a maximum size of 28MB.

WARNING   You should always specify a maximum size for data and transaction log files that have an autogrowth feature. If you do not, it is possible for the file to fill the entire hard-disk partition. If this happens, Windows NT will no longer allow you to use that partition. If the partition also has the Windows NT system files on it, you will no longer be able to use Windows NT until the situation is remedied.

Now that you have successfully created a couple of databases, it is time to learn how to gather more information about them. Using the Enterprise Manager, you can gather a wealth of information about your database. This includes the size of the database, its current capacity, any options that are currently set, etc. If you click your database in the console tree, you will receive summary information in the right pane, as shown in Figure 4.1.

You can also use system stored procedures to gather information about your database. The sp_helpdb stored procedure used by itself will give you information about all databases in your SQL Server. You can gather information about a particular database by using the database name as a parameter.

Now that you know how to create databases, you are ready to learn how to manage them.

Managing Database Options

The first step in managing databases is understanding the options that, when set, will change the way your database behaves in given situations. You can view and modify database options using the Enterprise Manager or the sp_dboption stored procedure, which includes options that are not available through the GUI.

FIGURE 4.1: The Database Information pane

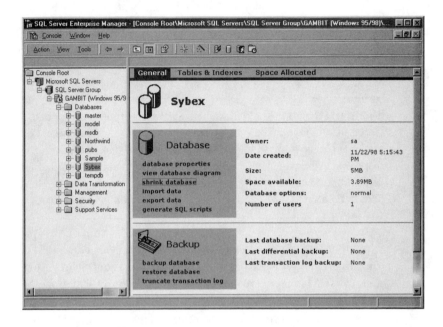

To view the options on a database in Enterprise Manager, you right-click your database and choose Properties. From the Database Properties dialog box, click the Options tab, as shown in Figure 4.2.

The database options are broken into separate categories for Access and Settings. Here is what the different settings mean:

DBO Use Only: Only members of the db_owner fixed database role have access to this database. This option is frequently used when performing a restoration or other tasks where you do not want to allow nonowners in the database.

Single User: Only one user at a time can access the database and with only a single connection. This is useful when renaming or restoring a database.

Read Only: This option marks the database as read only. No changes to the database will be allowed. Since no locking occurs

FIGURE 4.2: The Database Options tab

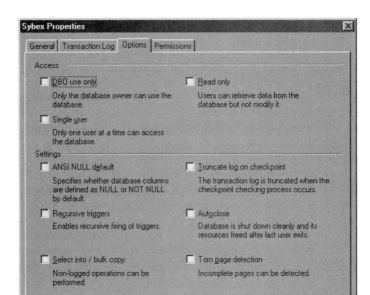

when Read Only is set, it is useful on databases where no changes are made to the data.

ANSI NULL Default: This option specifies that new columns created or added to tables have a default value of NULL. Although this is a default setting for the entire database, you can override this value by specifying either NULL or NOT NULL when you create your columns.

Recursive Triggers: This option allows recursive triggers to fire. *Recursive triggers* occur when one trigger fires a trigger on another table, which in turn fires another trigger on the originating table.

Select Into/Bulk Copy: This option allows you to perform non-logged operations. This includes the use of the bcp (bulk copy) command-line program as well as statements that create or fill tables using the SELECT INTO SQL statements.

Truncate Log on Checkpoint: This option specifies that the inactive portion of the transaction log should be truncated at the checkpoint process. Every minute, the checkpoint process is activated and checks each database in SQL Server. If it finds a database with five minutes worth of changes, it flushes the modified data pages in cache to the hard disk. When dirty pages have been written to disk as well as to the transaction log, you have a known point of consistency. This option is useful if you do not want to keep an active transaction log. You use it often during the development stages of a database.

Torn Page Detection: This option allows SQL Server to detect when a partial-page write to disk has occurred. Because this is a form of data corruption that should be avoided, you should enable this option.

Autoclose: This option safely closes your database when the last user has exited from it. This can be a useful option for optimization. It decreases the amount of resources that SQL Server needs to consume to maintain user information and locks.

Autoshrink: This option will automatically shrink both data and log files. Log files will be shrunk after a backup of the log has been made. Data files will be shrunk when a periodic check of the database finds that the database has more than 25 percent of its assigned space free. Your database will then be shrunk to a size that leaves 25 percent free.

Auto Create Statistics: This option will automatically generate statistics on the distribution of values found in your columns. The SQL Server query optimizer uses these statistics to determine the best method to run a particular query.

Auto Update Statistics: This option works with the auto-created statistics mentioned above. As you make changes to the data in your database, the statistics will be less and less accurate. This option periodically updates those statistics.

Use Quoted Identifiers: This option allows you to use double quotation marks as part of a SQL Server identifier (object name).

This can be useful in situations in which you have identifiers that are also SQL Server reserved words.

The sp_dboption stored procedure includes the following additional database options that are not available through the Enterprise Manager:

Concat Null Yields Null: This option specifies that anything you concatenate to a NULL value will return a NULL value.

Cursor Close on Commit: This option automatically closes any open cursors when the transaction that created the cursor completes. (*Cursors* are a subset of the results from a query.)

Default to Local Cursor: This option creates cursors that are local in nature and available only to the local batch, trigger, or stored procedure that generated the trigger. This option can be overridden by using the GLOBAL keyword when creating the cursor.

Merge Publish: This option allows a database to be a Publisher as part of merge replication.

Offline: This option takes a database offline and shuts it down. When a database has been taken offline, it can be placed on removable media such as a CD-ROM.

Published: This option specifies that the database is allowed to publish data for use in replication.

Subscribed: This option specifies that the database can participate in the Subscriber side of replication.

Managing Database Size

It is possible that your database may be so popular that it is filled with data much faster than anticipated and becomes too small. Fortunately, you can fix this problem by expanding the database. This expansion is accomplished by expanding the existing data file or adding secondary data files.

The main disadvantage of having multiple database files (as opposed to one large file) is administration. You need to be aware of these different files, their locations, and their use. An advantage is that you can place these files on separate physical hard disks (if you are not using striping) and avoid disk contention, thereby improving performance. When you use database files, you can back up individual database files rather than the whole database in one session. If you also take advantage of filegroups, you can improve performance by explicitly placing tables on one filegroup and the indexes for those tables on a separate filegroup. A *filegroup* is a logical grouping of database files used for improving performance and administration on VLDBs (very large databases). Filegroups will be discussed later in this chapter.

If you find that your database is taking up too much space on the disk, you can shrink it. In Enterprise Manager, this is done by right-clicking the database and selecting Shrink Database. The other way to do this is by running the DBCC SHRINKDATABASE command, which will attempt to shrink all files in the database, or the DBCC SHRINKFILE command, which will attempt to shrink a specific database file. When you run DBCC SHRINKDATABASE(*db_name*)by itself, it will tell you how much your database can be shrunk. Here is the syntax of the SHRINKDATABASE command:

```
DBCC SHRINKDATABASE {
(db_name,
[target_percent],
[{NOTRUNCATE | TRUNCATEONLY}])}
```

The following list presents the arguments and their meanings:

db_name: The logical name of the database that you wish to shrink.

target_percent: The percentage of free space left in the database after it has been shrunk. If, for instance, you have a 100MB database and wish to have 10MB of free space, you would enter 10 as the target percentage (10 percent of 100). The end result cannot be larger than the current database or smaller than the current data size.

NOTRUNCATE: This option just consolidates the data into one area and the free space into another area without releasing any free space back to the operating system. It is akin to defragmenting the database. For obvious reasons, NOTRUNCATE ignores the *target_percent* parameter.

TRUNCATEONLY: This clause will ignore the *target_percent* parameter and shrink the database to the size of data. Afterward, it releases all of the freed-up disk space back to the operating system.

When you no longer need a database, you can drop it from your server, freeing up disk space for other database files. Only the owner of a database has the authority to drop a database. Dropping a database is a very simple task, which can be accomplished through either Enterprise Manager or the T-SQL statement DROP DATABASE. Although the process is easy, you must remember that dropping a database is permanent. If you need to recover your database later, you will need to restore it from a backup.

NOTE   Master, Model, and Tempdb cannot be dropped.

WARNING   The MSDB database can be dropped, but doing so will render the SQLServerAgent service and replication completely unusable. It will also cause errors whenever you do a backup or restoration, because the system will attempt to write information to the detail and history tables in the MSDB database.

Working with Filegroups

As discussed in Chapter 1, filegroups are used for explicitly placing database objects onto a particular set of database files, which can improve performance and simplify backups.

The two basic filegroups in SQL Server 7 are the primary, or default, filegroup that is created with every database and the user-defined filegroups created for a particular database. The primary filegroup will always contain the primary data file and any other files that are not specifically created on a user-defined filegroup. You can create additional filegroups using the ALTER DATABASE command or the Enterprise Manager.

Filegroups have several rules that you should follow when you are working with them:

- The first (or primary) data file must reside on the primary filegroup.

- All system files must be placed on the primary filegroup.

- A file cannot be a member of more than one filegroup at a time.

- Filegroups can be allocated indexes, tables, text, ntext, and image data.

- If the primary filegroup runs out of space, it will not automatically start using space from a user-defined filegroup.

When you use filegroups, you may find that just one file in the database has grown too large and must be reduced. You can shrink that one file using the SHRINKFILE command:

```
DBCC SHRINKFILE {
  (filename | file_id}
  [, target_percentage]
  [, {EMPTYFILE | NOTRUNCATE | TRUNCATEONLY}])}
```

The *filename* or *file_id* parameters are used to specify the individual database file you wish to shrink. The *file_id* can be found by first running an **sp_helpdb** stored procedure.

The other new parameter is the EMPTYFILE option, which is used in conjunction with a filegroup. You can use this option to move all data stored on a particular file to other files in the filegroup. EMPTYFILE will then mark the file as empty. Once a file has been marked empty, you can remove it from the filegroup using the ALTER DATABASE command with the REMOVE FILE parameter.

Necessary Procedures

You will need to know a few procedures for the exam. The first, how to create data files and the corresponding transaction logs, will not be hit very hard. Since the next procedure, managing filegroups, is new in SQL 7, you will need to understand it well for the exam. Finally, the procedures for managing filegrowth (which you should have a firm grasp of for the exam, since they have been completely revamped for SQL 7) will be explored.

Creating Data Files and Transaction Log Files

As with nearly everything in SQL, there are two methods to create these files: graphically and with T-SQL. Creating data and transaction log files in Enterprise Manager is done using the following steps:

1. Expand your Databases folder.

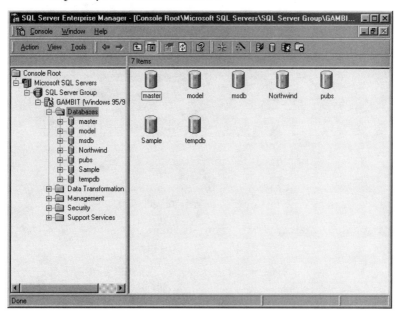

2. Right-click either the Databases folder in the console tree or the white space in the right pane, and choose New Database from the context menu.

3. On the General tab of the Database Properties dialog box, you can type in the name of your new database. When you enter the name, notice that the database filename automatically fills in.

4. Set the first data file's initial size.

5. If you want to have the file grow automatically, set the Automatically Grow File option to true (checked).

6. If your database will grow automatically, set the File Growth increment in either MB or percentage.

7. If your database will autogrow, you should set Restrict Filegrowth to the largest size you can afford. If you don't, the database will grow to take the entire hard disk.

8. Click the Transaction Log tab and set all of the same options. Note that the size of the transaction log should be 10 to 25 percent of the size of the data file.

9. When finished, click OK.

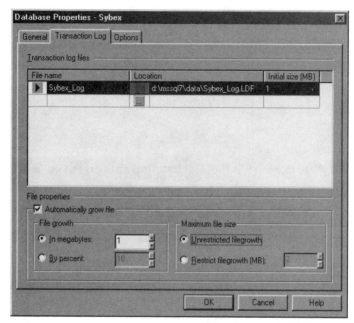

The alternate method for creating data and transaction log files is by using the CREATE DATABASE statement. To create a 4MB database named Sample that can grow to 10MB (in 10-percent increments) and a corresponding 1MB transaction log file that can grow to 4MB (in 10-percent increments), use the following code:

```
CREATE DATABASE Sample
ON [PRIMARY]
(NAME = 'SampleData',
 FILENAME = 'C:\MSSQL7\Data\SampleData.MDF',
 SIZE = 4,
 MAXSIZE = 10,
 FILEGROWTH = 10%)
LOG ON
(NAME = 'SampleLog',
 FILENAME = 'C:\MSSQL7\Data\SampleLog.LDF',
 SIZE = 1,
```

```
MAXSIZE = 4,
FILEGROWTH = 10%)
```

Managing Filegrowth Characteristics

The time will come when you need to expand or shrink your database. There is not a great deal of work involved with this, and it should not happen very often, but it is still necessary to know how to do it.

Expanding Databases

To work this miracle through Enterprise Manager, you just right-click the database and select Properties. In the subsequent dialog box, you can add additional data and log files. Simply click in a new box and fill in the new logical name, physical location, initial size, and other properties.

Expanding databases using T-SQL is just as simple. In the following example, you will see how to add a secondary file to a database named Sample using the ALTER DATABASE statement. The secondary file here is 4MB with the capacity to grow to 10MB in 2MB increments:

```
ALTER DATABASE Sample
ADD LOG FILE
(NAME = Sample_Log2,
 FILENAME = 'C:\MSSQL7\Data\Sample_Log2.ldf',
 SIZE = 4MB,
 MAXSIZE = 10MB,
 FILEGROWTH = 2MB)
```

Shrinking Databases

Shrinking a database using the Enterprise Manager is not particularly intuitive. Right-clicking your way to the Properties sheet and entering a smaller value for the Initial Space option will not shrink the database. The following steps will shrink a database in Enterprise Manager:

1. Open the Enterprise Manager.

2. Drill down to the Database folder and click the database you want to shrink.

3. Right-click the Sample database in the console tree and choose All Tasks ➤ Shrink Database.

4. Click Shrink Database by (%) and change the value. If, for example, you want to shrink a 13MB database down to 7MB, you would enter 50.

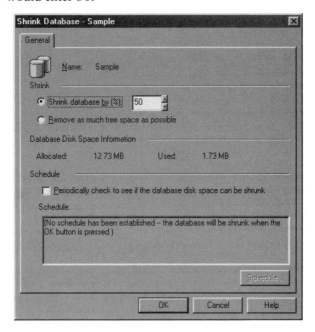

5. Click OK when you are finished.

6. You should get a confirmation message that tells you that the database has been successfully shrunk.

To shrink a database with T-SQL, you need to use the DBCC SHRINKDATABASE statement. To shrink a database named Sample leaving only 10 percent free space in the database, you would execute:

```
DBCC SHRINKDATABASE (Sample, 10%)
```

Working with Filegroups

Creating filegroups is a relatively straightforward task and will not be tested on a great deal. In fact, for the exam, it is better to understand what filegroups are used for rather than the mechanics of creating them. Nonetheless, it is still necessary to understand the procedures involved.

Creating Filegroups with the Enterprise Manager

You can create the filegroups when you create a new database or when you alter an existing database. The following steps outline the creation of a new filegroup with a new database file added to it:

1. Drill down in the console tree and right-click the database you want to modify, then choose Properties.

2. Just under the data file information, add a new data file, and then add a name for the new filegroup in the File Group box.

3. Click OK when you are finished. Your database Properties screen should look similar to the graphic shown here:

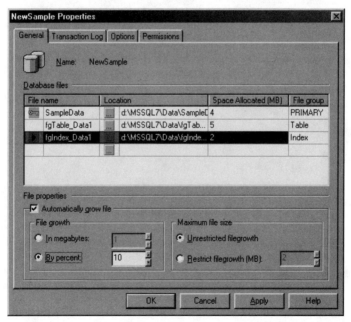

Creating Filegroups with T-SQL

As you might expect, using T-SQL to create a filegroup is a bit trickier. To add a filegroup and then add data files to the filegroup, you need to use the ALTER DATABASE statement.

In this example, you will create a new filegroup called Testing on the Dummy database. You will also see the results of the query.

```
ALTER DATABASE Dummy
ADD FILEGROUP Testing
GO


The command(s) completed successfully
```

Then, once you have created the filegroup, you are ready to add files to it. The following code will create a new table called fgTable_Data2, which will be 2MB in size and a part of the Sales filegroup:

```
USE NewSample
GO
ALTER DATABASE Sample
ADD FILE
(NAME = fgTable_Data2,
 FILENAME = 'C:\MSSQL7\Data\fgTable_Data2.ndf',
 SIZE = 2MB)
TO FILEGROUP Sales
```

Removing a Filegroup

To remove a filegroup, you must first ensure that all the files that make up the filegroup have been removed. Once the files have been removed, you can remove the filegroup using the ALTER DATABASE statement. The following steps demonstrate how to do this:

1. Run the following query to remove the files from the filegroup:

```
USE Sample
GO
ALTER DATABASE Sample
REMOVE FILE fgTable_Data1
GO
```

```
ALTER DATABASE Sample
REMOVE FILE fgTable_Data2
GO
```

2. Now that the data files have been removed, you can remove the
   filegroups themselves. Run the following query:

```
USE NewSample
GO
ALTER DATABASE NewSample
REMOVE FILEGROUP Sales
GO
```

Exam Essentials

This section will not be heavily tested on, but you can expect to see a
question or two regarding the following points.

Know how to manage file growth.   Since managing file growth
has been completely reworked in SQL 7, you can be sure to see a few
questions on the exam. You should be familiar with how to set autogrowth as well as manually changing the size.

Know how to put files in a filegroup.   You will need to have a firm
grasp of the methods for putting files into filegroups, because (as with
all new features) you will see exam questions on this topic.

Key Terms and Concepts

Data file: The data file is where all database objects, such as
tables and indexes, are stored.

Filegroup: A filegroup is a logical grouping of database files used
for improving performance and administration.

Transaction log file: Transaction log files are used to record
transactions that make modifications to the data. They are used
for up-to-the-minute recoverability in the event of a disaster.

Sample Questions

1. You have created a business-contact database that has been filled to capacity, leaving no room on the disk for further expansion. How can you allocate more space for this database?

   A. By using the DBCC EXPANDDB statement to create a secondary file for the database.

   B. By using the ALTER DATABASE statement to create a secondary file for the database.

   C. By moving the database to a larger hard drive.

   D. There is no way to accomplish this.

   Answer: B. ALTER DATABASE or Enterprise Manager can be used to add a secondary file to the database. Once that is done, you will have more room for the data. Incidentally, the statement in answer A does not even exist.

2. When you use T-SQL to create a 100MB database, but do not specify the transaction log parameters, what happens?

   A. No transaction log is created.

   B. A 10MB transaction log is created in the same directory as the data file.

   C. A 25MB transaction log is created in the same directory as the data file.

   D. The CREATE DATABASE statement fails when the transaction log information is not specified.

   Answer: C. A transaction log that is 25 percent of the size of the data file will be created in the same directory as the data file.

Load data by using various methods. Methods include the INSERT statement, the SELECT INTO statement, the bcp utility, Data Transformation Services (DTS), and the BULK INSERT statement.

O nce you have successfully created your database, it is important to fill it with data. Several methods for filling your databases, each one having its own strengths—the INSERT statement, the SELECT INTO statement, the bcp utility, Data Transformation Services (DTS), and the BULK INSERT statement—will be examined.

Under ordinary circumstances, you will need to fill your databases with new data only when the database is first created—but not all circumstances are ordinary. Some databases will need to be completely cycled on a regular basis, such as a catalog database that needs to be updated with brand-new data every quarter. Because such circumstances are becoming so commonplace, Microsoft has deemed it necessary to make this topic an exam objective.

This section is not just useful for the exam, though—you need this information in the real world as well. Not only will inserting massive amounts of data at one time be covered, but also how to insert small amounts—just one record. All of this is very important to you as an administrator and test taker, so watch closely as the secrets of loading data are uncovered.

Critical Information

In this section, the various methods for loading data, either in vast amounts or one record at a time, will be discussed. How to enter vast amounts will be covered a little later on; first, let's discuss how to update small amounts of data with the INSERT statement.

Loading Data with the INSERT Statement

The INSERT statement is used to add a single row of data to your table. Before you can use the INSERT statement, you need to know the structure of the table into which the data are being inserted. Specifically, you should know the number of columns in the table, the data types of these columns, the column names, and any defaults or constraints (e.g., IDENTITY) that are on a particular column. You can gather this information by using the sp_help tablename stored procedure or by right-clicking a table in Enterprise Manager and choosing Properties.

The easiest way to work with the INSERT statement is to specify data for each column in the table that requires data, in the same order in which the columns were defined.

NOTE When you are inserting character data, you must enclose the characters in single quotation marks. When you are inserting numeric data, you do not use quotation marks.

There is much more information that could be covered regarding the INSERT statement, but that is useful much more to the SQL Server developer than it is to the administrator. For the exam, you really need to know when it is appropriate to use the INSERT statement rather than the SELECT INTO statement, DTS, bcp, and so on.

Remember these facts about the INSERT statement:

- It generally adds a single record at a time.

- The inserted record is a logged transaction.

- If there is an index, it will be updated as well.

- You must have INSERT permission on the table to which you wish to add records.

Copying Tables with SELECT INTO

Essentially a copy-table command, the SELECT INTO statement is used to create new permanent tables or new temporary tables filled with data from another table.

To use the SELECT INTO command to create a permanent table in your database, you must first enable the Select Into/Bulk Copy database option. This can be done either in the Enterprise Manager or through the sp_dboption stored procedure. When you set the Select Into/Bulk Copy database option, you are specifying that you are about to perform a nonlogged insert of data. This is very important to know because it means that as soon as you are done with the operation, your database is vulnerable and needs to be backed up right away.

Keep the following things in mind when you are working with the SELECT INTO statement:

- To create a permanent table, you must have the Select Into/Bulk Copy database option enabled.

- To create local temporary tables, you must prefix your table name with an octothorp (#).

- To create global temporary tables, you must prefix your table name with two octothorps (##).

- To run the SELECT INTO command, you must have CREATE TABLE permissions in the database.

- Running a SELECT INTO statement performs a nonlogged operation—you should ensure your data by backing them up.

Copying Data with Bcp

Bulk copy, or bcp, is a lightning-fast command-line utility for moving data between a text file and your SQL Server 7 database. The upside of bcp is its speed and compatibility. If you do not have indexes created on your tables and you have the Select Into/Bulk Copy database option set, reading an ASCII file into your server is very quick (better than 2000 rows per second on average).

There are disadvantages, however. First, because bcp is a command-line utility, it requires you to remember a number of different switches and is case-sensitive. Another disadvantage is that bcp transfers data only, not other database objects such as tables, views, and schema. The last downside is the fact that bcp cannot do data transformations such as converting a text string to a numeric value or splitting a Name field into a FirstName and a LastName field.

To use bcp, you must have the appropriate permissions. When you wish to move data from a text file into SQL Server 7, you must have READ permissions on the file itself (if using NTFS), and you must have INSERT permissions on the SQL Server table into which you would like to move the data.

To use bcp to move data from SQL Server to a text file, you must have NTFS permissions for either Change or Full Control on the directory and the file. Within SQL Server, you must have SELECT permissions on the table or view from which you want to pull your data.

Here is the syntax for bcp:

```
Bcp [[dbname.]owner.]tablename | view_name | "Query"}
{in | out | queryout | format } datafile
[/6]
[/a packet_size]
[/b batchsize]
[/c]
[/C code_page]
[/e errfile]
[/E]
[/f formatfile]
[/F firstrow]
[/h "hint [,...n]"]
[/i inputfile]
[/k]
[/L lastrow]
[/m maxerrors]
[/n]
```

```
[/N]
[/o output_file]
[/P password]
[/q]
[/r row_term]
[/S server_name]
[/t field_term]
[/T]
/U login_id
[/v]
[/w]
```

The following list explains each parameter. Note that the only required parameters are `tablename`, `in/out/queryout/format`, `datafile`, and `login ID '/U'`.

dbname.owner.tablename or *view_name* or *query*: Specifies the name of the table view or query you want to export from or import to. If you don't specify the database name or the owner, these values will default to the current database and the user name of the person who is running the bcp command.

in/out/queryout/format: Specifies whether you are loading data into SQL Server 7 or extracting data out to a file.

datafile: Specifies the name of the file with which you wish to work. If you do not specify the full path name with your file, it will default to the local directory from which you run the bcp program. If you do not specify a filename at all, bcp will go into Format File mode. This allows you to create a format file that can be reused later. The format file is simply a template for bulk copying data into or out of SQL Server 7.

/6: Specifies that you are working with data from a SQL Server 6.*x* file.

/a packet_size: Allows you to specify the size of the packets you are going to be transferring across the network. The default is 4096 bytes.

/b *batchsize*: Specifies how many records you are going to transfer in a single batch. SQL Server will treat each batch as a separate transaction. If this option is not specified, the entire file will be loaded as a single batch.

/c: Specifies that the data being moved will all be converted to the character data type rather than the internal SQL Server data types. When used for export, it will create a tab-delimited flat file.

/C *code_page*: This option (note the capital C) allows you to specify a code page for the data file. For example, you can generate a file with the code page 850, which was the default code page for SQL Server 6.

/e *errfile*: Creates a path and filename containing the rows of data that bcp could not import or export properly. This can be very useful when you are troubleshooting your bcp operation. If you do not specify an error file, none will be generated. It is suggested that you use the .ERR file extension.

/E: The capital *E* specifies that identity columns in your SQL Server 7 table should be temporarily turned off. This allows the values in the source file to replace the automatically generated identity values in the SQL Server table during the bulk copy. Identity columns are similar to the autonumber feature in Microsoft Access.

/f *formatfile*: Allows you to specify the path and filename of the format file you wish to use during an insertion to or extraction from SQL Server 7. If you do not specify the format-file portion of this option, bcp will prompt you for formatting information and then create a format file called bcp.fmt.

/F *firstrow*: The capital *F* and firstrow value allow you to specify a row, other than the first row, to begin reading into SQL Server 7.

/h *"hint"*: Allows you to specify any hints you wish to use. For example, you might create hints about check constraints or sort orders.

/i *inputfile*: Allows you to specify all these input parameters and store them in a file. When you run bcp again, all you need to do is specify this input file—all the stored parameters will be used. As always, specify the full path and filename.

/k: Specifies that empty columns will retain their NULL values rather than having some default value applied to them.

/L *lastrow*: Specifies the last row to load from the data file into SQL Server. If this is not specified, SQL Server will load all rows from the data file.

/m *maxerrors*: Allows you to specify the maximum number of errors SQL Server will allow before the bulk copy process is canceled. You should specify this option if you are importing large data files. The default value is 10 errors.

/n: Specifies that the data being transferred are in native format. In other words, the data being moved around retain their SQL Server 7 data types. This option is especially useful when you are moving data from one SQL Server to another SQL Server.

/N: Specifies that you will be using Unicode for character data and native format for all noncharacter data.

/o *output_file*: Specifies the name of the file that will receive any messages generated by the bulk copy. This option is useful when you run bcp from a batch file and later want to review what was processed.

/P *password*: Specifies the password you wish to use when logging into SQL Server from bcp. If you do not specify a password, bcp will prompt you for one.

/q: Specifies that quoted identifiers are being used. When this option is set, all identifiers (table name, column names, etc.) must be specified within double quotation marks.

/r *row_term*: Specifies the value that bcp will use to determine where one row ends and the next row begins. You can use the following common characters as either field or row terminators:

   \0: Specifies an ANSI NULL.

   \n: Specifies a new line.

\r: Specifies a carriage return.

\t: Specifies a tab.

\\: Specifies a backslash.

/S *server_name*: Specifies the SQL Server to which you are connecting. If you don't specify a servername, bcp will assume that it is the local SQL Server.

/t *field_term*: Specifies the field terminator. In many cases, this will be a comma or tab character.

/T: This capital *T* specifies that the bulk copy utility will connect to SQL Server over a trusted connection.

/U *login_id*: Specifies the login ID that you will use to gain access to SQL Server and is a required parameter.

/v: Reports which DB-Library version is being used for the bulk copy process.

/w: Specifies that the data will be transferred using Unicode.

You should keep a few other items in mind when you are using bcp. Character mode is the most flexible method of bulk copy because all data are treated as characters. This means that SQL Server and most other applications can work with the data. When you use Character mode to export data, they will be stored as an ASCII text file. Native mode uses the internal SQL Server data types and can be faster for data transfers from one SQL Server to another SQL Server database. In fact, when you use the Transfer Manager (discussed later in this chapter), it uses bcp to move data from one SQL Server 7 computer to another SQL Server 7 computer.

When you perform a bulk copy to import data, you can do it in Normal mode, which means every insert is logged, or in Fast mode, which means inserts are not logged. To operate in Fast mode, you must enable the Select Into/Bulk Copy database option and drop all indexes that are affected by the data transfer. Once you have done this, you can quickly add your data using bulk copy. When you do a bulk copy, you should also be aware that defaults and data types will always be enforced, and rules, triggers, and constraints will always be ignored.

Since rules, triggers, and constraints are ignored during a Fast bulk copy, you should check the validity of your data by running queries or other stored procedures. A simple way to check your constraints is to run an UPDATE statement and set a particular field equal to itself. This will force all constraints to be checked against the new data. It will also fire off any update triggers associated with the table.

Once you are happy with your data, you should re-create your indexes and then back up your database because it is now unrecoverable.

Using BULK INSERT

You can be sure to see a question or two on the test regarding BULK INSERT because it is new to SQL Server 7. The BULK INSERT command treats data files like OLE-DB recordsets. Since SQL Server thinks the file is an OLE-DB recordset, it can move multiple records per step. You can move the entire file in one batch or in several batches.

One major difference between bcp and BULK INSERT is that BULK INSERT cannot move data from SQL Server to a file. Essentially, BULK INSERT gives you bulk copy capabilities through the use of T-SQL. Since bcp is a command-line utility, it can be placed into batch files; BULK INSERT cannot. You must be a member of the sysadmin server role to use the BULK INSERT command.

It is important to read through the BULK INSERT syntax and parameters at least once before the exam:

```
BULK INSERT [[database_name.][owner].]{table_name
FROM data_file}[WITH (
[BATCHSIZE = batch_size]]
[[,] CHECK_CONSTRAINTS]fa
[[,] CODEPAGE [= 'ACP' | 'OEM' | 'RAW' | 'code_page']]
[[,] DATAFILETYPE [= {'char' | 'native'| 'widechar' |
'widenative'}]]
[[,] FIELDTERMINATOR [= 'field_terminator']]
```

```
[[,] FIRSTROW [= first_row]]
[[,] FORMATFILE [= 'format_file_path']]
[[,] KEEPIDENTITY]
[[,] KEEPNULLS]
[[,] KILOBYTES_PER_BATCH [= kilobytes_per_batch]]
[[,] LASTROW [= last_row]]
[[,] MAXERRORS [= max_errors]]
[[,] ORDER ({column [ASC | DESC]} [,…n])]
[[,] ROWS_PER_BATCH [= rows_per_batch]]
[[,] ROWTERMINATOR [= 'row_terminator']]
[[,] TABLOCK])]
```

Here are the parameters:

database_name.owner.table_name: The fully qualified table
into which you BULK INSERT data.

data_file: The path and filename from which you wish to import.

CHECK_CONSTRAINTS: Specifies that constraints will be
checked during the BULK INSERT.

CODEPAGE: Specifies which codepage was used to generate the
data file.

DATAFILETYPE: Specifies in which format the data in the file
have been stored. This could be character data, bcp native, Unicode character, or Unicode native.

FIELDTERMINATOR: Specifies which character has been used
as a field terminator. As with bcp, the default is a tab character
(often shown as \t).

FIRSTROW: Specifies the row with which you want to begin the
BULK INSERT process. The default is the first row.

FORMATFILE: Specifies the full path and filename of a format
file to be used with BULK INSERT.

KEEPIDENTITY: Specifies that IDENTITY values copied from
the file will be retained rather than having SQL Server generate
new values.

KEEPNULLS: This option is similar to the KEEPIDENTITY option. It specifies that NULL values in the data file will remain NULL values when loaded into the table.

KILOBYTES_PER_BATCH: Allows you to specify the number of kilobytes to be moved in each step. By default, this is the size of the entire file.

LASTROW: Specifies which row you to want to use to end the BULK INSERT process. By default, it is the last row in the file.

ORDER: Allows you to specify a sort order in the data file. This can improve performance in situations where the data file and SQL Server use different sort orders.

ROWS_PER_BATCH: Specifies how many rows of data to move in each step of the batch. If you use the BATCHSIZE option, you do not need to use this option. By default, all rows are moved in a single batch.

ROWTERMINATOR: Allows you to specify the end of a single row of data. The default value is the new-line character (\n).

TABLOCK: Specifies that a table lock, which will lock the entire table, should be used during the BULK INSERT procedure. No other users may make changes to data in the table during the upload. This can improve the BULK INSERT performance, but it will decrease performance for the other users.

Using Data Transformation Services (DTS)

Most companies store their data in a variety of locations and formats. SQL Server can move data through any of them as long as they are OLE-DB or ODBC compliant by using DTS. When you are working with data from two SQL Server 7 computers, you can even transfer database objects and schema, including stored procedures, views, permissions, table layouts, etc. DTS does this by running a package, which can be created through Wizards or the DTS Designer.

DTS Packages

DTS packages are a set of tasks designed into a work flow of steps. These steps and tasks are then grouped together into a package. You can create packages using the Import and Export Wizards, through a scripting language, from the command line using `dtswiz` and `dtsrun`, or visually through the DTS Designer.

Once you have created a package, it becomes a completely self-contained COM object, which you can interact with through the Enterprise Manager Task Scheduler, the command line, or COM-compliant languages (such as VBScript). The components that compose a package are as follows:

Task objects: Each task in a package defines a particular action that should be taken or some type of processing that should be done. Task objects can be used to perform activities such as running a T-SQL statement or sending e-mail.

Step objects: Step objects are used to coordinate the flow of tasks, giving structure to the work flows. While task objects are self-contained units, a task object that does not have an associated step object will not be executed. Steps can run in parallel or one after the other.

Connection objects: DTS uses connection objects to connect to both a data source and a destination. All of the information necessary to make a connection, including the login IDs, passwords, filenames, locations of the data, format of the data, etc., is contained in a connection object. Connection objects can be either data file (a text file) or data source (a database).

Data-pump object: The DTS data-pump object is an OLE-DB service provider that takes care of importing and exporting, and the data transformation.

Once created, these DTS packages can be stored in one of three locations: the MSDB database, the SQL Server repository, or as a COM-based object. Each of these has advantages:

MSDB database: Packages stored here take less space than in the repository, and other SQL Servers can connect to the packages and use them.

Repository: Storing packages here makes them available to other SQL Servers and, unlike the MSDB database, tracks metadata. The metadata are a lineage, or history, of how many times a package has been run and the changes it has made to the data.

COM file: When saved as COM-structured storage, packages are stored as data objects and data streams. A data object is similar to a folder, while a data stream is similar to a file within that data object. Any COM-compliant programming language can manipulate the DTS package when it is stored as a COM file.

Since security is a very pressing issue, you will most likely get a question on how to secure your packages once they're created. Two levels can be set:

DTS Owner passwords: A user or application with the DTS Owner password has complete access to the package. By default, you store a package with an Owner password.

DTS Operator passwords: Any user or application with this password has the ability to execute the package, but cannot modify or view the package components.

DTS Import and Export Wizards

Perhaps the easiest way to create packages is by using the Import and Export Wizards. While these tools do not allow a great deal of complexity in the packages they create, you can use them to perform the following tasks:

- Copy tables

- Copy query results, including the ability to create queries with the Query Builder Wizard

- Specify data-connection objects for both the source and destination

- Create and schedule DTS packages

- Transform data

- Run scripting languages

- Save packages in SQL Server, the repository, and COM-structured storage

- Transfer database schema and objects using Transfer Manager from one SQL Server 7 database to another SQL Server 7 database

DTS Designer

If you want to create complex data-transformation packages, DTS Designer is the tool for you. DTS Designer is a GUI-based utility you can use to create and edit your DTS packages. If you are familiar with programming in Access or Visual Basic, you should have no problems picking up the interface for the DTS Designer. Due to the sheer magnitude of the Designer, all of its aspects can't possibly be covered here (in fact it should have its own book), but you should definitely take a look at it.

Necessary Procedures

From this section, it is important to know how to use all of the tools listed. You do not need to memorize each of the options and the case sensitivity, but rather, you should have a general understanding of what each tool is and how it functions.

Using the INSERT Statement

Using the INSERT statement is so simple that it does not even require steps. To add a single row to a table, just use the following code:

```
Use database
GO
INSERT INTO table VALUES
('col_one_value', 'col_two_value', 'col_three_value')
```

Using the SELECT INTO Statement

To use this statement, the Select Into/Bulk Copy option must be set on your database. To set this option from Enterprise Manager:

1. Navigate through the console tree to the database of your choice.

2. Right-click the database and choose Properties.

3. From the Properties window, click the Options tab.

4. On the Options tab, check the box next to Select Into/Bulk Copy.

You may also set this option via T-SQL code. Execute your SELECT INTO statement and immediately set the Select Into/Bulk Copy option to false again as follows:

```
USE database
GO

EXEC sp_dboption 'database_name', 'select into/
  bulkcopy', True
GO

SELECT * INTO new_table_name
FROM existing_table_name
GO

EXEC sp_dboption 'database_name', 'select into/
  bulkcopy', False
GO
```

Using Bcp

Even though bcp is used primarily for backward compatibility, it is still advisable to know how to use it. Used from a command prompt, the following code will transfer data out of a database to a text file (it wraps here for readability only):

```
bcp database..table out
c:\mssql7\data\filename.txt -c -SServerName -Usa -P
```

Using BULK INSERT

As with the other T-SQL commands that have been discussed thus far, the BULK INSERT statement is simple to use. The following T-SQL code can be used to insert data into a table from a text file:

```
BULK INSERT database.owner.tablename
FROM 'c:\mssql7\data\filename.txt'
```

Using the Import and Export Wizards

Since both of these Wizards look identical, only the Import Wizard needs to be discussed. The following steps can be used to import a table using the Wizard:

1. Open the Enterprise Manager and connect to your SQL Server.

2. Right-click the Data Transformation Services folder and choose All Tasks ➤ Import Data from the context menu.

3. You should now be at the Import Wizard welcome screen. Click Next to continue.

4. You are now presented with the Choose a Data Source screen. Choose the source server. Choose your authentication type (Windows NT or Standard) and the source database from which to import. If the database you want does not show up in the drop-down list box, click the Refresh button and try again.

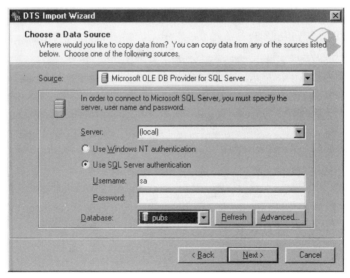

5. Clicking the Advanced button will display the Advanced Properties that you can work with (as shown below).

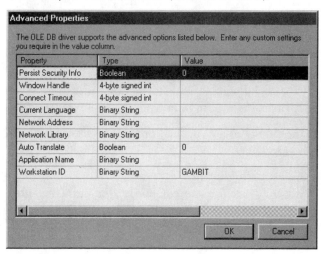

6. Click Next to work with the Choose a Destination screen. Fill in the options as you did earlier. Click Next to continue.

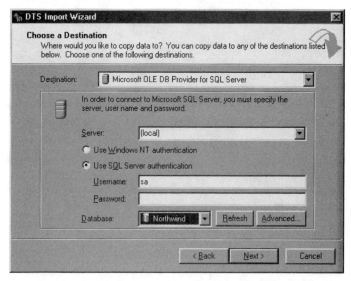

7. You are now presented with the Specify Table Copy or Query dialog box. If you choose Table Copy, it will move an entire table. The Query option will allow you to specify a query and use the query builder. If you selected a SQL Server 7 data source and destination, the Transfer Objects option will also be available. Click Next to continue.

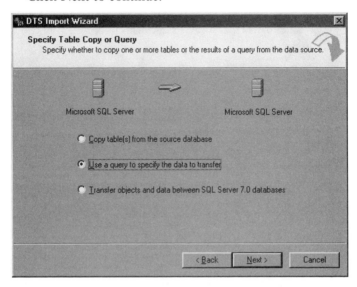

8. If you selected the Query option previously, you are now presented with the Type SQL Statement screen (as shown below). You can type in a query, use the Query Builder button, or load a query stored in a file. Once a query has been added, you can check it for syntax by clicking the Parse button. Click Next to move on.

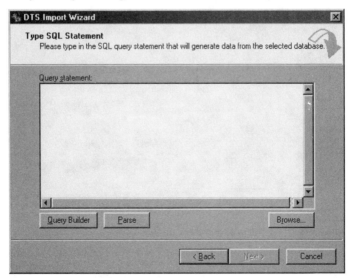

9. You should now see the Select Source Tables screen pictured below. Notice that the Source Table is Query and the Destination Table is called Results. You can change that if you like. There is also an ellipsis (...) in the Transform field, which takes you to the Transformation dialog box when clicked.

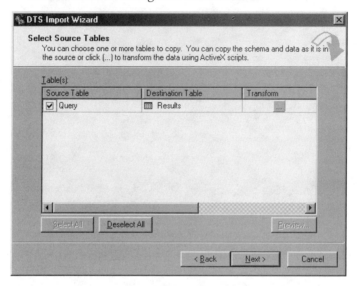

10. If you are making changes, you should now be presented with the Column Mappings and Transformations screen shown below:

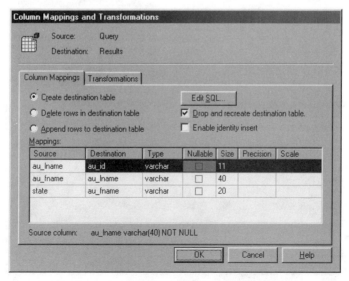

11. If you click the Transformations tab and then choose the Transform Information as It Is Copied to the Destination option, you can specify your own custom transformations using one of three scripting languages (as shown below).

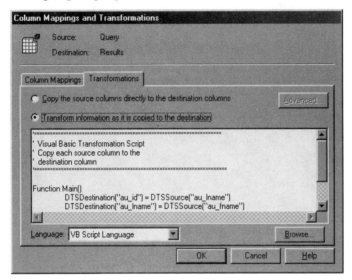

12. Click the OK button to return to the Select Source Tables screen. Click Next to continue processing.

13. You are now presented with the Save, Schedule and Replicate Package screen shown next. The Run Immediately option will run the package as soon as it has completed. You can also choose to make the package available for replication and set up a schedule for automatic execution. When you are finished, click Next to continue.

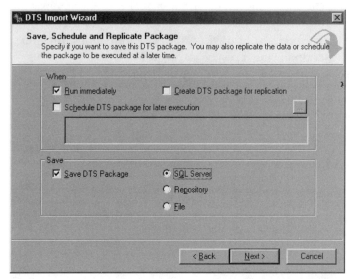

14. You are now presented with the Save DTS Package screen. Fill in the package name and description. This is also the place to secure your package with Owner and Operator passwords. Click Next to continue.

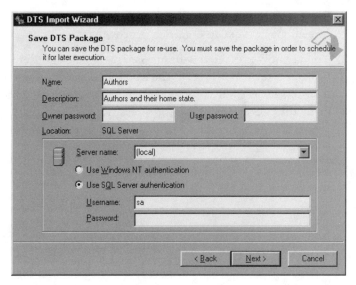

15. Finally, you are presented with the finish screen. Click Finish. You will see the package executing. You may be prompted with another dialog box informing you that the package ran and completed successfully.

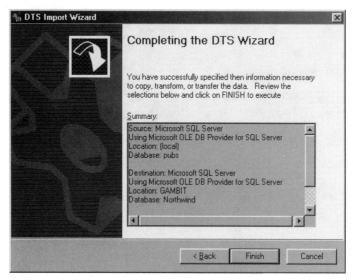

Using the DTS Designer

To access the Designer, follow the steps outlined here:

1. Open the SQL Enterprise Manager.

2. Drill down through the console tree into the Data Transformation Services folder.

3. Click the Local Packages icon, right-click an existing package, then choose Design Package.

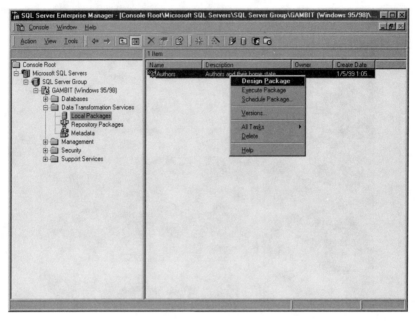

4. You should now see the DTS Designer screen (it should look similar to the graphic displayed below).

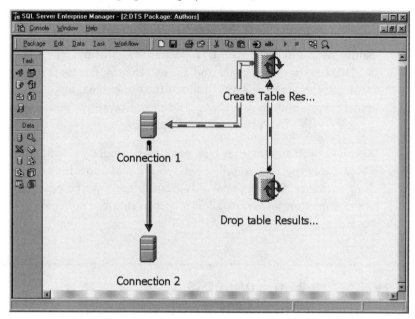

5. Right-click any of the objects or connections to view their information.

6. Close the DTS Designer when you are finished.

Exam Essentials

You should expect a few questions from this section since databases are useless if they don't have data in them—not to mention that DTS is a new feature, so Microsoft wants to make sure you know how to use it. Here are a few key points for the exam.

Know the various methods of importing data. Several methods of importing data were discussed here. It is important to understand all of them, knowing what they are used for and how to use them.

Know what DTS is capable of. You should know that DTS is capable of a great deal more than just moving data. DTS can move data from SQL to any ODBC source and vice versa. It can also manipulate the data so that they are not in the same structure at the destination.

Know where to store your DTS packages. Storing data in the MSDB database saves space and allows other SQL Servers to access your packages. The repository allows the same thing, but also stores data lineage about each package. The file option allows you to use the package with other programming languages.

Know how to secure your DTS packages. Since you will get asked about this topic on the exam, you should know how to secure your packages. Owner passwords grant full access to a package, while Operator passwords allow a user to run, but not change, the package.

Key Terms and Concepts

DTS package: This is a DTS object that defines a series of tasks to be executed in sequence for importing, exporting, and transforming data.

Repository: This is a metadata storage container. When a DTS package is stored here, its data lineage is maintained.

Sample Questions

1. Your company has just bought out a smaller company that is using an Access database to store critical information. You need to import this data into an SQL table for use by your users. What is the easiest way to do this?

    A. Export all of the data from the Access database to a text file, then import the text file into SQL using the INSERT statement.

B. Export all of the data from the Access database to a text file, then import the text file into SQL using the BULK INSERT statement.

C. Export all of the data from the Access database to a text file, then import the text file into SQL using bcp.

D. Use the DTS Import Wizard.

Answer: D. Answers B and C would have worked, but they require you to use Access to create the text file. The DTS Wizard will access the Access database for you via ODBC.

2. You have just created a DTS package and want to be certain that only members of the MIS department can run the package and that only administrators in the MIS department can change it. How should you protect the package?

A. Put Owner and Operator passwords on the package. Give the Owner password to everyone in MIS.

B. Put Owner and Operator passwords on the package. Give the Owner password to the administrators in MIS and the Operator password to everyone else in MIS.

C. Put an Operator password on the package and give it to everyone in MIS. The administrators will not require a password as long as an administrator creates the package.

D. There is no way to protect the package.

Answer: C. The Operator password will allow everyone in MIS to run the package without being able to change it. Giving the Owner password to the administrators ensures that only administrators can make changes.

Back up system databases and user databases by performing a full database backup, a transaction log backup, a differential database backup, and a filegroup backup.

As an administrator, one of the most important duties of your career is backing up your data. Why is this so important? Imagine what would happen if your sales database went off-line for a few hours—you could lose thousands of dollars in revenue, not to mention operating costs. You need to be sure that doesn't happen by performing backups. Since this topic can, and will, save you from disaster, you need to pay special attention not only for the real-world application, but for the exam.

Four different types of backups will be examined here: full, transaction log, differential, and filegroup. Each of these has its own strengths and weaknesses that can be exploited to your benefit.

Critical Information

The first step in backing up your data is creating a *backup device* (called a *dump* in earlier versions), which is where SQL stores backups. Backup devices can be permanent, which are reusable, or temporary, which can be used only once. The temporary variety is useful for emergency backups or backups that need to be shipped off for storage off-site. Permanent backup devices will be discussed in this section. These backup devices can point to files, or you can back up directly to tape.

If you use a tape, you can leave a single tape in the computer for both SQL and Windows NT backups, since SQL Server 7 uses the same tape format as Windows NT Backup. The problem with using a tape is that it needs to be installed physically in the SQL Server computer—it cannot be remote.

TIP   If you want to use a remote tape drive, you need third-party software such as Arcserve or Backup Exec.

Since the majority of people back up to a file and then back the file up to tape as part of their Windows NT backup, the focus in this section will be primarily on backing up to files. Most of the principles for backing up to tape are the same.

If you have multiple backup devices, you can perform what is called a *parallel striped backup*. This speeds up the backup process by backing up to multiple devices at the same time. For example, backing up a database to tape may take an hour. If you have three tape drives in the SQL Server box and back up the database across all three devices, the backup would take approximately 20 minutes.

Another feature of striped backups is that they don't have to be restored simultaneously. A database that has been backed up on three different tape devices can be restored onto a SQL Server that has only one tape drive. You would restore the tapes in order: first, second, and third.

Once you have created the backup device, you can start the backup process. There are four types: full, transaction log, differential, and filegroup—all of which are dynamic and can be performed while users are accessing the database.

NOTE   A backup device is essentially a pointer that SQL Server uses so that it knows where to put the backup file when the backup is actually done. Because of this, files are not created until the backup is actually performed.

Performing Full Database Backups

When a database backup is started, SQL Server will first do a checkpoint of the database and bring it up to date with all the completed transactions. SQL Server then takes a *snapshot* of the database and backs up the entire database. If users are trying to update pages, they will be temporarily blocked by SQL Server as it jumps ahead of the updates.

Any transactions that were not completed when the backup started will not be in it. Because of this, even though backups can be done during normal business hours, backing up the databases at night will help ensure that there is a clear understanding of what is in the backup as well as what didn't make it.

Databases can be backed up by either issuing T-SQL commands or using Enterprise Manager. The syntax for the command that backs up databases is as follows:

```
Backup Database <name> to <device> (with init)
```

Backing Up Transaction Logs

If the database is not set to Truncate Log on Checkpoint, the transaction log can be backed up and restored apart from the database.

The transaction log is a running total of all the transactions that have occurred in that particular database. One of the features of SQL Server is that the transaction log is truncated (cleaned out) only after a successful backup of the log. Many companies have run SQL Server for two or three months with no problems, until they suddenly find that no new transactions can be recorded because the transaction log is filled up.

The good news is that the transaction log will be cleaned out by SQL Server as part of a normal transaction log backup. The bad news is that SQL Server doesn't do this by default—all backups (and thus the cleaning, or truncating, of the log) must be configured by the administrator.

WARNING Although the Truncate Log on Checkpoint option will automatically keep the log clean, it is not recommended for production environments because you cannot recover transactions that happened between database backups. You will also not be able to perform transaction log backups. If you do use the Truncate Log on Checkpoint option, make sure you perform frequent (at least nightly) database backups.

Another advantage of backing up the transaction log is that it can be restored up to a certain point in time. For example, if you have a backup of the transaction log for Wednesday and you later discover a major error had occurred at 4:05 P.M., you could restore the data up to 4:04 P.M.

You can back up the log by issuing the following command:

    Backup log <database> to <device>

This command backs up the log and cleans it out.

Various switches can be added to the command to change the way the backup works:

Truncate_Only: This switch is used to clean out the log without backing it up. If you perform a full database backup every night, maintaining a backup of the log would be redundant, yet the log still needs to be cleaned out. Truncate_Only would perform this task.

No_Log: Since a transaction log backup writes a record to the transaction log, it will fail if the log fills to capacity. This switch will not record the backup in the log.

No_Truncate: This switch does the opposite of the Truncate_ Only switch—it backs up the log without cleaning it out. The main purpose of this switch is to make a new backup of the transaction log when the database itself is either too damaged to work or completely gone.

WARNING Note that with SQL Server 7, you must have at least one .MDF file (database file) still working for the **No_Truncate** switch to back up data successfully from the transaction log.

Performing Differential Database Backups

SQL Server 7 adds the ability to create a differential database backup, which records the final state of any added, edited, or deleted rows since the last full database backup.

NOTE Differential backups, unlike transaction log backups, cannot be restored to a particular point in time, since only the final state of the data is recorded. You may wish to combine differential backups with transaction log backups so that you have the advantages of both types of backups.

To perform a differential backup using T-SQL syntax, simply open a Query Analyzer window and issue the following command:

```
Backup Database <database> to <device> with
    differential
```

Performing Filegroup Backups

SQL Server 7 also allows you to back up files and filegroups independent of the database. For example, suppose you have three data volumes (N:, O:, and P:) and three filegroups (Employees, Customers, and Orders), each residing on a different data volume. If the entire database took too long to back up, you could back up the Employees files on Monday, the Customers files on Tuesday, and the Orders files on Wednesday. Because backing up files or filegroups does not back up the transaction log, make sure you also perform a transaction log backup after backing up the filegroup.

To perform the filegroup backup using T-SQL, issue the following command:

```
Backup database <database>
file=<filename>,filegroup=<filegroup> to <device>
```

Necessary Procedures

For the test, you will need to know how to perform backups using Enterprise Manager and T-SQL. Since you need to have a backup device before you can perform those backups, you will also need to know how to create backup devices. The mechanics of backups will not be tested a great deal—it is more important to spend time on what they can do as opposed to how to make them do it. Even so, these procedures are very important to you.

Creating Backup Devices

Backup devices can be created with the `sp_addumpdevice` command. The syntax for the command specifies the logical name for the device and the path to the file that will be created after the backup is completed:

```
Sp_addumpdevice 'type', 'logical name', 'path'
```

Another, perhaps easier, method for creating these devices is through Enterprise Manager. To create a backup device, follow the steps below:

1. Open the Backup folder (under Management) inside Enterprise Manager.

2. Right-click and choose New Backup Device, or choose Action ➤ New Backup Device.

3. Add a name for your new device and point it to a file on disk. Alternatively, you could create the device on tape.

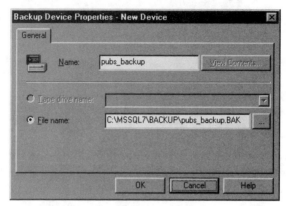

4. Choose OK to make the device.

5. Verify that your device was made by looking in the Backup folder.

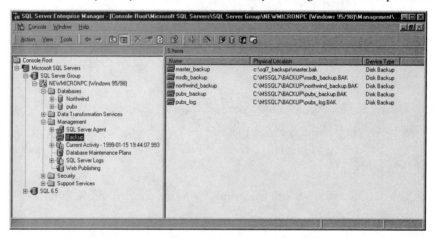

Performing Full Backups

Performing a full backup using T-SQL is quite simple—just use the following code:

```
Backup Database dbname to backup_device with init
```

The with init statement is used for overwriting any exisiting data in the backup device; if no switch is specified, the backup will be appended to any existing data.

To perform a full backup through Enterprise Manager, use the following steps:

1. Highlight the database you want to back up.

2. Go to the Backup screen by either right-clicking and choosing All Tasks ➤ Backup Database, or choosing Tools ➤ Backup Database.

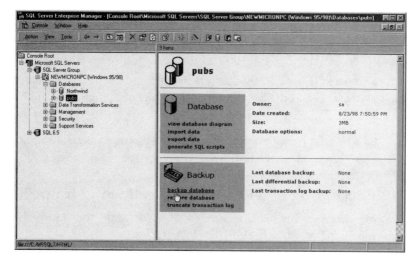

3. In the Backup dialog box, select the database to back up, then enter a name and description for the backup.

4. For a full backup, you need to select the Database—Complete radio button under Backup.

5. Under Destination, select either tape or disk, then select a device. If your device is not listed, click Add.

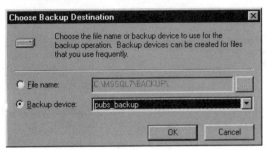

6. If you wish to erase all other data in the device, select the Overwrite Existing Media option from the Overwrite portion of the screen. If not, select Append.

7. Select OK to start the backup. You should see blue bars go across the screen as the backup proceeds. The Pubs database should take only a few seconds to back up.

8. After the backup completes, choose OK from the confirmation screen to close the Backup screen.

Backing Up and Restoring Directly to or from Files

SQL Server 7 can back up or restore directly to or from a file without having to specify a backup device first.

The syntax in SQL Server 7 to back up directly to a file is an extension of the Backup Database command, using a To keyword in front of the specified path and file instead of the device name. For example, to back up Pubs2 to a file, enter the following line:

```
Backup Database Pubs2 to C:\MSSQL\Dumps\Pubs2.dmp
```

Enterprise Manager can also be used to back up to a file directly. Instead of selecting a backup device, simply enter the path of the file you wish to use (as shown next).

Backing Up Transaction Logs

The following steps demonstrate how to back up transaction logs:

1. Go to the Backup screen by highlighting the database in Enterprise Manager; select Backup Database, or right-click and choose Backup Database.

2. Back up the transaction log by selecting Transaction Log for the backup type; select a device to back up to and click OK to start the backup.

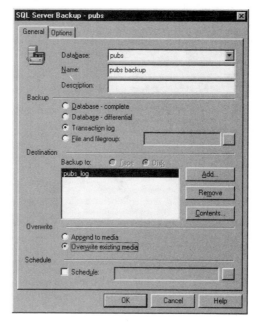

Performing Differential Backups

You can also use Enterprise Manager to perform differential backups, as demonstrated by the following steps:

1. Start Enterprise Manager and go to the Management/Backup folder.

2. You should create a separate device for the differential backups using *differential* somewhere in the naming scheme (i.e., pubs_ diff_backup).

3. Highlight the database you want to back up and choose Backup Database from the Tools menu.

4. Select Differential Backup, choose the backup device, and click OK to start the backup.

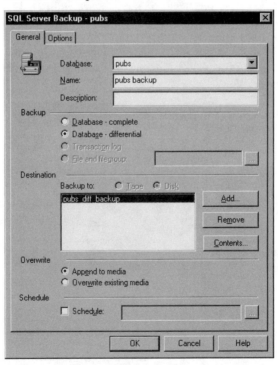

Performing Filegroup Backups

To perform filegroup backups through Enterprise Manager, do as follows:

1. Highlight the database to back up and choose Backup Database from the Tools menu.

2. Select To Do a File and Filegroup Backup and select the Primary (default) filegroup. Choose OK.

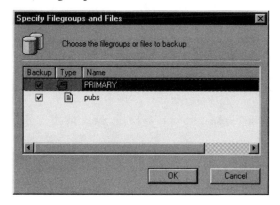

3. Select a backup device and click OK to start the backup.

4. Choose OK to close the Backup screen.

Backup Device Information

Once you have backed up your data, there are several different ways to get information about the backup devices and the dates and contents of the backups stored on them. One way is by using the sp_ helpdevice command with the particular database device specified. You can also use Enterprise Manager to see the contents of backup devices, as shown here:

1. Start Enterprise Manager.

2. Go to the Management ➤ Backup folder.

3. Highlight a backup device, right-click, and choose Properties.

4. Select the View Contents button.

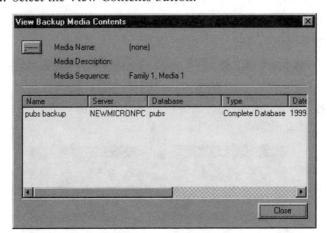

5. Choose Close and Cancel to go back to Enterprise Manager.

Exam Essentials

Backups are a very important part of your life as a database administrator—without them, you could lose very important data. It is because of this that Microsoft is going to ask you questions regarding backups on the exam. Specifically, pay attention to the following key points.

Know the difference between differential and transaction log backups.   Differential backups will back up only records that have changed since the last full backup. Transaction log backups will record the entire lineage of changes.

Know when and how to use a filegroup backup.   Filegroup backups are best used with VLDBs since they capture only a small section of the database. Do not forget that you must still back up the transaction logs after performing this type of backup.

Know when the transaction log is cleared.   The transaction log is cleared only when a transaction log backup is performed or the Truncate Log on Checkpoint option is set on the database.

Key Terms and Concepts

Backup device: This is a pointer telling SQL where the backup files are stored. This can be either disk or tape.

Differential backup: Backs up all records that have changed since the last full backup.

Filegroup backup: Backs up only a single filegroup at a time instead of an entire database.

Full backup: Backs up the entire database.

Transaction log backup: Backs up and clears the transaction log. This is the *only* backup that will clear the transaction log.

Sample Questions

1. You have been performing full backups once a week and differential backups every night for the last two months. When is your transaction log cleared?

   A. Never.

   B. When the full backup is performed.

   C. When the differential backup is performed.

   D. SQL will clear it automatically when it gets too full.

   Answer: A. If you do not perform transaction log backups, your transaction log will not be cleared. The only way to have a transaction log cleared automatically is by setting the Truncate Log on Checkpoint option to true (which should be done only on a development system).

2. When your transaction log fills to capacity, how can you clear it so that users can access the database?

   A. Back up log with `No_Truncate`.

   B. Back up log with `Truncate_Only`.

C. Perform a full backup.

D. Back up log with No_Log.

Answer: D. Backing up with No_Log is the only way to clear a transaction log that has filled to capacity.

Restore system databases and user databases from a full database backup, a transaction log backup, a differential database backup, and a filegroup backup.

Backups and restorations go hand in hand—one serves no purpose without the other. If you have a solid backup strategy and back up every night, those backups will be useless without the capability to restore.

In this section, the methods used to restore your data from backups will be discussed—how to restore from full, differential, transaction log, and filegroup backups. There will also be some discussion of how to restore your system databases, whether or not you have a valid backup.

This section is going to prove invaluable to you when you're out in the real world simply because of this: Bad things happen. Your power may go out, you may get a hacker, or your building may burn down. In any of these instances, you will need to know how to restore. You should watch for a few restoration questions on the exam—since this topic will one day save your databases, Microsoft has wisely decided that SQL DBAs need to be tested on these concepts.

Critical Information

The process of restoring SQL databases can be summed up in the following steps:

1. Attempt to back up the transaction log.

2. Find and fix the cause of the failure.

3. Drop all the affected databases.

4. Restore the database from a database backup, or from a file or filegroup backup.

5. Restore the transaction log from a log backup, or restore the differential database backup.

NOTE   The older syntax of Load Database and Load Transaction can be used in place of the Restore Database and Restore Log commands, but they are not recommended because support for these older commands could be dropped with any newer version of SQL Server.

Attempting to Back Up the Transaction Log

You should always try to create a transaction log backup after a database failure to capture all the transactions up to the time of the failure. You should use the No_Truncate switch, which backs up the log when the database is unusable. If you successfully back up transactions to the point of the failure, simply restore this new transaction backup set after you restore the other transaction log backups.

Finding and Fixing the Cause of the Failure

This step involves troubleshooting NT and/or SQL Server to determine the cause of the failure. There are two basic reasons for determining the cause—obviously, the first is to fix the problem, and the second is to take the appropriate steps to prevent it from happening in the future.

Dropping the Affected Databases

Before the database can be re-created, it must first be dropped. You can delete it using either Enterprise Manager or the T-SQL Drop Database <*database*> command.

Restoring the Database

Enterprise Manager can restore databases quickly. Simply highlight the database to be restored, select the backup, and choose Restore. You can also restore a database without having to re-create it, because the restoration procedure will create the database if it doesn't already exist. To automatically re-create the database, simply choose a backup set to restore from—if the database doesn't exist, it will be re-created. If a database by the same name as that in the backup set already exists, it will be overwritten. If you wish to restore a backup set to a differently named database, use the Replace option (discussed below).

Although the syntax to do a restoration starts out simple, many options let you control exactly what is restored from which backup set.

The syntax to do a restoration is as follows:

Restore Database <*database*> from <*device*> <*options*>

The most common options are as follows:

Dbo_only: Tags the restored database as read only.

Recovery: Recovers any transactions and allows the database to be used. This is the default if none is specified and should be used on the last file restored.

No_recovery: Allows additional transaction logs to be restored and does not allow the database to be used until the Recovery option is used. This should be used when you have other files to be restored to the database.

TIP   If you use this option by mistake (or end up not having any logs to restore), you can issue the command Restore Database <*data-base*> Recovery to activate the database.

Replace: Required when the name of the database being restored is different than the one that was backed up.

Standby: Allows the database to be read only between log restorations. This is used for standby servers or other special purposes, such as testing the data contained in each transaction backup set.

Restart: Usually used with tape backups. Restart allows you to restart an operation at the point of failure. For example, suppose you have five tapes, and on the last tape, you insert the wrong one. By using the Restart switch, you can simply insert tape five and quickly finish the job.

WARNING   SQL Server wipes out the old database when you restore a full backup of a database—there is no merging of data.

Restoring the Transaction Log

Enterprise Manager or the `Restore Log` command can be used to restore transaction logs. Restoring transaction logs can be thought of as reapplying all the transactions in the order they occurred.

The T-SQL command to restore the log is as follows:

```
Restore Log <database> from <device> <options>
```

All the options that apply to the `Restore Database` command also apply to the `Restore Log` command, with the exception of the Replace option, which is not supported for log restorations.

Unlike restoring the entire database, restoring transaction logs literally reapplies all the transactions that took place between the time of the full database backup and the time of the transaction log backup, appending any changes to the database. It is because of this that SQL Server can restore transaction log backups up to a certain point in time.

For example, suppose your accounting department comes to you and asks you to bring the accounting data back to the state it was in at 3:02 P.M. yesterday. With the point-in-time restoration capability given to you by the transaction log, you can do just what they ask. To make it happen, just choose a date and time from the Point in Time Restore window, as shown in Figure 4.3.

FIGURE 4.3: Restoring to a certain point in time

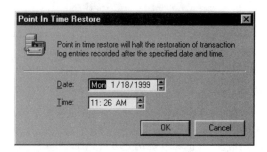

Restoring Differential Backups

Restoring a differential backup works very much like restoring transaction log backups. You must first do a full database restoration, then select the most recent differential backup to restore.

The T-SQL syntax to restore a differential backup is the same as for restoring the entire database.

Restoring Filegroups

Restoring filegroups can be done by using either Enterprise Manager or T-SQL syntax. It is done in Enterprise Manager in much the same fashion as full database restorations.

The T-SQL syntax for restoring files and filegroups is as follows:

```
Restore Database <database> from <device> File=<logical
    filename> Filegroup=<logical filegroup name>
```

Restoring the Master Database

Because the Master database contains all the settings for SQL Server, restoring the Master database is not only more complicated, but impossible to do accidentally. To restore the Master database, you must start SQL Server with the -m switch, which causes SQL Server to start in Single User mode.

NOTE When you rebuild the Master database, the MSDB, Model, and Distribution databases also are rebuilt (reset). You should restore these databases from your most recent backups so that the scheduled jobs, alerts, operators, and ongoing replication don't disappear.

If the Master database becomes corrupt and, much to your chagrin, a current backup is unavailable, there is a procedure that will allow you to re-create the Master database so that you can gain access to the system again. The steps are as follows:

Find and fix the cause of the failure: Just as noted above, you will need to find and fix the hardware or software failure that caused the Master database to become corrupted.

Rebuild the Master database: Use the Rebuildm.exe program to rebuild the Master database.

TIP Expect to see a test question about the use of Rebuildm.exe.

WARNING Rebuilding the Master database does not fix the existing one; it creates a completely new Master database—just as though you reinstalled SQL Server.

Attach valid database files to the Master database by running the sp_attach_db command for each file: You can attach databases without losing the data therein by using the sp_attach_db procedure. Because a newly rebuilt Master database will not know about any of your previous databases, you will need to run sp_attach_db for each of them.

Re-create the settings for SQL Server: Because the rebuilt Master database holds all the settings for SQL Server, they will revert to the defaults. You will need to reconfigure SQL Server with its previous settings, and probably stop and restart SQL Server to have them take effect.

Re-create the users and security for each database: Because the rebuilt Master database will have only the default SQL logins, you will need to re-create all of the logins.

Restore the MSDB, Model, and Distribution databases: Rebuilding the Master database also rebuilds the MSDB database. Any tasks, alerts, and operators you have created will have to be re-created by hand if a current backup of the MSDB database is unavailable.

Necessary Procedures

These procedures will save your data when disaster strikes—and don't think it won't strike. Many administrators are lulled into complacency, and they don't take the time to learn the procedures for restoring their data. Because of that lack of knowledge, the restoration time can be twice as long, if it happens correctly at all. In this section, the procedures for restoring from a full, differential, transaction log, and filegroup backup will be examined.

Restoring from a Full or Differential Backup

Since the steps for restoring from a full or differential backup are exactly the same, the following steps will guide you through the restoration process for both:

1. Right-click the database you wish to restore and choose All Tasks ➤ Restore Database.

2. Select the backup you wish to restore from the list of available backups.

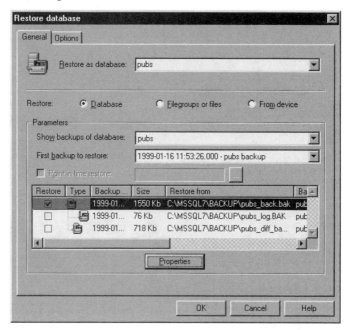

3. If this is not the last backup you will be restoring, go to the Options tab and make sure that the Recovery Completion State is set to Leave Database Nonoperational. If this is the last file you will be restoring, make the database operational.

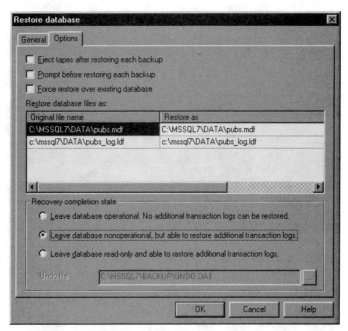

4. Select OK to start the restoration. Select OK at the Restoration Confirmation screen.

5. Go back to the Databases folder. The database you are restoring should be grayed out with "Loading" next to it.

Restoring from a Transaction Log Backup

To restore transaction logs using Enterprise Manager, follow the steps below:

1. Restore the database in question by highlighting it and selecting Restore Database from the right screen, or by right-clicking and choosing All Tasks ➤ Restore Database.

2. Select the device to restore from—it should be the one containing the transaction log backups.

3. Make sure you select Transaction Log from the Restore Backup Set menu.

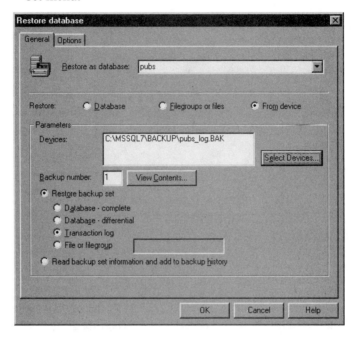

4. Select OK to restore the transaction log. Select OK to close the confirmation window.

Restoring the Master Database

In this set of steps, you will see the procedures for restoring the Master database when you have a valid backup available:

1. Stop SQL Server.

2. Open a command prompt.

3. Start SQL Server in Single User mode by opening a command prompt and issuing the following command:

```
SQLSERVR -m
```

4. Minimize the command prompt.

5. Start Enterprise Manager (SQL Server will show a red stoplight, even though it is running).

6. Highlight the Master database.

7. Go to the Restore screen.

8. Select the device Master was backed up to and choose Restore Now.

9. After the Master database is restored, the command prompt should automatically stop SQL Server and return to a regular C:\ prompt.

10. Restart SQL Server normally.

Exam Essentials

Since backups are completely useless without the ability to restore them, you will be asked a restoration-related question or two. Take the following restoration-related knowledge into the test center with you.

Know the restoration procedures.   Even though the procedures themselves will not be tested to a great extent, there is the chance of a question or two. The real importance of knowing the procedures comes in the real world when you need to restore your own data.

Understand point-in-time recovery.   Since point-in-time recovery can be quite useful in the real world, you will need to understand it for the test. You must remember that point-in-time recovery is possible only with transaction log restorations, nothing else.

Know how to restore the Master database.   Since the Master database is the heart of SQL Server, you need to know how to bring it back in case it crashes. You need to know how to perform this feat whether or not you have a good backup. If the backup you made is corrupt, you will use Rebuildm.exe.

Know the effects of Rebuildm.exe.   When you use Rebuildm.exe, not only is the Master database rebuilt, so are the Model, MSDB, and

Distribution databases. That means if you repair one, you must repair them all.

Key Terms and Concepts

Point-in-time recovery: When restoring from transaction logs, this is the capability of SQL to restore data up to a certain date and time.

Rebuildm.exe: This utility is used to re-create the Master, Model, MSDB, and Distribution databases when there is a system crash and no good backup is available.

Sample Questions

1. One of your users has discovered some malicious updates to your data that occurred the day before at about 2:00. How can you bring the database back to the state it was in just before the update occurred?

   A. Perform a full database restoration with point-in-time recovery.

   B. Perform a differential database restoration with point-in-time recovery.

   C. Perform a transaction log restoration with point-in-time recovery.

   D. You cannot bring the database back to the previous state.

   Answer: C. Transaction log restorations can be restored up to a point in time. This means that you can bring the database right back to the state it was in just before the update.

2. True or false. When performing a full database restoration with subsequent transaction log restorations, you must specify the Recovery option after each restoration is complete.

   A. True

B. False

Answer: B. You must specify No_Recovery for every restoration except the final one. It is only on the final restoration that you will use the Recovery option.

Manage replication.

- Configure servers, including Distributor, Publisher, and Subscriber.
- Create publications.
- Set up and manage subscriptions.

Many companies in today's world have multiple database servers in their organizations, and those servers require much of the same data. For example, suppose you have several thousand users in your organization that all need access to a very popular sales database—you would not want them accessing that database from one lone server because that would cause several bottlenecks on the network. Rather than having everyone come to one server, you can replicate the data to other servers in the organization and have everyone gain access to a local copy.

In Chapter 1, there was a discussion of how this works, and you even created a plan for replication. But how do you set it up? In this section, that topic will be discussed—the mechanics of setting up and managing replication. The first thing you will need to do for the sake of replication is configure your Distributors, Publishers, and Subscribers. Once that is done, you can create publications, which is what the servers in your organization subscribe to in order to get the data they need.

If you have only a few servers in your organization, you may not see the need to read through this section, feeling that it does not apply to you. That could not be further from the truth. If you don't know what

SQL is capable of, you will not be prepared to make necessary changes in the future—what if you get several more servers that need the same data just a few months from now? By reading this section, you'll be ready to manage the replication. Be aware that the concepts of replication get hit pretty hard on the exam because Microsoft wants to be sure that you know how to administer small and large networks.

Critical Information

To successfully install and enable replication, you must install a distribution server, create your publications, and then subscribe to them. Before any of this can take place, you must first configure your SQL Server. The computer itself must meet the following requirements:

- All servers involved with replication must be registered in the Enterprise Manager.

- The replication agents use the same Windows NT account that the SQLServerAgent uses. This account must have administrative rights and be a member of the Administrators group.

- The SQLServerAgent account must have the Log On as a Service advanced user right (this should have been assigned during setup).

- If the servers are from different domains, trust relationships must be established before replication can occur.

- Any account that you use must have access rights to the Distribution working folder on the distribution server.

- The server must have a minimum of 32MB of RAM with 16MB allocated for SQL Server 7.

- You must enable access to the Distribution working folder on the distribution server. For an NT Server, this is the \\Server-Name\C$\MSSQL7\ReplData folder. On a Windows 95/98 computer, you must use the share name C$ for the defaults to operate properly. (The $ means that only accounts with administrative rights can access that particular share.)

TIP It is suggested that you use a single Windows NT domain account for all of your SQLServerAgents. Do not use a LocalSystem account, because this account has no network capabilities and will therefore not allow replication.

Installing a Distribution Server

Since installing distribution and publication are taken care of through the same Wizard, the actual setup will be covered in the "Necessary Procedures" section to follow. Before you jump in and start swimming in the pool of replication, though, you should be aware of a few things. For example, before you can enable a Publication database, you must be a member of the sysadmin fixed server role. Once you have enabled publishing, any member of that database's db_owner role can create and manage publications.

Keep the following points in mind when you choose your Distributor:

- Ensure that you have enough hard-disk space for the Distribution working folder and the Distribution database.

- You must manage the Distribution database's transaction log carefully. If that log fills to capacity, replication will no longer run, which can adversely affect your Publication databases as well.

- The Distribution database will store all transactions from the Publisher to the Subscriber. It will also track when those transactions were applied.

- Snapshots and merge data are stored in the Distribution working folder.

- Be aware of the size and number of articles being published.

- Text, ntext, and image data types are replicated only when you use a snapshot.

- A higher degree of latency can significantly increase your storage space requirements.

- Know how many transactions per synchronization cycle there are. For example, if you modify 8000 records between synchronizations, there will be 8000 rows of data stored on the Distributor.

- Consider using a remote Distributor to minimize the impact of replication on your publishing servers.

Adding a Publication

Once you have enabled distribution and publishing, you can add publications and articles to your server. When you add a new publication, you need to determine the type of replication that will be used, the snapshot requirements, and Subscriber options such as updating or anonymous Subscribers. You can also partition your data and decide whether you will allow push or pull subscriptions.

In the "Necessary Procedures" section, you will be walked through the Create Publication Wizard, but before you get there, you need to consider a few options:

- You should consider how often to publish a new snapshot for refreshing the Subscriber databases.

- Consider which tables and stored procedures you wish to publish before running the Wizard.

- If you will be using two-phase commit or the Microsoft Distributed Transaction Coordinator, you may want to allow updating Subscribers.

- Think about whether to allow pull subscriptions. If you have a large number of Subscribers or Subscribers over the Internet, this will be the way to go.

- Replicate only the data you need. Use filters to send only the fields and records that you need.

- Use primary keys on replicated tables to ensure entity integrity. If you don't have primary keys, you can perform only snapshot replication.

Creating a Subscription

As part of the process of creating a subscription, you will be able to specify the Publishers you wish to subscribe to and a destination database to receive the published data, verify your security credentials, and set up a default schedule. While you will see more detail on this when you step through the Wizard in the "Necessary Procedures" section, you should check these points first:

- You can use pull subscriptions to off-load the work from the Distributors to each Subscriber.

- You should use updating Subscribers rather than merge replication if possible.

Managing Replication

Managing and maintaining replication can be very intensive work for an administrator. Fortunately, Microsoft SQL Server 7 has included many tools in the Replication Monitor to make this job a lot easier. Before the use of these tools is discussed, however, one of the most important tasks in replication administration—backing up—must be examined.

Replication Backup Strategies

When you perform backups of your replication scenario, you can make backups of just the Publisher, the Publisher and Distributor, the Publisher and Subscriber, or all three. Each of these strategies has its own advantages and disadvantages. The following list highlights these distinctions:

Publisher only: This strategy requires the least amount of resources and computing time, since the backup of the Publisher does not have to be coordinated with any other server backups to stay synchronized. The disadvantage is that restoration of a Publisher or Distributor is a slow and time-consuming process.

Publisher and Distributor: This strategy accurately preserves the publication as well as the errors, history, and replication agent information from the Distributor. You can recover quickly because there is no need to reestablish replication. The disadvantages of this strategy are the coordination of the backups, and the amount of storage and computing time necessary to perform a simultaneous backup.

Publisher and Subscriber(s):   This strategy significantly reduces the recovery time by removing the initialization process (running a snapshot). The main disadvantages of this strategy manifest themselves when you have multiple Subscribers. Every Subscriber will have to be backed up and restored.

Publisher, Distributor, and Subscriber(s):   This strategy preserves all of the complexity of your replication model. The disadvantages are storage space and computing time. This scenario also requires the most time for recovery.

WARNING   It is essential that the Distribution database and log do not get filled to capacity. When this database or log gets filled to capacity, it can no longer receive publication information. When this occurs, the logged transactions at the Publisher cannot be removed from the log (unless you disable publishing). Over time, your Publishing database's transaction log will also get filled to capacity, and you will no longer be able to make data modifications.

Using the Replication Monitor

Once you have installed distribution and publication, you will notice a new icon in the console tree of your SQL Server—the Replication Monitor icon. This tool will allow you to monitor and maintain each and every part of replication. You can look at agent properties and histories, and even set replication alerts.

The Replication Monitor resides on the computer where the distribution server has been installed and gathers replication information about the different replication agents. Through the Monitor, you can edit the various schedules and properties of the various agents. This includes the agent history, which keeps track of everything that has happened during the replication, including information about inserts, updates, deletions, and any other transactions that were processed.

After a successful log is read and moved to the Distributor and the Subscriber pulls the transaction, the distribution server needs to be cleaned up. Once a transfer has been successfully completed, a clean-up job will run.

There is at least one clean-up job for every Subscriber. In other words, if you have 20 Subscribers to your database, you will have at least 20 clean-up jobs on the Distributor. If you click the Miscellaneous Agents folder in the console tree, you will see some of the clean-up jobs that have been created (shown in Figure 4.4). These are explained below.

F I G U R E 4.4: Miscellaneous Agents' clean-up jobs

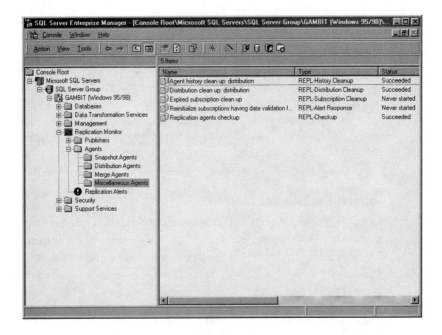

Agent History Clean Up: Distribution: This job cleans up the historical information in the Distribution Agents History tables after they have aged out.

Distribution Clean Up: Distribution: This job cleans up the Distributor by removing transactions from the Distribution database after they have aged out.

Expired Subscription Clean Up: This job removes expired subscription information from the Subscription database.

Reinitialize Subscriptions Having Data Validation Failures: This job reinitializes all subscriptions that failed because of problems with data validation.

Replication Agents Checkup: This job watches for replication agents that are not actively adding information to their history logs.

Working with Replication Scripts

Now that you have replication set up and working properly, you may wish to save all your hard work in the form of a replication script. This can save you a great deal of time in the event of a system crash, since, with a script in hand, you will not need to completely re-create your replication setup. You can just run the scripts and have replication right back to the way it was. Here is a list of even more advantages that this brings you:

- You can use the scripts to track different versions of your replication implementation.

- You can use the scripts with some minor tweaking to create additional Subscribers and Publishers with the same basic options.

- You can quickly customize your environment by making modifications to the script and then rerunning it.

- Scripts can be used as part of your database recovery process.

TIP As with all timesaving devices, you should expect at least one test question on this subject.

Getting Information about Replication

There are many stored procedures that are used to create and install replication on your computer. Here is a short list of stored procedures that are at your disposal for gathering administrative information about your SQL Server replication configuration:

sp_helpdistributor: This gathers information about the Distribution database, the Distributor, the working directory, and the SQLServerAgent user account.

sp_helpdistributiondb: This gathers information about the Distribution database, its files, and their location as well as information regarding the distribution history and log.

sp_helppublication: This gathers publication information and configuration options.

sp_helpsubscription: This gathers information associated with a particular article, publication, Subscriber, or set of subscriptions.

sp_helpsubscriberinfo: This gathers information about the configuration settings of a Subscriber, including information regarding frequency of the subscription, retry delays, and much more.

Necessary Procedures

The procedures here will not be tested as much as your understanding of the underlying concepts, but they will still be tested. In this section, you will be walked through a number of Wizards: the Distribution and Publishing Configuration Wizard, the Publishing Wizard, and the Subscribing Wizard. It is important that you understand them all.

Enabling Distribution and Publishing

To replicate your data, you need to enable distribution and publishing:

1. Using Enterprise Manager, connect to your SQL Server.

2. Highlight your SQL Server and then choose Tools ➤ Replication ➤ Configure Publishing and Subscribers.

3. You are now presented with a welcome screen. If you take a closer look at the welcome screen, you'll see that you can create your local computer as the Distributor. Click Next to continue.

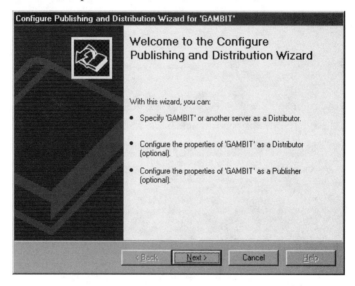

4. You are now presented with the Choose Distributor screen. Here, you will decide where the distribution server is going to be installed. Only SQL Servers that are already registered in the Enterprise Manager will be available from here.

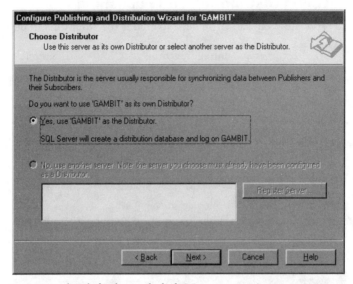

5. Leave the defaults and click Next to continue.

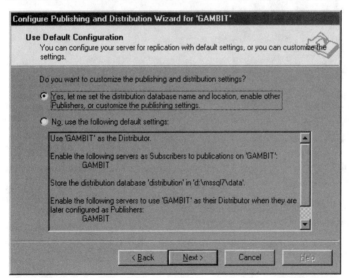

6. You can now decide whether you want to use all the default settings for your Distributor. Under normal conditions, this is not a problem at all. Since you are seeing this for the first time, let's take a look at the customizable settings. Choose the Yes, Let Me option and click Next to continue.

7. You are now presented with the Provide Distribution Database Information screen. You can supply a name for the Distribution database as well as location information for its database file and transaction log. Keep the defaults and click Next to continue.

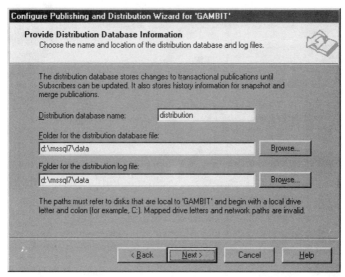

8. The Enable Publishers screen shows all registered SQL Servers. You can pick and choose which servers you wish to configure as publishers. The ellipsis (...) allows you to specify security credentials such as login ID and password as well as the location of the snapshot folder. Be sure to place a checkmark next to your local SQL Server and then click Next to continue.

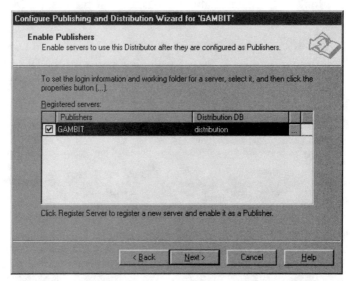

9. You are now looking at the Enable Publication Databases screen. You can select the databases on the newly enabled Publisher from which you wish to allow publishing. Next to the database you wish to replicate, select the checkbox for the type of replication you desire and click Next to continue.

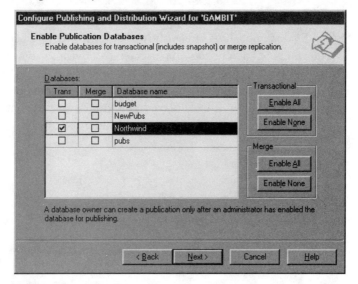

10. You are now presented with the Enable Subscribers screen. This is very similar to the Enable Publishers screen. For this example, you are going to use the same SQL Server for publishing, distribution, and subscribing. If you have additional SQL Servers, feel free to implement replication to them now.

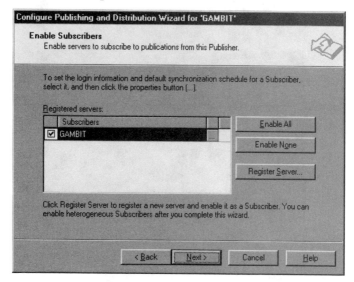

NOTE If your server isn't listed here, you can click the Register Server button to register another Microsoft SQL Server computer. You must set up non-Microsoft SQL Servers through the Configure Publishing and Distribution screen.

11. Click the ellipsis to modify the security credentials of the subscription server.

12. You are now looking at the General tab of the Subscriber Properties screen. Let's take a closer look at the Schedules tab shown below.

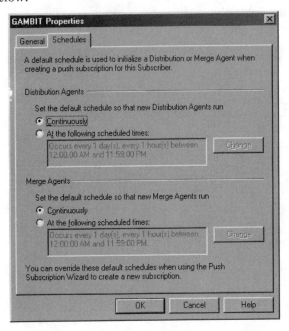

13. You can specify the replication schedule for both the merge and distribution agents. The default for these values is Continuously, but you can set the schedule to anything you like (just as when creating and scheduling SQL Server jobs). Click OK to return to the Enable Subscribers screen.

14. Click Next to continue. You are now given a summary of the configuration options you have chosen. Click Finish to implement these configurations and enable the distribution server.

15. Now that you have successfully installed the Distribution database and distribution server, you should see the Replication Monitor icon up in the Enterprise Manager console tree.

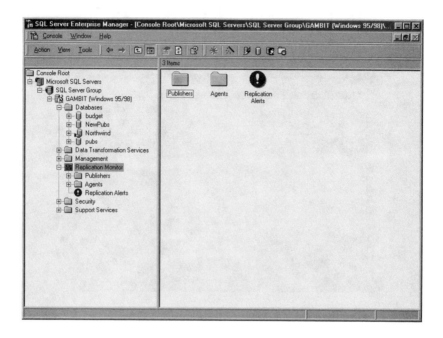

Creating a Publication

In the following walkthrough, you will create a new publication:

1. Connect to your SQL Server in the Enterprise Manager. If you expand the Databases folder, you will now see a hand icon on the database you have set up for replication. This indicates that the database has been marked for replication.

2. Highlight the database with the hand icon and then go to Tools ➤ Replication ➤ Create and Manage Publications. You will now be presented with the Create and Manage Publications dialog box.

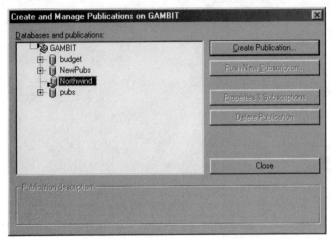

3. Highlight the database to publish and click Create Publication.

4. The Create Publication Wizard now starts with a welcome screen. Click Next to continue.

5. You can now specify what type of publication you wish to create—Snapshot, Transactional, or Merge. For this example, select Transactional and click Next to continue.

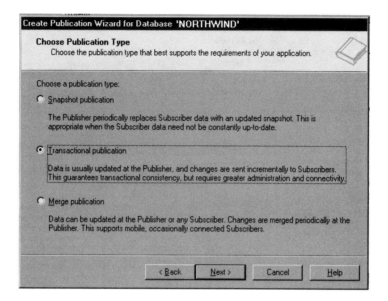

NOTE Transactional replication on the Desktop edition of SQL Server running on Windows 95/98 is supported as Subscriber only. This is because the server-side network libraries for Named Pipes are required for this type of replication and are not available on Windows 95/98. Windows 95/98 Named Pipes on the client side is supported, however.

6. You can now specify whether you wish to enable updating Subscribers. As you might recall, updating a Subscriber makes changes at both the subscription server and the publishing server, using a two-phase commit. Either both servers are updated or neither of them is. For this example, keep the default No, Do Not Allow and click Next to continue.

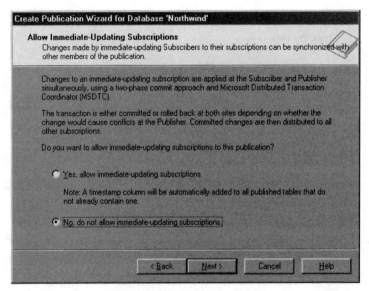

7. The following graphic shows the Specify Subscriber Types screen. When you were working on the Distribution database installation, you learned that you could specify only Microsoft SQL Servers as Subscribers. Although you can enable non-Microsoft SQL Servers as Subscribers from here, you are not going to do that in this walk-through. Leave the default All Subscribers Will Be and click Next to continue.

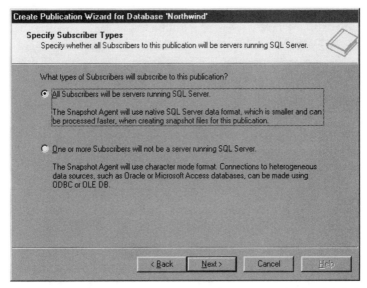

8. Here, you can determine which tables you wish to publish from. In essence, you are creating your articles. Click the checkbox next to the Categories table.

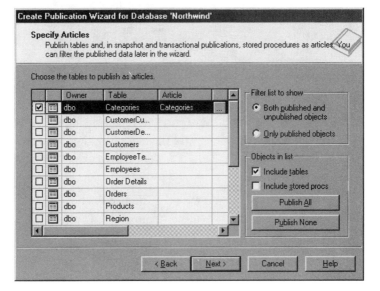

9. Selecting an article creates the ellipsis button. Click the ellipsis.

10. You are now presented with the Categories Properties pages. The General tab allows you to specify the Article Name, a Description, the Destination Table Name, and the Destination Table Owner. Change the Destination Table Name to rtblCategories and be sure to specify the owner as dbo.

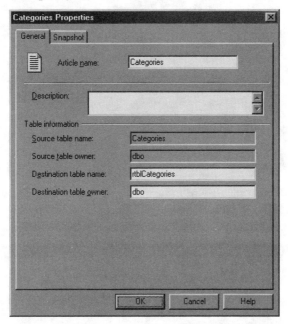

11. The Snapshot tab allows you to specify what will happen during the snapshot process. Will you drop the existing table? Will you truncate the data in it? Leave the default options and click OK to return to the Specify Articles screen. Once back at the Specify Articles screen, click Next to continue.

12. You are now presented with the Choose Publication Name and Description screen. When you are finished, you should have something similar to what is shown below. Click Next to continue.

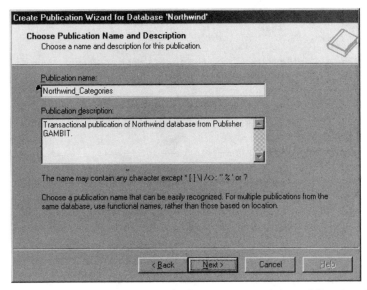

13. You now see the Use Default Properties of the Publication dialog box. From here, you can accept the default filtering and partitioning options, or you can customize them. Although you will not make changes to these options, let's take a look at them. Click the Yes, I Will Define option and then click Next to continue.

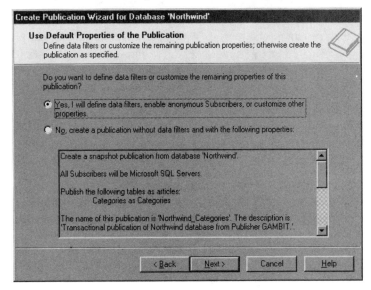

14. When you see the Filter Data screen, you can choose to filter your data or leave them alone. Click the Yes, I Want to option, then click Next to continue.

15. From the Filter Table Columns screen, you can select which columns you wish to exclude from your replication. Click Next to continue.

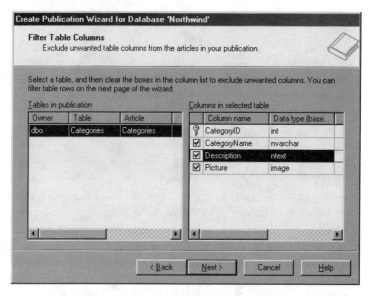

16. You can now filter the rows. If you click the ellipsis, you can create a new filter by filling in a Where clause. When you are finished, click Next to continue.

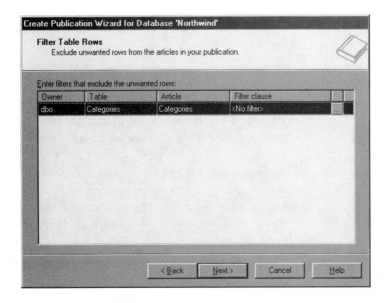

17. You are now asked whether you wish to allow anonymous Sub-scribers. If you have many Subscribers or you are allowing subscriptions across the Internet, you may wish to allow anony-mous Subscribers. Anonymous Subscribers reduce some of the administration of your replication. Note, however, that this choice does not compromise security. Leave the default No, Only Known and click Next to continue.

18. You are now presented with the Set Snapshot Agent Schedule screen. Remember that before replication can begin, a snapshot of your data must be moved to the Subscriber to set a baseline for all future replication. Click the checkbox to indicate that you want the Subscriber to create the first snapshot immediately. Click the Change button to set up your snapshot schedule. A snapshot schedule (formerly referred to as a *scheduled table refresh*) is useful when you have nonlogged operations running on the Publisher. If an operation is not logged, it won't be replicated. This can come in handy if you are replicating text, ntext, or image data types. Click Next to continue.

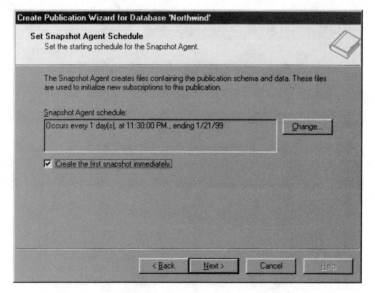

19. You are now at the finish screen. You can review the options you have chosen and, when you are ready, click Finish to complete the creation of your publication. After some processing takes place, you will return to the Create and Manage Publications screen, but with changes: Your new publication—Northwind_Categories— should be listed.

20. From here, you can push this publication to Subscribers, or you can look over its properties and subscriptions by clicking the Properties & Subscriptions button. When you do this, you will see much of the information you entered displayed in a set of pages. When you are finished, click OK to return to the Create and Manage Publications screen.

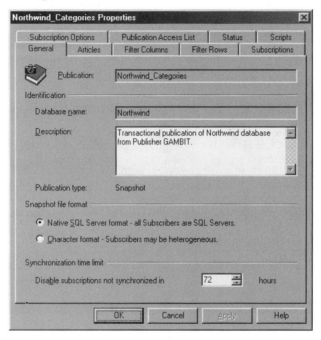

21. From the Create and Manage Publications screen, you can also delete your publications. Click Close to finish.

Creating Subscriptions

Once you have created a publication, the other servers in your organization can subscribe to the data you are publishing. Here are the steps for creating a pull subscription:

1. Connect to your SQL Server, highlight the server, and choose Tools ➤ Replication ➤ Pull Subscription to *Your Server Name*.

2. You are now looking at the Pull Subscription to *Your Server Name* dialog box.

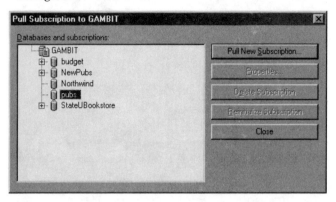

3. Click the Pubs database and then click Pull New Subscription.

4. As always, you are presented with a welcome screen. Click Next to continue.

5. You can now see a list of Publishers. By expanding the Publishers, you can see the publications that they have made available. If you do not see your publishing server here, you can click the Register Server button to register another server. Expand the server you want to pull from and select a publication. Click Next to continue.

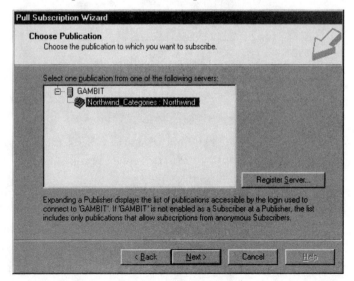

6. You must now specify the security credentials that your synchronization agent will use for the synchronization process. Fill in **sa** and no password. Click Next to continue.

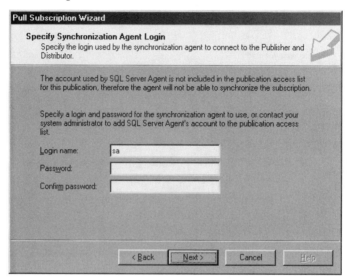

7. You must now choose your destination database. This is where the subscribed data will be stored on your server. Click Next to continue.

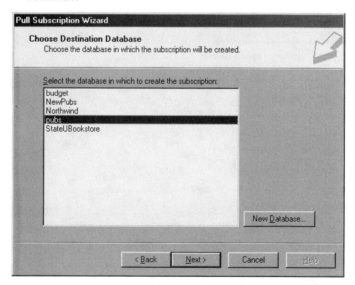

8. If the schema and tables don't already exist at the Subscriber, they must be initialized there. Take the default value as shown below and click Next to continue.

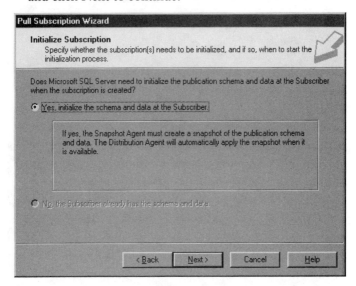

9. You can now set the synchronization schedule. For snapshots, it might be wise to set up some type of regular schedule. For merge replication, you will most likely use a manual form of synchronization called *on demand*. Click Next to continue.

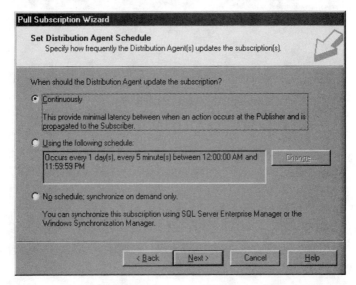

10. You are now looking at the Start Required Services screen. Because all your agents use the SQLServerAgent service to interact with the various servers, the SQLServerAgent must be running. If it is not, click the checkbox to force the service to start. Once you have it running, click Next to continue.

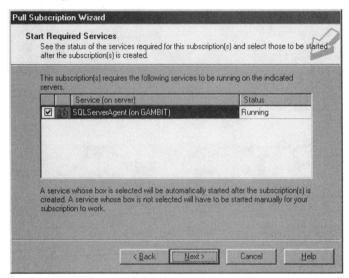

11. You are now at the finish screen again. As with other screens of this type, you can review your subscription. When you are satisfied, click Finish to create the subscription.

12. You should now be back at the Pull Subscription to *Your Server Name* screen, but this time your subscription should be displayed. Here, too, you can choose your subscription and look at its Properties pages. You can also delete the subscription or reinitialize it. When you are finished, click Close.

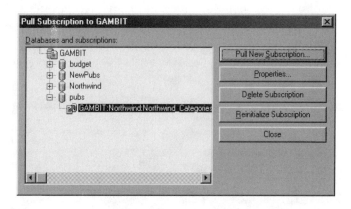

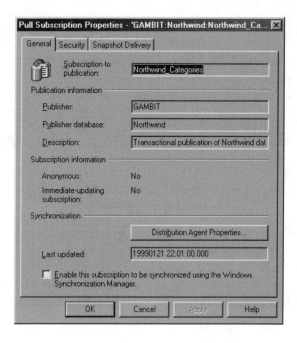

13. If you expand your destination database folder, you will notice that there is now a Pull Subscriptions folder in it. There is also a Publications folder under the published database. You can highlight these items and then double-click the publication or subscription in the right pane for additional information about them.

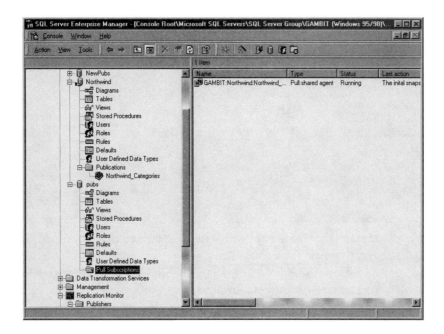

Working with Replication Monitor

Follow these steps to work with the various agents:

1. Open the Enterprise Manager on the SQL Server where the distribution server was installed.

2. Expand the Replication Monitor icon, then the Agents folder, and finally, highlight the Snapshot Agents.

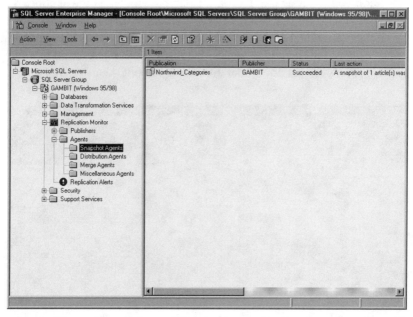

3. If you right-click a publication in the details pane, you will see that you can view the agent history, properties, and profile. You can also start or stop the agent. There are options to modify the refresh rate and choose the columns to view. Right-click and choose Agent History.

4. You are now presented with the Snapshot Agent History. You can filter the list to show information based on all sessions; sessions in the last 7 days, the last 2 days, or the last 24 hours; or sessions with errors. You can also look at the Agent Profile and its settings as well as the Monitor Settings. The Monitor Settings allow you to specify how often the items in the Replication Monitor will be refreshed.

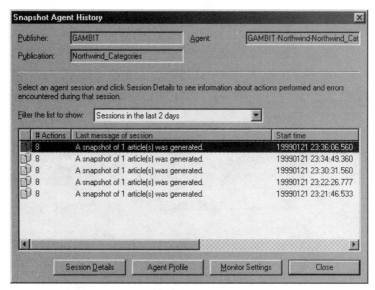

5. You can look at the details of a particular session. Session details include information about all the different processes that took place during the session.

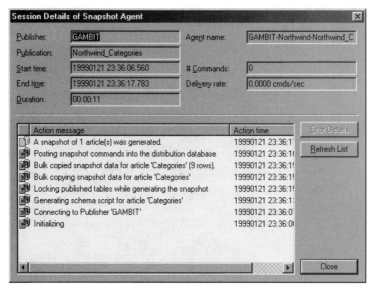

6. Close the Snapshot Agent History. Right-click a publication and choose Agent Properties. You are now looking at the Properties sheets. These operate in the same fashion as the scheduled jobs that you have already worked with. When you are finished browsing, close the Snapshot Agent History.

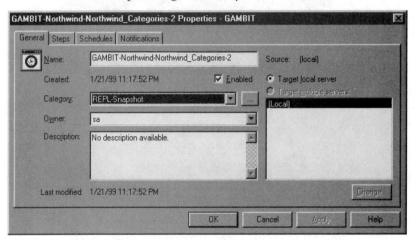

Using Replication Scripts

In this walkthrough, you will create some replication scripts for your current setup:

1. Highlight your server in the console tree and then choose Tools ➤ Replication ➤ Generate Replication Scripts.

2. You are now presented with the Generate SQL Scripts pages. You can script the Distributor and the publications for the various replication items stored with this distribution server. The File Options tab allows you to save your script to several different file types. The default storage location for your scripts is C:\MSSQL7\Install. This particular folder holds many other scripts that are used to create and install your SQL Server and several databases.

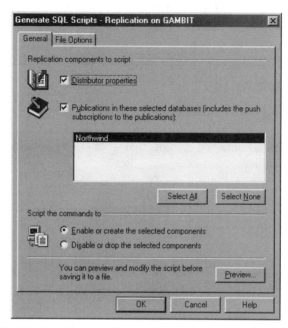

3. The Preview button allows you to view the scripts themselves.

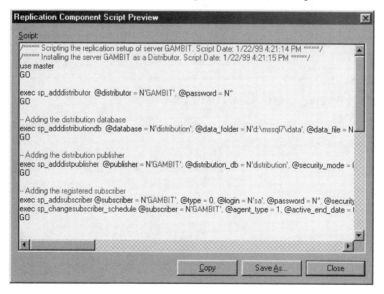

4. When you are finished viewing the scripts, click Close. You can now close the replication-scripting property pages.

Exam Essentials

Replication is a very important part of the exam, although most of the replication questions will be about the concepts rather than the mechanics. Some of the points that will help you with these questions are listed here.

Know how to use replication scripts.   Replication scripts are going to rescue you from a great deal of extra effort if your system ever crashes—it is a good idea to know how to create them. You should also know where to store them, preferably off-site.

Know when to use a pull as opposed to a push subscription. You should use push subscriptions when you want control over who gets your data and there are few Subscribers. If there are a great number of Subscribers or your Distributor does not have generous resources, you should use pull subscriptions to off-load the processing burden from the Distributor and the administrative burden of pushing the subscriptions.

Key Terms and Concepts

Replication agents: Scheduled tasks in SQL Server that perform the work of replication.

Replication scripts: Transact-SQL scripts that can be used to completely re-create the replication scheme on a SQL Server.

Sample Questions

1. You have been successfully replicating data to several of your servers for over a month when suddenly replication stops functioning. What is the most likely cause?

   A. The distribution agent has been disabled.

   B. The transaction log on the Distribution database has filled to capacity.

   C. The Publication database has become corrupt.

   D. The Subscription database has become corrupt.

   Answer: B. Like any other database, the Distribution database has a transaction log that must be cleared through a regular transaction log backup. If that does not happen, the log will fill, and replication will cease.

2. Your organization has close to 60 SQL Servers scattered throughout the world, and you need to replicate three separate databases to each of those servers. Your distribution server has 512MB of RAM and three 18.2GB hard drives in a RAID 5 array dedicated to the Distribution database. Should you configure the subscriptions as push or pull?

   A. Push

   B. Pull

   Answer: B. While the distribution server could easily handle the processing load of pushing the subscriptions, you would want to use pull subscriptions just because of the administrative load of configuring and managing 180 (60×3) push subscriptions.

Automate administrative tasks.

- Define jobs.
- Define alerts.
- Define operators.
- Set up SQLAgentMail for job notification and alerts.

Many years ago, if people wanted to wear clothes made from cotton, they had to pick and process the cotton by hand. This was an extremely time-consuming and repetitive process, almost mind numbing. That is why a rather creative man named Eli Whitney came up with the idea of the cotton gin to help automate the process. He wasn't the first to automate something, and he certainly wasn't the last—other people through the years have also seen the value of automating repetitive tasks so that they could be freed up to perform more complex and challenging duties.

Microsoft has followed suit by giving us automation in SQL Server. In this section, the discussion will involve not only how to automate repetitive tasks by defining jobs, but how to automatically warn someone when something goes wrong by defining alerts and operators. Finally, one of the handiest tools in SQL Server—SQLAgent-Mail, which allows you to send e-mail to operators when there is a problem—will be examined.

The information in this section is definitely going to save you time, lots of time. Learn this not just for the test, but for the real world. Let SQL take care of those repetitive tasks so that you can go home at a reasonable hour and come back in the morning to find your tasks have been completed by SQL Server automation.

Critical Information

To use SQL Server's automation capabilities, you must have the SQLAgent properly configured. Here is a checklist to make sure this is done:

- SQLAgent must log on using a user account, with administrative rights.

- The service should be configured to start automatically (if it is set to manual, you will have to start it by hand every time you reboot your server).

- While most services don't require a user account assigned to them to function correctly, services that go beyond the physical box and connect to other servers on the network (as the SQLAgent may do) usually need a user account assigned. This is so they have an account with which to be authenticated on the remote server. Otherwise, they connect with NULL security credentials and by default will be denied access.

NOTE When using the Desktop version of SQL Server with Windows 95/98, you cannot assign an account to the SQLAgent. Not assigning an account to the agent will not affect any jobs or alerts on the local computer. The major limitation on Windows 95/98 computers is that they cannot be assigned as job managers for other servers.

Defining Jobs

Earlier versions of SQL Server (4.21a and earlier) could schedule backups, but that was the extent of their scheduling capabilities. Beginning with version 6, SQL Server's scheduling capabilities have been greatly expanded. In SQL Server 7, you can define jobs to perform just about any task you can think of and schedule those jobs to run at regular intervals or when an alert is triggered. SQL Server supports four general types of jobs:

TSQL jobs: These jobs are written using T-SQL commands. They are often used to back up the database, rebuild indexes, and perform other various routine database maintenance activities.

CmdExec jobs: These jobs literally open a command prompt and run some sort of batch file or executable file. Common CmdExec jobs are those created by the Database Maintenance Plan Wizard or by the SQL Server Web Assistant.

Replication jobs: These jobs deal with replication. Normally, you would use the Replication Wizards and prompts to help set up replication jobs, although monitoring these jobs is an important step in maintaining replication.

Active Script jobs: These jobs can run Visual Basic or Java script at a regular interval.

These jobs that you create do not even have to be local. SQL Server 7 allows you to create what are called *multiserver jobs*. In a multi-server scenario, you have a master server, where the jobs are created, and target servers, where those jobs are run. Using this method, you can ease the administrative burdens of creating jobs since you need to create the job only once, at a single server, and have it run on multiple servers in your organization. Since the target servers upload the job status to the master server, you can even view the job history from one server (the master). To create multiple server jobs, you must do as follows:

- Ensure that all servers involved are running SQL Server 7 on Windows NT.

- Make certain that all SQLAgent services are logging on with a domain account.

- Designate one server as the master server (MSX).

- Designate a master server operator (MSX operator) to be notified in case a multiserver job fails.

- Designate one or more servers as target servers when you create the job.

NOTE   A target server can report to only one master server at a time.

When you actually create the job, you need to supply the name, schedule, and command to be executed during one or more steps. Once you've told SQL what to do, you need to tell it *when* by selecting one of four schedule settings:

When the SQLAgent starts: A job can be created that automatically executes whenever the SQLAgent starts. This would be good for an automated system of some kind.

When the CPU is idle: A job can be scheduled to start after the CPU has been idle a certain amount of time, which is configurable in the Properties screen of the SQLAgent.

One time only: A one-time-only job is usually created for a special purpose; it executes only once on its scheduled date and time.

Recurring: A recurring job happens on a regular basis. The job's frequency can be daily, weekly, or even monthly.

Defining Alerts

A SQL event that is written to the Windows NT application log can have an alert defined for it. When you define an alert, you are really telling SQL to watch for errors in the Windows NT application log and match those errors to entries in the sysalerts table. If an event is matched to an entry in sysalerts, SQL follows whatever actions are prescribed by the alert, such as firing a job or sending an e-mail.

There are two types of alerts to create: SQL error-message and performance alerts. Error-message alerts are based on predefined messages that are stored in the sysmessages table—you can use the SQL messages (all 2000+ of them), or you can create your own. If you do create your own, you should call the new error message from within your T-SQL script or program by using the following command:

```
Raiserror (error_number, severity, state)
```

The performance alerts are used to warn you when one of the performance counters reaches a certain value; for example, when the transaction log of a database reaches 75 percent full. There are a few basic options to consider before creating an alert:

- If based on a SQL Server error message, define the error to look for. Alerts can be based on a generic error-message number, the error's severity, or an error happening in a specific database.

- Optionally, define the database in which the error must happen. An alert can filter error messages based on the database. For instance, an alert can be created to watch the Pubs database in case it fills up. This alert would operate only on the Pubs database; if any other database filled up, the alert wouldn't do anything.

- If based on a Performance Monitor counter, define which counter to monitor and the threshold that will trigger the alert.

- Define the response of the alert. Alerts can be set up to trigger jobs automatically and/or to warn operators that the alert was activated.

- Alerts are usually designed to perform a job when the alert is fired, so you need to define (or select) the job to be done. This is a standard job, so you are not limited in the tasks that it can perform.

- If the alert is meant to notify someone, define who will be notified and how this will be done. You can specify operators and whether they should receive an e-mail message and/or be paged when an alert is triggered.

- Activate the alert by selecting the Enabled box inside the Edit Alert dialog box (it is selected by default, but can be deselected to temporarily disable an alert).

If you have more than one system running SQL Server, you can define a central server that will receive from other servers events for which you have (or have not) defined alerts. The server that receives these events is called an *unhandled event forwarding server*. The server that is designated as the unhandled event forwarding server must be registered in Enterprise Manager.

NOTE Windows 95/98 cannot forward events to, or act as, an unhandled events server.

Defining and Managing Operators

When you define an alert in SQL, it is probably because you want to notify someone that the alert has fired. The person that you will notify is called an operator in SQL Server. Operators can receive messages about alerts in one of three ways:

Net send: This a standard Windows NT net-send message that pops up a dialog box on the user's computer screen.

E-mail: This method will actually send a message to the user's mailbox. To use this, you must have SQLAgentMail configured and a MAPI-compliant messaging server (such as Exchange).

Pager: This will send the alert to an alphanumeric pager. The pager must be able to accept text messages sent over the Internet for this to work.

Configuring SQLAgentMail for Job Notification and Alerts

You may have figured out by this point that to define a fully functional operator, you must have SQLAgentMail configured. There are four basic steps to installing MAPI support for Windows NT 4:

1. Make certain that the SQLAgent service is logging on with a domain account (this step was most likely completed during setup).

2. Create a mailbox for the SQL user account on the MAPI-compliant mail server.

3. Log into the SQL Server computer as the SQL user account and create an Exchange profile that points to the Exchange Server and post office box created in step 2.

4. Assign the profile (created in step 3) to the SQL Mail portion of SQL Server. Start the SQL Mail session.

After you have configured and tested e-mail, you can start sending e-mails and pages to your operators whenever an alert fires or a job completes.

Necessary Procedures

You should understand how to complete all of the procedures presented in this section. You must know how to configure jobs so that you can automate repetitive tasks. Alerts need to be configured so that they can warn operators when things go wrong. To warn an operator via e-mail or pager, you must have SQLAgentMail configured and running. Since having a firm understanding of these tasks can save you a great deal of time on your own networks, you need to understand these tasks for the exam.

Defining Jobs

In this series of steps, you will create a job and make it recurring:

1. In Enterprise Manager, open the Management window and open the Jobs window. This should show you any jobs you have previously made.

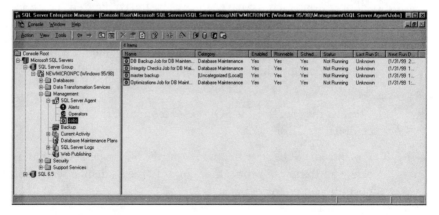

2. Click the New button (it looks like a star) on the toolbar, or right-click the Jobs folder and choose New Job.

3. In the New Job Properties dialog box, enter a descriptive name for the job.

NOTE You can pick target servers for this job if you have enlisted this server as a master server and have designated one or more target servers from the bottom right of the screen.

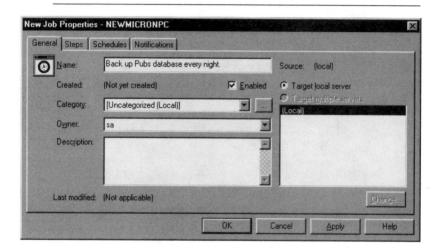

4. Go to the Steps tab.

5. Create a new step by selecting the New button at the bottom of the screen.

6. Enter a name for the step name, select the type (T-SQL, command, or Active Script), and then enter the command.

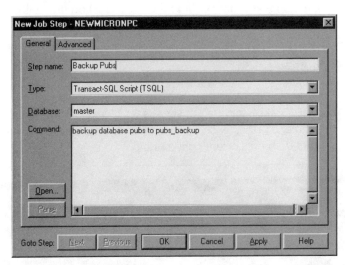

7. If the command is T-SQL, use the Parse button to check the command for syntax errors. You should get an OK box. If not, fix the command until it works.

8. Select the Advanced tab and change any necessary settings, such as what to do when the step fails, how many times to retry, etc.

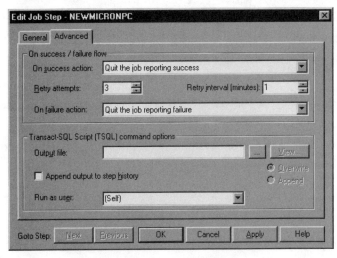

9. Go to the Schedules tab in the New Job Properties dialog box.

10. Choose New Schedule.

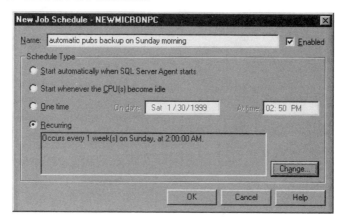

11. Enter a descriptive name for the schedule.

12. Change the schedule for the job by selecting the Change button.

13. Set the schedule to whatever your needs may be—weekly, monthly, daily, hourly, etc. Choose OK to save the changed schedule.

14. Make sure the schedule is enabled and choose OK to save it.

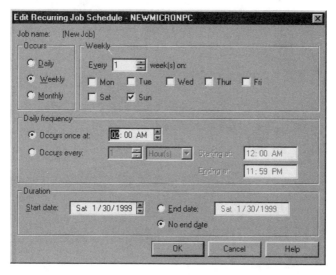

15. Choose OK to save the new job. The job should now be listed in the Jobs folder.

Defining Alerts

There are two types of alerts to configure: error-message and performance alerts. The differences between the two are subtle, but enough to require two sets of steps. This first set of steps will outline the method for creating an error-message alert:

1. In Enterprise Manager, open the Management window and open the Alerts window. You should see nine predefined alerts.

2. To add a new alert, click the New button on the toolbar, choose Action ➤ New Alert, or right-click and choose New Alert.

3. You'll see the New Alert dialog box. In the ID: New Name field, enter a name for the new alert.

4. In the Event Alert Definition section, select the Error Number option button and enter a number in the associated box—if you don't know the number you want, you can search for it by clicking the Find button next to the error-number text box.

5. Select a specific database to report on or allow the message to be fired for all databases.

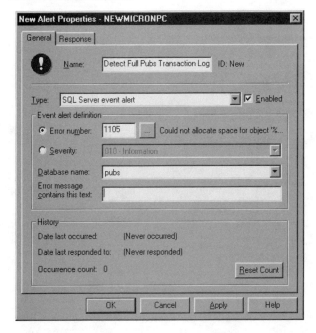

6. Go to the Response tab and select Execute Job if you wish to have a job run when the alert fires.

7. If you have operators defined, you may specify whether and how to alert them on the Operators tab at this time.

8. Click OK to save the alert. Your alert should now be listed with the default alerts.

This next series of steps will show you how to create an alert based on a performance counter:

1. In SQL Enterprise Manager, open the Management window and open the Alerts window. You should see nine predefined alerts (as well as any you have made).

2. To add a new alert, click the New button on the toolbar, choose Action ➤ New Alert, or right-click and choose New Alert.

3. You'll see the New Alert dialog box. In the ID: New Name field, enter a descriptive name for the new alert.

4. Change the Type to SQL Server Performance Condition Alert.

5. Select the object you want to monitor.

6. Select the appropriate counter.

7. Select whether the alert should fire if the value is equal to, over, or under the defined value.

8. Define a value for the alert to watch for.

9. Choose OK to save the alert.

If you find that the predefined SQL error messages don't suit your needs, you can create your own. In this set of steps, you'll do just that:

1. In SQL Enterprise Manager, highlight the server and select Action ➢ All Tasks ➢ Manage SQL Server Messages, or highlight the server, right-click, and choose All Tasks ➢ Manage SQL Server Messages.

2. Choose New to create a new message.

3. Add a custom message to an error number equal to or higher than 50,001 with the text you want to see when the alert is fired. You must also check the Always Write to Windows NT Eventlog box; otherwise, you will never receive an alert on the message.

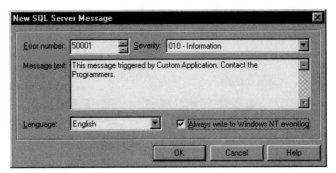

4. Click OK, then OK again, to close the window.

5. To test the message, start the Query Analyzer.

6. Enter and execute the following query:

   ```
   raiserror (50001,10,1)
   ```
   The error message that you just created should appear in the Results window.

7. Open the Windows NT event log (select Programs ➤ Administrative Tools ➤ NT Event Viewer) and select Log ➤ Application to display the application log. The message that you entered should appear.

8. Double-click the message for more details. You should see the Event Detail dialog box with information about the error and your message.

Defining Operators

Here are the steps to create an operator:

1. In Enterprise Manager, go to the Operators folder under the SQL Agent and Management folders.

2. Click the New button, right-click and choose New Operator, or go to Action ➤ New Operator.

3. In the Edit Operator dialog box, enter an operator name, then the e-mail, pager, and/or net-send addresses for the person you want to notify.

4. If you have SQLAgentMail configured, you can click the Test button to send mail to the user. SQL Server should report that the message was sent successfully.

5. On the Notifications tab, select all the alerts you wish to have go to this operator.

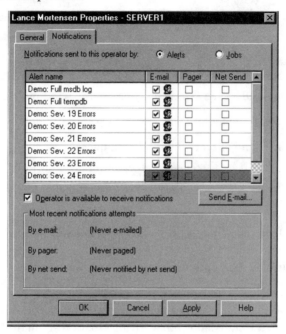

6. Select OK to save the operator.

After you've set up your operators (defining their working hours), you can designate a fail-safe operator in case no other operators are on duty when an alert is triggered:

1. In Enterprise Manager, highlight the SQL Server Agent folder under the Management folder.

2. Select Action ➤ Properties, or right-click and choose Properties to bring up the Properties screen.

3. Go to the Alert System tab. In the Fail-Safe Operator drop-down list box, select an operator you have already set up, as shown below. Check the E-Mail box as well.

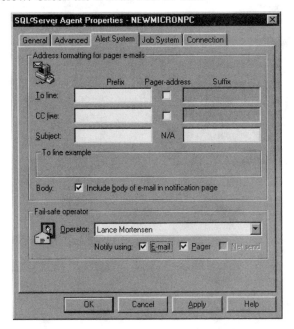

4. Click OK to save your changes.

Setting Up SQLAgentMail

In this series of steps, you are going to configure SQLAgentMail. This is very similar to the steps in Chapter 2 for configuring SQL Mail, but notice the subtle differences:

1. On your mail server, create a mailbox for your account if one does not already exist.

2. Log in to Windows NT as the user you created for the SQLAgent account.

3. Go to Control Panel ➤ Mail and Fax, and select Add under the Profile section.

4. Assuming that you use Exchange Server for e-mail, leave Microsoft Exchange Server selected and clear all the other selections. Select Next.

5. Enter the name of the Exchange Server and the mailbox. Select Next.

6. Select No when asked if you travel with the computer. Select Next.

7. Take the default path to the Address Book. Select Next.

8. Do not choose to add Outlook to the Startup Group. Select Next.

9. Select Finish at the final screen.

10. Note the name of the profile. You will need to know this name for later steps.

11. Go to Enterprise Manager.

12. To configure the SQLAgentMail, right-click SQL Mail (under SQLAgent under Management) and select Configure.

13. Enter the name of the profile from step 10, then click OK.

14. To start the SQL Mail session, right-click the SQL Mail icon and choose Start. The session should start, and the arrow should turn green.

The Maintenance Wizard

While the Maintenance Wizard is not a specific exam objective, it is a marvelous tool for scheduling backups. It fits best here since it is used for automation. The time will not be taken to go through every step of the Wizard, but you should know its purpose and how to get to it.

There are two ways to start the Wizard: by right-clicking the database you want to maintain and selecting All Tasks and then Maintenance Plans, or by selecting Database Maintenance Plans under the Management icon. The Wizard is capable of scheduling:

- Error checking and repair
- Index rebuilding
- Full and transaction log backups

Once you have configured a maintenance plan, you can edit it by going to the Maintenance Plan icon under Management, right-clicking the plan in the Contents pane, and making your changes.

Exam Essentials

Since automation can save you a lot of time as an administrator, you can be certain to expect some test questions on it. Here are a few key points that will help you with the automation questions.

Understand the types of commands used in jobs. It is good to remember that there are four types of commands used in jobs: Transact-SQL, CmdExec, active scripting, and replication. You will not configure a replication job directly—that is done automatically when you configure replication.

Know how to configure multiserver jobs. Since this is going to save you time in a large network, you should be familiar with how to set up a job designed to run on multiple servers.

Know what it takes to make an alert fire. There is one very important point here: An alert won't fire if it is not written to the Windows NT application log. This is especially important if you are creating your own alerts. You should also remember that if you create your own alert, it must start with number 50,001.

Know the limits on tasks and schedules. Simply put, there are none. A job can have multiple tasks that run under multiple schedules.

Key Terms and Concepts

Alert: A response to an event in the database engine that is useful as a method of warning an administrator when something goes awry.

Job: A series of tasks combined with associated schedules.

Operator: The representation of an administrator's e-mail, pager, and net-send addresses in SQL Server.

Schedule: A timer in a job that executes tasks.

Task: A command, either T-SQL, command line, or active script, that occurs when it is scheduled to do so.

Sample Questions

1. You have just created an error message–based alert in SQL that does not seem to be firing. What is the most likely cause?

   A. The alert is not being written to the Windows NT application log.

   B. The alert is not above 50,001.

   C. The alert does not have an associated job.

   D. The alert was not enabled after it was created.

   Answer: A. The alert must be written to the application log or it will never fire. Answer D may be correct, but not likely, since the default setting for a new alert is enabled.

2. You have configured several operators that are scheduled to be paged throughout the week and on the weekend. There is, however, no one scheduled to be paged on Sunday morning from 12:00 A.M. to 8:00 A.M. What happens if there is a critical error during that time?

   A. SQL will page the last person who was on duty.

   B. No one will be paged.

   C. If there is a fail-safe operator, that person will be paged.

   D. The error message will be queued until the next operator is scheduled to be paged.

   Answer: C. If you have a fail-safe operator, they will be paged; otherwise, no one will be paged.

Enable access to remote data.

- Set up linked servers.
- Set up security for linked databases.

In a replication scenario, your users require access to the same data stored on multiple servers. They may also need access to different data stored on multiple servers. For example, suppose that you have multiple regions around the continent that have their own sales databases. When the purchasing department runs their reports to find out who is low on inventory, they need to access the data that are stored on all of those servers. That is what this section is all about—giving them access to those distributed data. In this brief section, what is necessary to give your users access to linked databases will be discussed.

Critical Information

When your users need access to data stored on multiple servers in one query, it is called a *distributed query*, which returns result sets from databases on multiple servers. Although you might wonder why you would want to perform distributed queries when you could just replicate the data between servers, there are practical reasons for doing the former.

Don't forget that because SQL Server is designed to store terabytes of data, some of your databases may grow to several hundred megabytes in size—and you really don't want to replicate several hundred megabytes under normal circumstances.

The first step is to inform SQL that it will be talking to other database servers by running the `sp_addlinkedserver` stored procedure. The procedure to link to a server named AccountingSQL looks something like this:

```
sp_addlinkedserver @server='AccountingSQL',
@provider='SQL Server'.
```

Your users can then run distributed queries by simply specifying two different servers in the query. The query `select * from SQLServer .pubs.dbo.authors, AccountingSQL.pubs.dbo.employees` would access data from both the SQL Server (the server the user is logged in to, or the sending server) and the AccountingSQL server (the remote server) in the same result set.

The security issue here is that the sending server must log in to the remote server on behalf of the user to gain access to the data. SQL can use one of two methods to send this security information: security account delegation or linked-server login mapping. If your users have logged in using Windows NT authentication and all of the servers in the query are capable of understanding Windows NT domain security, you can use account delegation.

Once you have configured this, it is essential to monitor your office to be sure that no one is trying to bypass security; this can be done with the SQL Profiler.

Necessary Procedures

You should definitely understand how to make remote access work on your networks. The following steps will show you how to configure security account delegation:

1. If the servers are in different domains, you must make certain that the appropriate Windows NT trust relationships are in place. The remote server's domain must trust the sending server's domain.

2. Add a Windows NT login to the sending server for the user to log in with.

3. Add the same account to the remote server.

4. Create a user account for the login in the remote server's database and assign permissions.

5. When the user executes the distributed query, SQL will send the user's Windows NT security credentials to the remote server, allowing access.

If you have users who access SQL with standard logins, or if some of the servers do not participate in Windows NT domain security, you will need to add a linked login. Here's how to do it:

1. On the remote server, create a standard login and assign the necessary permissions.

2. On the sending server, map a local login to the remote login using the `sp_addlinkedsrvlogin` stored procedure. To map all local logins to the remote login RemUser, type:

```
sp_addlinkedsrvlogin @rmtsrvname='AccountingSQL', ~CA
@useself=FALSE, @locallogin=NULL, ~CA
@rmtuser='RemUser', @rmtpassword='password'
```

3. When a user executes a distributed query, the sending server will log in to the AccountingSQL (remote) server as RemUser with a password of *password*.

Exam Essentials

You will not get tested very much on linked servers, if at all. However, they are an important subject since they are being found in more and more networks. It is a good idea to remember the following points in the exam center.

Know what linked servers are for. Linked servers allow you to run a query against databases stored on more than one server.

Know the types of linked-server security. There are two types of linked-server security: account delegation and linked-server login mapping. Account delegation can be used only if the user who is accessing the query is logged in with Windows NT authentication. If the user is logged in with standard security, you will need to configure a linked login.

Key Terms and Concepts

Account delegation: The act of sending the current user's Windows NT security credentials to log in to a server; in this case, for accessing a SQL database.

Linked login: A login that allows users who are using standard security to perform distributed queries.

Sample Questions

1. You have configured your servers to perform distributed queries using account delegation. Who can run the distributed query?

   A. Only people who are logged in using a standard login

   B. Only people who are logged in with a Windows NT login

   C. Anyone who has logged in and been validated

   D. Only members of the db_execlinked role

   Answer: B. Only users who have logged in with a Windows NT account will be able to access the distributed query when the servers are configured to use account delegation. Incidentally, D is a trick answer.

2. What is the correct stored procedure to use for configuring a linked login?

   A. sp_addsrvlogin

   B. sp_addlinkedlogin

   C. sp_addlinked

   D. sp_addlinkedsrvlogin

   Answer: D. sp_addlinkedsrvlogin with the proper parameters will configure a linked-server login.

CHAPTER

5

Monitoring and Optimization

Microsoft Exam Objectives Covered in This Chapter:

▶ **Monitor SQL Server performance.** *(pages 265 – 292)*

▶ **Tune and optimize SQL Server.** *(pages 292 – 299)*

▶ **Limit resources used by queries.** *(pages 299 – 301)*

Imagine for a moment that you are the chief operating officer of a rather sizable company. It is your job to make sure that the company runs smoothly and that everything gets done efficiently. Rather than just guessing what needs to be done, you would ask for reports from the various department managers and base your decisions on those reports. You might discover, for instance, that the accounting department has too much work and could use some help. Based on this report, you could hire more accountants.

SQL Server is much the same in that you need to make certain everything is getting done efficiently. Rather than randomly assigning tasks, which is an invitation to disaster, you need to get reports from your "department managers": the CPU, the disk subsystem, the database engine, etc. Once you have these reports, you can assign tasks and resources accordingly.

Most systems administrators don't perform monitoring and optimization functions because they believe they don't have the time. Most of their time is spent on fire fighting—that is, troubleshooting problems that have cropped up. It's safe to say that if they had taken the time to monitor and optimize the systems, those problems might never have arisen in the first place. That makes monitoring and optimization *proactive* troubleshooting, not *reactive*, as is the norm. Due to this fact, Microsoft hits this objective pretty hard on the test—they want to be sure that you are performing monitoring and optimization.

In this chapter, the various methods and tools for getting the reports you need from your SQL Server will be discussed. How to use Performance Monitor to check on not only SQL Server, but Windows NT as well, will be covered. Then, a great deal of time will be spent working with Profiler, which is a very powerful tool for monitoring.

After the tools for monitoring have been discussed, how to optimize the system, specifically RAM and CPU usage, will be examined. Then, the Query Governor, which will limit the resources that are used up by queries, will be introduced.

Monitor SQL Server performance.

When your systems run at top speed, your users are generally happy. When your users are happy, they make less support calls. When you get less support calls, you are a happier person. It is because of this that you need to optimize your SQL Server. However, you can't just make some changes to the system and hope that they pan out—you need to monitor your system first and see what changes are needed.

This section will cover the tools available for monitoring and how to use those tools. Performance Monitor, which is useful for monitoring Windows NT as well as SQL Server, will be discussed. Then, Profiler, which is designed to monitor only SQL Server and therefore does a very comprehensive job of it, will be examined. A number of statistics as well as methodology for using the tools that you should become familiar with for the exam and your own edification will also be presented in this chapter.

Critical Information

SQL cannot function properly if it does not have available system resources, such as memory, processor power, fast disks, and a reliable network subsystem. If these subsystems do not work together, the system as a whole will not function properly. For example, if the memory is being overused, the disk subsystem will slow down because the memory will have to write to the pagefile (which is on the disk) far too often. To keep such things from happening, you will need to get reports from the subsystems; you can do this by using Performance Monitor.

Performance Monitor

Performance Monitor comes with Windows NT and is located in the Administrative Tools folder on the Start menu. Four views are available for your use:

Chart: This view displays a graph of system performance. As values change, the graph will spike or dip accordingly.

Report: The report view looks more like what you might get on a piece of paper, except that the values here change with system use.

Alert: With alert view, you can instruct Performance Monitor to warn you when something bad is looming on the horizon, perhaps when CPU use is almost—but not quite yet—too high. This type of warning gives you time to fix potential problems before they become actual problems.

Log: This view is for record keeping. With log view, you can monitor your system over a period of time and view the information later, as opposed to viewing it in real time (the default).

With each of these views, you monitor objects and counters. An *object* is a part of the system, such as the processor or the physical memory. A *counter* displays a number that tells you how much that object is being used. For example, the % Processor Time counter under the Processor Object will tell you how much time your processor spends working. Not only does Windows NT have several such objects and counters, the most common of which are listed in Table 5.1, but SQL Server provides some of its own. The SQL counters you will be using most often have been preset for you and can be accessed through the Performance Monitor icon in the SQL Server 7 menu on the Start menu. Table 5.2 describes each of the counters in the preset Performance Monitor.

T A B L E 5.1: Common Counters and Values in Performance Monitor

Object	Counter	Recommended Value	Use
Processor	% Processor Time	Less than 75 percent	Monitors the amount of time the processor spends working.
Memory	Pages/Sec	Fewer than 5	Monitors the number of times per second that data had to be moved from RAM to disk and vice versa.
Memory	Available Bytes	More than 4MB	Monitors the amount of physical RAM available. Since Windows NT uses as much RAM as it can for file cache, this number may seem low—as long as it is above 4MB, it is acceptable.
Memory	Committed Bytes	Less than physical RAM	Monitors the amount of RAM committed to use.
Disk	% Disk Time	Less than 50 percent	Monitors the amount of time that the disk is busy reading or writing.
Network Segment	% Network Utilization	Less than 30 percent	Monitors the amount of network bandwidth being used.

NOTE To see the Network Segment: % Network Utilization counter, you must install the Network Monitor Agent from Control Panel ➤ Network ➤ Services.

WARNING If you don't enable the disk counters by executing diskperf -y (or -ye when using RAID), all disk counters will read zero.

TABLE 5.2: Preset SQL Counters in Performance Monitor

Object	Counter	Use
SQLServer:Buffer Manager	Buffer Cache Hit Ratio	This tells you how much data are being retrieved from cache instead of disk. This number should be high.
SQLServer:Buffer Manager	Page Reads/Sec	Monitors the number of data pages that are read from disk each second.
SQLServer:Buffer Manager	Page Writes/Sec	Monitors the number of data pages that are written to disk each second.
SQLServer:General Statistics	User Connections	Monitors the number of user connections. Each of these will take some RAM.
SQLServer:Memory Manager	Total Server Memory (KB)	Monitors the total amount of memory that SQL has been dynamically assigned.
SQLServer:SQL Statistics	SQL Compilations/Sec	Monitors the number of compilations per second.

Profiler

Once the system is functioning efficiently, you can move up a rung and start monitoring the database engine by using Profiler. You will accomplish this by performing a *trace*, which is a record of data that have been captured about events. Stored in a table, a trace log file, or both, traces can be either shared (viewable by everyone) or private (viewable only by the owner).

The actions you will be monitoring, or tracing, are called *events* and are logically grouped into *event classes*. Some of these events are useful for maintaining security, and some are useful for troubleshooting problems, but most of these events are used for monitoring and optimization.

Possibly the easiest way to create a trace is by using the Trace Wizard, which is a very handy tool for creating a quick-and-dirty trace to get some standard information. You can create a total of six traces with this Wizard:

Find the Worst Performing Queries: This trace will help identify which queries are the slowest by grouping the output according to the duration of each query.

Identify Scans of Large Tables: This trace will identify scans of large tables. If you find such scans, you may need to create some indexes.

Identify the Cause of a Deadlock: Deadlocks, caused by multiple users trying to access the same data at the same time, can slow all users down. This trace will show the chain of events leading up to the deadlock and the object that was being accessed.

Profile the Performance of a Stored Procedure: Stored procedures are T-SQL code that is stored at the server for clients to access. Improperly written stored procedures can slow the system down. This trace will help find improperly written stored procedures.

Trace Transact-SQL Activity by Application: This trace will show you which applications are being used the most to access SQL Server.

Trace Transact-SQL Activity by User: This trace will help you see which of your users are accessing SQL Server the most and what they are doing while logged in.

One issue to be concerned with when you create and execute a trace is that it returns a great deal of data that you don't necessarily want or need to see. For example, a great deal of information about system objects is returned, and every application you use to access SQL (e.g., Enterprise Manager) will be recorded in the trace. To get rid of the extraneous data, you should consider filtering the trace, which will remove the excess data.

After you create and execute the trace, you can use it to re-create problem-causing events by replaying it. Loading your saved traces into Profiler will allow you to replay them against the server and, in this way, figure out exactly where the problem occurred. An especially nice touch is that you don't have to play the whole trace all at once; you can take it step by step to see exactly where the problem lies.

One final feature of Profiler is the Index Tuning Wizard, which is used to keep your indexes in top shape. Some circumstances that may require the services of the Index Tuning Wizard include wrong columns being indexed from the beginning, or users that have started querying different data over time, requiring the creation of new indexes.

To run the Index Tuning Wizard, you will need a workload, which you get by running and saving a trace in Profiler. It is best to get this workload during times of peak database activity to make sure that you give the Wizard an accurate load. If you aren't sure about which events to trace, you can base your trace on the Sample 1 Trace SQL definition, which defines a standard set of events to capture.

Tips and Techniques for Both Tools

If you want the best results from SQL Server's monitoring tools, you need to know and use the proper techniques. If you don't, the end result will not be what you are hoping for—or what you need.

Since you will never know if your system is running slower than normal unless you know what normal is, you will need a measurement baseline that shows you what resources (memory, CPU, etc.) SQL consumes under normal circumstances. You create the baseline before putting your system into production so that you have something to compare your readings to later on.

To create an accurate measurement baseline, you should have a test network with just your SQL Server and one or two client machines—this will limit the broadcast traffic on the network, which can throw off your baseline. If you don't have a test network, you may want to consider shutting down as many machines as possible and generating your baseline off-hours on your production network. You can then start your baseline. The Windows NT counters mentioned at the outset as well as the preset SQL counters should provide an accurate baseline with which you can compare future readings.

Once you have completed monitoring your system, you should archive the data (probably to tape). One of the primary reasons to do so is to back up requests for additional equipment. For example, if you ask for funds to buy more memory for the SQL Server, but don't bring any proof that the system needs the RAM, you are probably not going to get the money. If you bring a few months worth of reports, however, and say, "After tracking SQL for a time, we've found this...," management may be far more willing to give you the money you need. Using archived data in such fashion is known as *trend tracking*.

One of the most valuable functions of using your archived data for trend tracking is proactive troubleshooting—that is, anticipating and avoiding problems before they arise. Suppose you added 50 new users to your network about three months ago and are about to do it again. If you archived your data from that period, you would be able to recall what those 50 users had done to the performance of the SQL Server, and you could compensate for it. On the other hand, if you have thrown that data away, you might be in for a nasty surprise when your system unexpectedly slows to a crawl.

Necessary Procedures

You should be familiar with several procedures for the test. The first thing you need to know is how to use Performance Monitor to check on the status of the server as a whole—how to use it to gather real-time data as well as log data to read later on. Then, you will read about how to use Profiler to the fullest, which includes creating traces manually and through the Trace Wizard. The final procedure is using the Index Wizard to optimize your system's indexes.

Using Performance Monitor

The following steps will help you monitor your system in real time using Performance Monitor:

1. From the Start menu, select Programs ➤ Administrative Tools ➤ Performance Monitor.

2. On the Edit menu, select Add to Chart to bring up the Add to Chart dialog box.

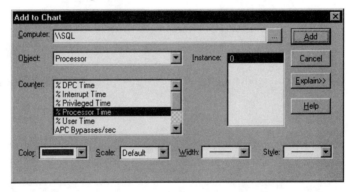

3. In the Object box, select the object you want to monitor (such as Processor).

4. In the Counter box, select a counter for the object.

5. Repeat steps 3–4 for any other objects you want to monitor.

6. Click Done and notice the graph being created on the screen.

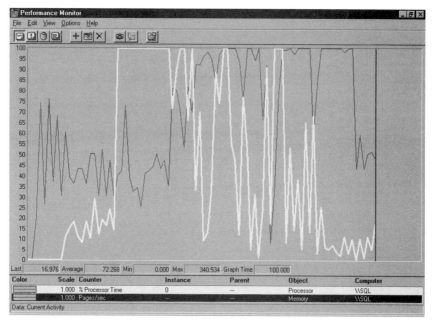

7. Press Ctrl+H and notice the current counter turn white. This makes the chart easier to read.

8. On the View menu, select Report.

9. On the toolbar, click the + button to bring up the Add to Report dialog box.

10. Add the counters and objects that you wish to view, then click Done. Notice the report displayed on the screen.

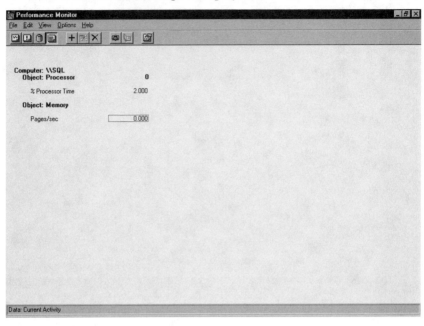

11. On the View menu, select Alert View and click the + button on the toolbar.

12. Select the object and counter you wish to be warned about.

13. Under Alert If, select either Under or Over, and in the box next to it, type a corresponding value.

14. Click Add; then click Done.

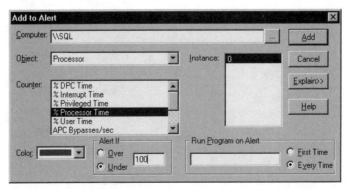

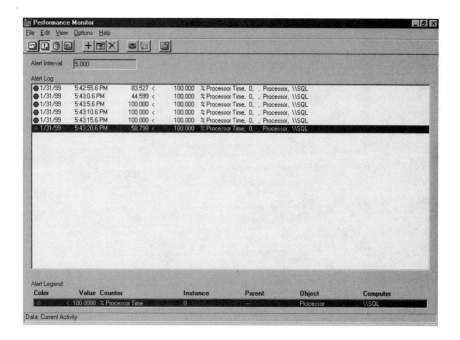

Logging with Performance Monitor

The next series of steps will show you how to store your performance information in a log file so that you can read it at your leisure, rather than needing to watch the screen the entire time.

1. Open Performance Monitor in the Administrative Tools menu.

2. On the View menu, select Log.

3. On the Options menu, select Log to open the Log Options dialog box.

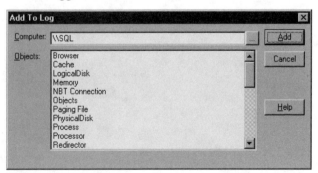

4. In the File Name box, type a log filename.

5. Under Update Time, set the seconds for Periodic Update (300 seconds, or 5 minutes, is average).

6. Click the Save button.

7. On the Edit menu, select Add to Log and notice that you are allowed to add only objects. All counters for each selected object will be logged.

8. On the Options menu, select Log to open the Log Options dialog box.

9. Click Start Log to start logging.

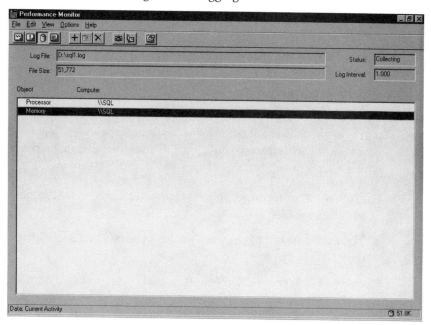

10. When you are done logging, on the Options menu, select Log. Then, click the Stop Log button.

11. On the View menu, select Chart.

12. On the Options menu, select Data From, then select Log File and enter the name of the log file in the text box.

13. On the Edit menu, select Add to Chart and notice that you are allowed to add only the objects that were logged.

14. Add your objects and click the Done button—notice the chart that has been created. Data are available for only the amount of time that you were logging.

15. Exit Performance Monitor.

Using Profiler

Now that you have mastered Performance Monitor, you are ready to move on to Profiler. The next few series of procedures will show you how to work with traces. You'll start by manually creating a trace with a filter applied:

1. From the Start menu, go to the SQL Server menu under Programs and click Profiler.

2. You may be asked to register a server—you must do so to create a trace.

3. On the File menu, select New, then click Trace to bring up the Trace Properties dialog box.

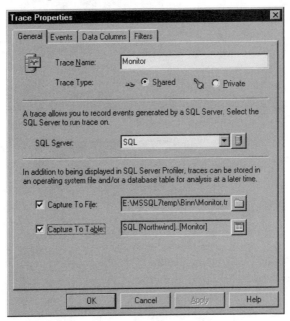

4. In the Trace Name box, type a name for your trace.

5. Select either Shared (accessible by all) or Private (accessible by the owner) as the Trace Type.

6. If you want to capture to a file on disk, check the Capture to File checkbox, and enter a name and location for the file.

7. To capture to a table, check the Capture to Table checkbox and fill in the server, database, owner, and table to capture to.

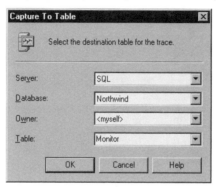

8. Click the Events tab.

9. Under Available Events, select the events you wish to monitor and click Add.

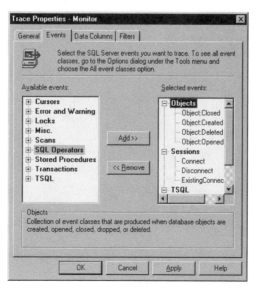

10. Click the Data Columns tab to change the data you see in the trace.

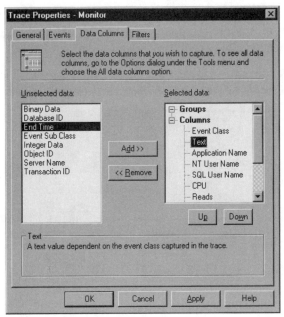

11. Click the Filters tab. You will notice that the only information filtered out is that which comes from Profiler.

12. To exclude system objects, select Object ID under Trace Event Criteria and check Exclude System Objects.

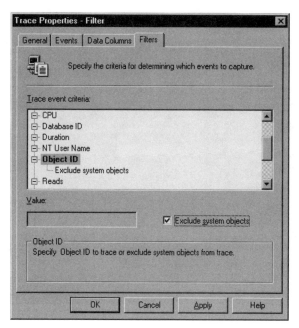

13. Click OK to start the trace.

Using the Trace Wizard

Fortunately, you don't have to create all of your traces manually—you can also use the Trace Wizard. This Wizard is great for creating a quick-and-dirty trace that can be fine-tuned later to your liking. You'll create a trace here for finding the worst performing queries:

1. Open Profiler, and on the Tools menu, select Create Trace Wizard.

2. In the Create Trace Wizard box, read through the checklist on the first screen and click Next.

3. On the next screen, select your server in the Server list.

4. In the Problem list, select Find the Worst Performing Queries, then click Next.

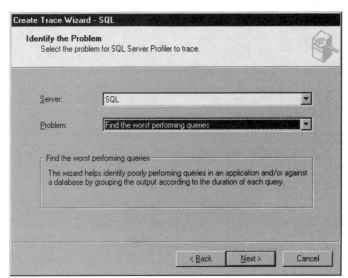

5. Select All Databases in the Database list.

6. In the Minimum Duration box, type a value for the number of seconds that a query must run to qualify to be shown.

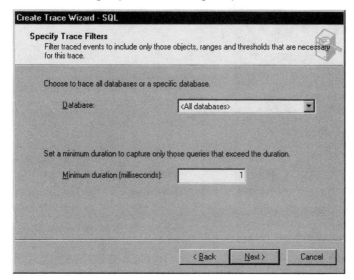

7. On the next screen, select Choose to Trace One or More Specific Applications.

8. Check the MS-SQL Query Analyzer checkbox and click Next.

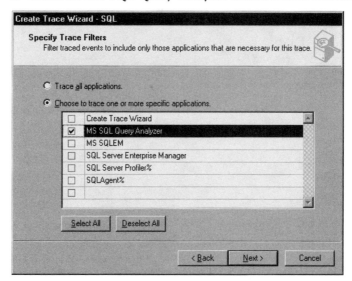

9. Leave the Trace Name set to Worst Performing Queries and click Finish. This will start the trace.

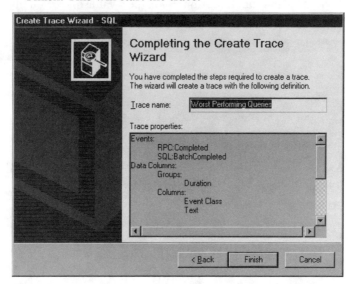

Using the Index Tuning Wizard

Now that you know how to create and filter traces both manually and through the Trace Wizard, you are ready to use the Index Tuning Wizard. Since this Wizard requires a workload, you need to create a trace first, then you can run the Wizard with the following steps:

1. Open Profiler.

2. On the Tools menu, select Index Tuning Wizard. This will open the welcome screen.

3. Click Next.

4. Select the local server in the Server drop-down list.

5. Select the database to tune.

6. Decide whether you wish to Keep All Existing Indexes.

7. Decide whether to Perform Thorough Analysis.

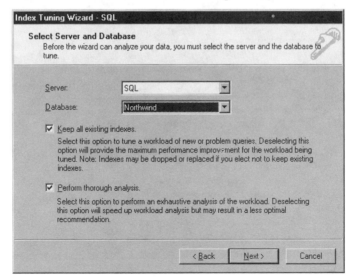

8. Click Next.

9. On the Identify Workload screen, select I Have Saved a Workload File.

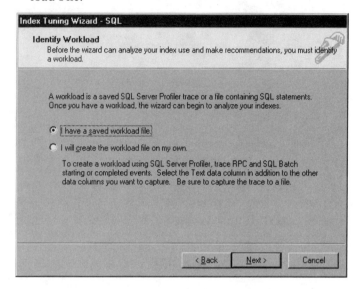

10. Click Next.

11. Click the My Workload File button.

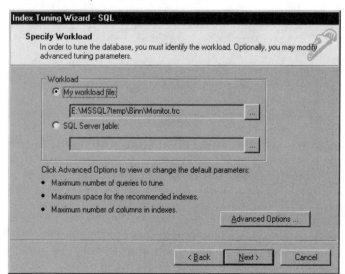

12. In the File Open dialog box, select a trace created earlier and click OK.

13. When returned to the Specify Workload screen, click the Advanced Options button, note the defaults, and click OK.

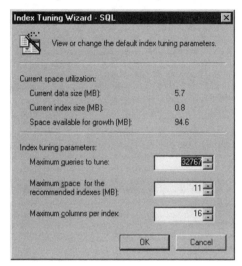

14. Click Next.

15. Select the Tables to Tune.

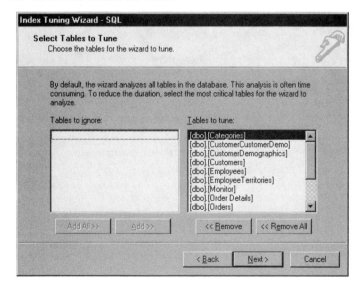

16. Click Next—the Wizard will now start tuning your indexes.

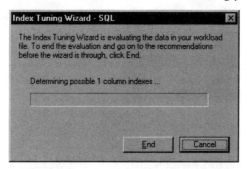

17. You will now be asked to accept the index recommendations; click Next.

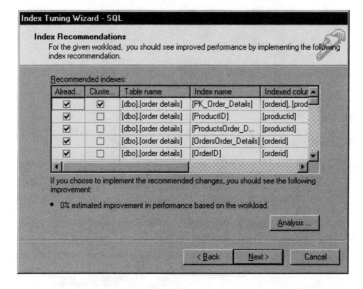

18. On the Schedule Index Update Job screen, select Apply Changes and Execute Recommendations Now, or schedule them for a later time.

19. Just below that, you can save the changes made to a script by checking Save Script File.

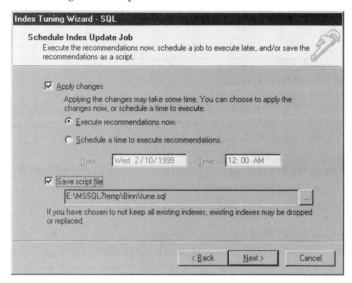

20. Click Next.

21. On the final screen, click Finish to apply the changes.

22. When you receive a message stating that the Wizard has completed, click OK.

23. Exit Profiler.

Exam Essentials

Since you cannot optimize your system without first monitoring it, you can expect some questions on the test about these concepts. Some points that you should pay special attention to for the exam are listed here.

Know what counters to monitor in Performance Monitor. Earlier in the chapter, two tables list the counters to look for in both Windows NT and SQL Server. It is a good idea to be familiar with them.

Know what Profiler is for and how to use it. Profiler is used for monitoring database engine activity. You should be familiar with how it works and when to use Profiler as opposed to Performance Monitor.

Key Terms and Concepts

Counters: Each object in Performance Monitor has counters that report specific statistics of the object. For instance, the % Processor Time counter of the Processor object would report the percent of time during which the processor is busy.

Event: This is an action taking place in the database engine, such as a DELETE statement or a user logging in.

Filter: Filters are set in Profiler to exclude extraneous data from being captured and displayed in a trace.

Object: In Windows NT Performance Monitor, an object is used to identify and monitor a system resource, such as the CPU or memory.

Trace: This is a record of events that is captured using Profiler.

Sample Questions

1. Your developers have just implemented a new database application that, according to your users, seems to slow down the system. What can you do speed it up?

   A. Analyze the new queries with Query Analyzer.

   B. Monitor the Physical Disk: Average Disk Queue counter in Performance Monitor during a period of peak activity to see if the disk subsystem can handle the new queries.

   C. Create a trace with Profiler and use the trace file with the Index Tuning Wizard to improve the indexes.

   D. Increase the size of `tempdb`.

   Answer: C. Since the tables and queries are new, any indexes involved most likely have not been stress tested. The Index Tuning Wizard will find and correct the problem indexes.

2. After using a trace in Profiler to monitor database activity, what should you do with the trace file?

   A. Delete it—it is useless.

   B. Save it on disk so you can use it later for trend tracking.

   C. Archive it to tape (or another backup medium) and keep it for trend tracking.

   D. Print out the trace summary, put it in a binder, and then delete the trace file.

   Answer: C. Archive the files to tape and keep them for as long as you can. They will prove very valuable when you need to track trends later on. Incidentally, there is no trace summary to print out.

3. You need to know if your SQL Server can handle the load that your users are placing on it. When should you monitor your server?

   A. In the morning, when your users first start up.

   B. Just after lunch, when your users are getting back.

C. There is no set time—monitor when activity is at its lowest.

D. There is no set time—monitor when activity is at its highest.

Answer: D. If you monitor when activity is at its highest, you will get an accurate reading of the stress your users place on the system.

Tune and optimize SQL Server.

If you really were the chief operating officer of a company receiving reports from your managers on a regular basis, you can be sure that your company wouldn't benefit from those reports if you did not act on them. The same is true with SQL—if you don't act on the reports you are getting from Performance Monitor and Profiler, your system will be doomed to run slow for all its days.

In this section, the various methods for acting on those reports to optimize SQL Server will be examined. You'll see how to make SQL use RAM most efficiently, then you'll see how to optimize the CPU usage. Both of these configurations will be considered not only for a dedicated machine, but for shared machines (i.e., SQL and Exchange) as well. Finally, even though it is not listed as an exam objective, you will get hit pretty hard with RAID questions. So, you will learn how to optimize disk usage for your server.

Critical Information

SQL Server can dynamically adjust most of its settings to compensate for problems. It can adjust memory use, threads spawned, and a host of other settings. In some cases, unfortunately, those dynamic adjustments may not be enough—you may need to make some manual changes. A few specific areas that may require your personal attention will be discussed.

Manually Configuring Memory Use

While SQL is capable of dynamically assigning itself memory, it is not always best to let it do so. A good example of this is when you need to run another BackOffice program, such as Exchange, on the same system as SQL Server. If SQL is not constrained, it will take so much memory that none will be left for Exchange. The constraint you need to put in place is the Max Server Memory setting—by adjusting it, you can stop SQL Server from taking too much RAM. If, for example, you set Max Server Memory to 102,400 (100×1024 [the size of a megabyte]), SQL will never use more than 100MB of RAM.

NOTE   These concepts will be tested quite a bit, so become one with them.

You could also set Min Server Memory, which tells SQL never to use less than the set amount—this should be used in conjunction with Set Working Size. Windows NT uses virtual memory, which means that data in memory that have not been accessed for a while can be stored on disk. The Set Working Size option stops Windows NT from moving SQL data from RAM to disk, even if it is idle. This can improve SQL Server's performance, since data will never need to be retrieved from disk (which is about 100 times slower than RAM).

If you decide to use this option, you should set Min Server Memory and Max Server Memory to the same size, then change the Set Working Size option to one. This configuration should be used only on a dedicated SQL Server, since it will take RAM away from other programs and never give it back.

WARNING   For the amount of memory that SQL requires, you will want to have 1MB of Level 2 cache on your system. If you don't have enough L2 cache, your system may actually slow down when you add RAM.

Optimizing CPU Usage

Since SQL uses the CPU to the hilt, you may want to change the way SQL uses it. Each program on the system has a priority assigned to it by the operating system. Programs with a higher priority get more CPU time than programs with lower priorities. On a dedicated SQL server, you can change the priority that is assigned to SQL from the default 7 to 15 (or from 15 to 24 on a multiprocessor system) by using the sp_configure stored procedure. Setting the priority boost setting to 1 will make the priority higher. The boost can be set from Enterprise Manager on the Processor tab of the Server Properties dialog box, or by executing sp_configure 'priority boost', '1'.

WARNING Priority boost is only for a dedicated machine—if you are running more than one program on the SQL Server, boosting the priority will take CPU time from the other programs.

NOTE The next two subsections may not seem like parts of the objective, but you need to know them for the exam.

Max Async I/O

It should go without saying that SQL needs to be able to write to disk, since that's where the database files are stored, but is SQL writing to disk fast enough? If you have multiple hard disks connected to a single controller, multiple hard disks connected to multiple controllers, or a RAID system involving striping, the answer is probably no. The maximum number of asynchronous input/output (Max Async I/O) threads by default in SQL is 32, meaning that SQL can have 32 outstanding read and 32 outstanding write requests at a time. Therefore, if SQL needs to write data to disk, it can send up to 32 small chunks of that data to disk at a time. If you have a powerful disk subsystem, you will want to increase the Max Async I/O setting.

The setting to which you increase it depends on your hardware. So, if you increase the setting, you must then monitor the server. Specifically, you will need to monitor the Physical Disk: Average Disk Queue Performance Monitor counter, which should be less than two (note that any queue should be less than two). If you adjust Max Async I/O and the Average Disk Queue counter goes above two, you have set it too high and will need to decrease it.

NOTE   You will need to divide the Average Disk Queue counter by the number of physical drives to get an accurate count. That is, if you have three hard disks and a counter value of six, you would divide six by three—which tells you that the counter value for each disk is two.

RAID

RAID (Redundant Array of Inexpensive Disks) is used to protect your data and speed up your system. In a system without RAID, data that are written to disk are written to that one disk. In a system with RAID, those same data would be written across multiple disks, providing fault tolerance and improved I/O. Some forms of RAID can be implemented inexpensively in Windows NT, but this uses such system resources as processor and memory. If you have the budget for it, you might consider getting a separate RAID controller that will take the processing burden off Windows NT. The types of RAID that you may want to consider for your SQL Server are listed here:

RAID 0 Stripe Set: This provides I/O improvement, but not fault tolerance.

RAID 1 Mirroring: This provides fault tolerance and read-time improvement. This can also be implemented as duplexing, which is a mirror that has separate controllers for each disk. This is the only way to provide fault tolerance for the operating system files and is best for the transaction logs.

RAID 0+1 Mirrored Stripe Set: This is a stripe set without parity that is duplicated on another set of disks. This requires a third-party controller, since Windows NT does not support it natively.

RAID 5 Stripe Set with Parity: This provides fault tolerance and improved read time. Since modifications to data are written initially in RAM and copied to disk later, you should not be overly concerned with write performance for the data files—that makes RAID 5 ideal for data files.

The ideal disk configuration is to have a combination of these forms. For instance, you may want to have your transaction logs on a mirrored (or duplexed) drive, and your databases on RAID 5 or RAID 0+1 array. No matter what fault tolerance you go with, you should consider getting a third-party RAID controller to take some of the burden off the system processor.

Necessary Procedures

If you want to set the memory and CPU usage, you will need to know how to do so.

Setting Memory and CPU Usage

This series of steps will show you how to configure the Max and Min Server Memory settings as well as the Set Working Size setting:

1. In Enterprise Manager, right-click your server and select Properties.

2. Select the Memory tab to change the settings.

3. To manually set the minimum memory that SQL will use, move the Minimum (MB) slider to the desired position.

4. To manually set the maximum memory that SQL will use, move the Maximum (MB) slider to the desired position.

5. To set both Minimum and Maximum to the same setting, move the Use a Fixed Memory Size (MB) slider to the desired position.

6. To set the Set Working Size option, check the Reserve Physical Memory for SQL Server checkbox and set the amount of RAM in bytes that SQL is allowed to use.

Setting the CPU to a higher priority is so simple that there is not even a series of steps for it. You simply open the Properties dialog box for the server you want to boost, select the Processor page, and check the Boost SQL Server Priority on Windows NT checkbox.

NOTE   Any of the procedures you've just performed in Enterprise Manager can also be accomplished with T-SQL by using the `sp_configure` stored procedure.

Exam Essentials

You are going to be hit hard with optimizing questions on the test, so know this topic well. Understanding the points listed here will help you tremendously on the exam, so eat, sleep, and breath them.

Know when to use the Max and Min Server Memory settings. There will probably be several questions on the test dealing with running SQL alongside another application (such as Exchange). You need to know when you should set the Min and Max Server Memory settings to make both programs run optimally.

Know when to configure the Set Working Size option.   You'll run into the same set of questions about multiple programs on the system here, but you need to remember that this option is only for dedicated machines.

Be familiar with RAID options.   Since RAID is a very useful tool for improving performance and gaining fault tolerance, you can be sure that there will be a fair share of questions about how to configure your arrays for use with SQL. You should know when to use each RAID level.

Key Terms and Concepts

RAID: This is an acronym for Redundant Array of Inexpensive Disks. RAID arrays are a series of hard disks that are seen by the system as one disk. They are used to improve I/O and give fault tolerance.

Working set: This is the amount of physical RAM an application is using at any given time.

Sample Questions

1. Your system is equipped with two 6.2GB drives and three 9GB drives. Without purchasing a separate controller, what is the optimal configuration for these drives for speed and fault tolerance?

   A. Mirror the two 6.2GB drives, and place the operating system and SQL binary files on them. Put the 9GB drives in a RAID 5 array, and place the databases and transaction logs there.

   B. Mirror the two 6.2GB drives, and place the operating system, SQL binaries, and transaction logs there. Put the 9GB drives in a RAID 5 array, and put the databases there.

   C. Mirror the two 6.2GB drives, and place the operating system, SQL binaries, and transaction logs there. Put the 9GB drives in a RAID 0 array, and put the databases there.

   D. Place all drives in a RAID 0+1 array, and do not worry about file placement.

   Answer: B. This will give the maximum I/O and fault tolerance without purchasing separate hardware, because data files work best on RAID 5 arrays, and transaction logs work best on a mirror or duplex (they require faster write times).

2. You are running both SQL Server and Exchange Server on the same computer due to budget constraints. How should memory usage be configured so that both programs run efficiently?

   A. In SQL Server, adjust the Min Server Memory setting.

   B. In SQL Server, adjust the Max Server Memory setting.

C. Set the Set Working Size option to one after setting both Min and Max Server Memory to the same size.

D. Do nothing—SQL will detect Exchange and automatically assign RAM accordingly.

Answer: B. By adjusting the Max Server Memory setting, you can instruct SQL not to take all available RAM—then, some RAM will be left over for Exchange.

Limit resources used by queries.

Surprising as it seems, not all queries are properly written and optimized. It is because of this fact that you will need to know how to keep SQL from wasting system resources on poorly written queries. The Query Governor is designed to do just that.

Critical Information

Right out of the box, SQL will run any query you tell it to, even if that query is poorly written. You can change that by using the Query Governor. This is not a separate tool, but part of the database engine, and is controlled by the Query Governor Cost Limit.

The Query Governor Cost Limit setting tells SQL not to run queries longer than x (where x is a value higher than zero). If, for example, the Query Governor Cost Limit is set to two, any query that is estimated to take longer than two seconds would not be allowed to run. SQL knows how long a query will take to complete even before it is executed, because it keeps statistics about the number and composition of records in tables and indexes.

NOTE If the Query Governor Cost Limit is set to zero (the default), all queries will be allowed to run.

Necessary Procedures

The only thing you need to know here is how to set the Query Governor Cost Limit setting. The Query Governor Cost Limit can be set by using the command `sp_configure 'query governor cost limit', '1'` (the *1* in this code can be higher). It can also be set on the Server Settings tab of the Server Properties page in Enterprise Manager.

Exam Essentials

There are not too many questions about the previous section on the exam, but it is good to know that SQL Server has the capability to limit resources used by queries. For the exam, you should know one thing in particular.

Know what the Query Governor is for and how to set it. The Query Governor is used for instructing SQL not to run long queries and is set via the `sp_configure` stored procedure or Enterprise Manager. While there won't be many questions on this topic, there will be a few, since this is a useful tool in the real world.

Key Terms and Concepts

Query Governor Cost Limit: This is a setting that affects the database engine by not allowing SQL to run long queries.

Sample Questions

1. You are concerned that some of your users are writing queries that are wasting system resources because they take too long to complete (on average, more than three seconds). How can you stop SQL from running queries that take longer than three seconds to execute?

   A. Use `sp_configure 'query governor cost limit', '3'`.

   B. Use `sp_configure 'query governor', '3'`.

   C. Use `sp_configure 'query limit', '3'`.

   D. Use `sp_configure 'query governor limit', '3'`.

   Answer: A. The other three options are all typos and would not function.

2. True or false. If you set the Query Governor Cost Limit to zero, no queries will run.

   A. True

   B. False

   Answer: B. All queries will be allowed to run if this is set to zero.

CHAPTER

6

Troubleshooting

Microsoft Exam Objectives Covered in This Chapter:

▶ **Diagnose and resolve problems in upgrading from SQL Server 6.x.**
(pages 305 – 308)

▶ **Diagnose and resolve problems in backup and restore operations.**
(pages 309 – 311)

▶ **Diagnose and resolve replication problems.** *(pages 312 – 317)*

▶ **Diagnose and resolve job or alert failures.** *(pages 318 – 320)*

▶ **Diagnose and resolve distributed query problems.**
(pages 321 – 323)

▶ **Diagnose and resolve client connectivity problems.**
(pages 323 – 328)

▶ **Diagnose and resolve problems in accessing SQL Server, databases, and database objects.** *(pages 329 – 333)*

In a perfect world, machines would never have problems, and this chapter would be unnecessary. However, since we don't live in a perfect world, we need a troubleshooting chapter. In fact, this may be the most important chapter in the book.

Imagine what would happen to your network if your SQL Server containing your sales database went down. Your sales department would not be able to make any sales—they would miss meetings and may even lose important customers if the database was down for an extended period. Now imagine what would happen to your paycheck if the sales database went down, and you could not bring it back—your paycheck would suddenly stop appearing. While this may seem a bit dramatic, it demonstrates the need for troubleshooting knowledge.

You will need to be familiar with some tools to perform successful troubleshooting—the SQL error log and the Windows NT Event Viewer. The SQL Server error log is a group of ASCII text files located in the \MSSQL7\Log folder—the most recent is named ERRORLOG. When a new log is created, the old log is renamed ERRORLOG.1, which in turn is renamed ERRORLOG.2, and so on, for up to six history logs. Note that the oldest log file—ERRORLOG.6—is not renamed, but is overwritten by ERRORLOG.5.

The error log is not the only place where errors are stored, though; you would be remiss if you did not check the Windows NT Event Viewer, since SQL Server stores errors in the application log as well. Once you are familiar with these tools, you can perform successful troubleshooting.

This troubleshooting knowledge will serve you well not only in the real world (where it will do the most good), but also for the test. The fact that the knowledge from this chapter will rescue you from disaster should assure you that there will be several questions on the exam designed to test your knowledge of these concepts. Unfortunately, all of the problems you can run into and how to fix them cannot possibly be listed in this one chapter—that knowledge will come with experience. What can be listed here, though, will one day save your data and exam score, so don't take this chapter lightly.

Diagnose and resolve problems in upgrading from SQL Server 6.*x*.

A lot of people out there will be upgrading from a previous version of SQL to version 7—you may even be one of them. Hopefully, you won't have any problems with your upgrade, but on the off chance that you do, this section can help you tremendously. You are going to read about the various problems that can occur when you upgrade a database to SQL 7 from a previous version and how to fix those problems. Since Microsoft is expecting a mass exodus from previous versions of SQL, you should be prepared for some questions on how to troubleshoot the upgrade.

Critical Information

The Upgrade Wizard will perform the actual work of morphing your 6.*x* databases into 7 databases. The first thing the Wizard needs to do is check the syscomments tables for inconsistencies, then it validates user permissions and logins. Once that is done, the Upgrade Wizard can transform your database schema and objects into a SQL 7 database, and fill that new database with your existing data.

If the Upgrade Wizard finds problems (heaven forbid) during the upgrade process, it will give you an error message saying, "One or more warnings have been logged. Please read the next screen carefully before you begin your upgrade." The Summary of Warnings screen is then displayed with the inconsistencies that the Wizard found. You can read about them right then or, if you want to view them later, you can read the error file. This is a text file with an err.out extension that is stored in the folder \MSSQL\Upgrade*server name_date_ time*. The error files themselves have a naming convention:

check65-<*dbid*><*dbname*>_err.out

For example, if the SQL Server is named Sybex and you did the upgrade on February 27, 1999, at 12:22:23 P.M. on the MySample database, the full path and filename for this output file would be as follows:

\MSSQL\Upgrade\Sybex_02-27-99_12:22:23\check65-
019MySample_err.out

While it is impossible to list every problem you could ever run into, the following list is a good summation of common problems and their associated solutions:

- If Tempdb is too small, you will have problems. For an upgrade, your Tempdb should be at least 10MB. However, it is recommended that you resize the database to 25MB or more for an upgrade.

- Ensure that the database users have valid SQL Server logins in the syslogins table on the Master database.

- If any objects have had their entries manually deleted in the syscomments table, you must drop and re-create the objects to re-create the syscomments entries.

- Since the upgrade process stops and restarts the SQL Server service, you should disable any stored procedures that are configured to execute at startup.

- If you have SQL Server 6.5 login accounts with a default database other than Master, that default database must exist in SQL 7; if not, the user accounts will not be upgraded.

- If you are using two computers to perform your upgrade, you cannot use the local system account, because it has no network capabilities. The user account that you do use should have administrative capabilities on both computers.

- Disable replication and clear the associated transaction logs.

- Do not try to upgrade to a different sort order or character set since SQL does not allow this.

Exam Essentials

Every section in this chapter is very important to you, both for the test and for the real world. In the upgrade section in particular, you should watch for the following items.

Know the potential problems with upgrades and how to fix them.   You should go over the list in this section and be sure that you understand the problems and solutions.

Know where to look for errors.   It seems like a small point, but it is important to know where the error logs are located. If several errors are printing out, the error log will give you something to refer to when you are making repairs.

Key Terms and Concepts

Syscomments: This is a table stored in each database that contains the original T-SQL code used to define each view, rule, default, trigger, CHECK constraint, DEFAULT constraint, and stored procedure.

Sample Questions

1. What steps should you take to prepare your server before running the Upgrade Wizard?

   A. Increase the size of Master to 25MB.

   B. Increase the size of Tempdb to 25MB.

   C. Disable automatic execution of stored procedures.

   D. Disable replication.

   Answer: B, C, D. Master cannot be less than 25MB in the first place; the other three options are requirements for upgrading.

2. True or false. Any errors encountered by the Upgrade Wizard are stored in the check65-<*dbid*><*dbname*>_err.out table in the Master database.

   A. True

   B. False

   Answer: B. This is not a table in the database; it is a file on disk.

Diagnose and resolve problems in backup and restore operations.

Backups and restorations are designed to rescue you in case of disaster. That means if you are having problems with backups and restorations, you need to get them back online right away. In this section, you will read about some of the common problems with backups and restorations, and how to fix them.

Critical Information

Some database activities are not allowed during a backup. If one of these activities is going on when you try to start a backup, you will get Error 3023. To fix this error, just wait until the illegal activity is complete and try your backup again. The activities that will cause this error are as follows:

- bcp
- CREATE INDEX
- Data file movement or resizing
- DBCC CHECKALLOC
- DBCC SHRINKDATABASE
- DBCC SHRINKFILE
- SELECT INTO

Two other errors that you may run into are Errors 3120 or 3149. These errors mean that you are trying to restore a database that was backed up from a server that is using a different character set or sort order than the system to which you are restoring. SQL Server can restore only databases that have the same character set and sort order as the backup. The best way to fix this error is to install another copy of SQL

Server 7 on another computer that has the proper character set and sort order, and restore to that computer. Once your database has been restored, you can use Data Transformation Services to move the restored database from the second server to your permanent database.

One error that will become fairly common actually stems from an excellent new feature in SQL Server 7—the ability to share tapes with Windows NT Backup. Since SQL and Windows NT now use the same tape format, it is possible to accidentally try to restore a non-SQL backup into SQL Server—that is what generates Error 3143. By using the RESTORE HEADERONLY command, you will be able to tell whether you are actually looking at a SQL backup.

Some other common errors include attempting to back up a transaction log when you have the Truncate Log on Checkpoint database option enabled. With that option enabled, there is no log to back up, so the backup fails. It is also good to note that if you try to restore transaction logs out of sequence, or if you have gaps between the logs, your restoration will fail.

Exam Essentials

Since backups and restorations are designed to save you in the event of an emergency, it is very important to understand how to make them work if they fail. While you do not need to memorize the error numbers for the test, here are some specific areas to pay special attention to.

Know what you can restore.   You cannot restore a backup that was made on a server that uses a different code page or sort order.

Remember to watch your tapes.   Since SQL and Windows NT can share tapes now, you need to watch the contents of the tapes to make certain you are not restoring the wrong one.

Key Terms and Concepts

DBCC: The Database Consistency Checker (DBCC) is used to ensure the physical and logical consistency of a database. Backups cannot be performed while it is running.

Sample Questions

1. You want to restore a database to your server. Your server is using case-insensitive sort order, and the backup was made on a server using binary sort order. Will the restoration work?

   A. Yes, the restoration will work.

   B. Yes, the restoration will work, but there will be warnings.

   C. Yes, the restoration will work, but only the data will be restored—the schema must be created first.

   D. No, the restoration will fail.

   Answer: D. You cannot restore a database that was backed up using a different sort order or code page.

2. Which activities are prevented during a backup?

   A. Users writing to the database

   B. DBCC SHRINKFILE

   C. Full-text searches

   D. Index creation

   Answer: B, D. Since backups are dynamic, users are still allowed to write to the database and search it for information.

Diagnose and resolve replication problems.

If you have a very popular database that all of the users in your company need access to, you are probably replicating that database. Databases are replicated so that users can access a local copy of the data without having to traverse slow WAN links and other bottlenecks to perform their queries. Once this replication is in place and working, your users come to depend on it for their data—if replication fails, your users will not be able to work.

Since so many companies today are finding use for replication and the employees are growing to depend on it so much, you need to know how to troubleshoot it when it fails. You will read about several areas where replication could break down, then you will look at some fixes. These areas will be covered quite extensively on the exam, so watch closely.

Critical Information

For replication to function the way it was intended, you need two SQL Servers connected via a network. Right away, you should see a potential problem: Since the SQLAgent takes care of replication, and that SQLAgent needs to talk to the SQLAgent on another computer, your SQLAgents need to be logged in using a domain account. Actually, all of the SQLAgents involved should be logging in with the *same* domain account, and that account should be an administrative account. Once SQL is configured properly, you can start working with replication.

Replication Will Not Run

Before replication can begin, an initial snapshot of the data must be copied to each subscriber. If the snapshot is not applied, replication cannot begin. If you suspect that the snapshot has not been applied, you need to first check that the snapshot agent is running; this can be done in Enterprise Manager under Replication Monitor.

If the snapshot agent is running, you need to check the agent history (as discussed in the "Necessary Procedures" section) and look for any errors that may have occurred. One of the more common errors in this situation is security; in the "Necessary Procedures" section, you'll read about how to verify that your distributor can log in to your subscriber or vice versa.

If your snapshot agent is not doing anything at all, make certain that your distribution server is online and available, and that you have the appropriate permissions on the working folder at the distributor.

No Subscribers Are Working

If none of your subscribers are getting replicated data, but the snapshot agent appears to be working, the problem is most likely with the logreader agent. If the logreader agent is not moving data from the transaction log of the Publishing database to the Distribution database, the distribution agent cannot move those records to subscribers. Since none of the subscribers are getting data, it is far more likely that the logreader, rather than the distribution agent, is not performing. To troubleshoot this, take a look at the history of the logreader agent in the Replication Monitor. Verify that the jobs are running as scheduled and that data are moving.

On the distribution server, you should verify that your Distribution database is large enough to hold the replicated transactions and that the Distribution-database transaction log is not full. Since this is a normal database, its transaction log can fill up just like any other if you do not perform transaction log backups regularly.

Several Subscribers of Many Are Not Working

When several subscribers of many are not working, it is almost definitely a problem with the distribution process. Because other subscribers are receiving replicated data, you know that the logreader process is working properly. You should check for the following problems:

- Check the distribution-agent histories for the failing servers.

- Ensure that the subscription server is online and has connectivity.

- Ensure that the Subscription database is available, not marked for DBO use only, and not set to read only.

- Ensure that the SQLAgent security credentials are set properly for the subscription servers; all SQLAgents should be using the same domain account.

- Ensure that the distribution agent is not waiting to perform a manual synchronization

Recovering Crashed Servers

Once you have repaired any other problems with replication, you can focus on another important area: recovery of crashed servers. When one of the servers in a replication scenario crashes, you need to know what to do to bring it back. Fortunately, in most cases, you don't need to do anything since SQL recovers itself well. Still, a time may come when SQL cannot recover itself and needs your help.

Recovering the Publishing Server

When your publisher goes down, your subscribers will not get updated data. SQL is actually pretty good at recovering from this, because the logreader agent places pointers (like bookmarks) in the transaction logs of published databases to track which transactions have been replicated already. If the publishing server crashes, the logreader agent will simply find the place where it stopped and continue once the system comes back online. If you have to restore the Publishing databases for some reason, your pointers and subscribers will be out of synch. To resynchronize them, you only need to run a snapshot, after which replication should proceed normally.

Recovering the Distribution Server

When your distribution server is down, replication halts. Since the distribution agent keeps track of which transactions have been applied to which subscribers, replication should continue from where it stopped when the system is brought back online. The real problem is when the distributor is down for an extended period. The distributor keeps transactions for only 24 hours (by default), then deletes them; this is known as the *retention period*. If this happens, just run a snapshot to resynchronize your subscribers.

Recovering the Subscription Server

When your subscription servers go down, you simply need to bring the servers back online. Replicated transactions on the distribution server will automatically be applied, and the subscriber will start running again normally. If the subscriber has been down for an extended period, you may want to run a snapshot just to be safe.

Necessary Procedures

You may have noticed that there are not many procedures when it comes to troubleshooting. There are two very necessary procedures, though—one is knowing how to read the agent histories; the other is knowing how to test security.

Reading Agent History

These steps will show you how to read agent history:

1. Open the Enterprise Manager and expand the Replication Monitor folder, then the Agents folder, and finally click the Snapshot Agents folder.

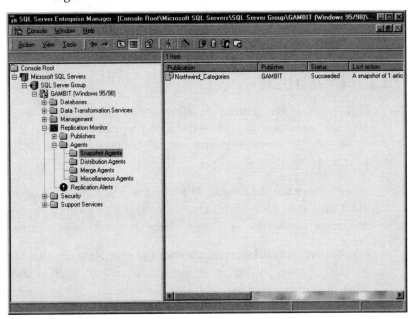

2. Right-click the agent in the right pane of the window and choose Agent History. This will give you information regarding how often the agent has run and what the agent accomplished.

3. Verify that the jobs are running as scheduled and that errors are not occurring.

Troubleshooting Security

This series of steps will show you how to test security between subscribers and distributors. First, if you are using a pull subscription, the distribution agent runs at the subscriber, so the subscriber must be able to log in to the distributor. Here's how to test it:

1. At the subscriber, log in to Windows NT as the SQLAgent service account.

2. Open Query Analyzer and connect to the distributor using Windows NT Authentication.

3. If you are successful logging in, your problem is not with security. If you fail, check your service account.

For a push subscription, the roles are reversed. All you need to do is follow steps 1 through 3, logging in at the distributor and connecting to the subscriber.

Exam Essentials

Since replication is designed to reduce network traffic and make data access faster in general, you need to know how to keep replication up and running at all times. Here are a couple of specifics that will help you do just that.

Know where the distribution agent runs.   In a pull subscription, the distribution agent runs on the subscriber; in a push subscription, it runs on the distributor. This will help you troubleshoot security.

Make sure your SQLAgents are configured.   Not only should your SQLAgents be logging on with a domain account, they should all be using the same account. If this is not the case, you can run into security problems.

Key Terms and Concepts

Logreader: This agent reads transaction logs on the publisher and moves transactions that are marked for replication to the Distribution database.

Snapshot: This is a complete copy of the database, copied from the publisher to the subscribers. It is used for initial setup and periodic refreshes.

Sample Questions

1. You have been successfully replicating one of your databases for some time. One day, your users complain that they are not seeing data that they know have been updated. What is the most likely cause?

    A. The Publisher database has become corrupt.

    B. The Subscriber database has become corrupt.

    C. The distributor has gone offline.

    D. The publication agent has stopped responding.

    Answer: C. Since you can access the databases at both the publisher and subscriber, you can be sure they are not corrupt. Incidentally, there is no such thing as the publication agent.

2. The distributor has been offline for two days due to a systems failure. What do you need to do to update the subscribers?

    A. Nothing—they will resynchronize themselves.

    B. From the publisher, run a snapshot for each of the subscribers.

    C. From the distributor, run the `sp_resynch` stored procedure.

    D. Delete and re-create the subscription at each subscriber.

    Answer: B. Running a snapshot after the distributor has been down for an extended period will resynchronize your subscribers.

Diagnose and resolve job or alert failures.

As an administrator, you are going to rely on jobs quite heavily to take over repetitive tasks such as backing up databases and performing routine maintenance. In fact, without the ability to schedule jobs, quite a bit of your time would be wasted doing menial work that could have been automated.

Alerts are another useful tool that warn you when something has gone wrong with your server and then fire a job to automatically fix whatever is wrong. Without alerts, you would have to get up from your chair, go to the server, and check for alerts yourself every few minutes just to be sure everything is OK; if there is a problem, you would need to repair it manually.

If you lose either of these capabilities, SQL Server administration is going to become a time-consuming nightmare, which is unacceptable. In this section, you will read about how to troubleshoot both jobs and alerts so that you do not lose automation capabilities.

Critical Information

For troubleshooting jobs, there are a number of important points to bear in mind:

- Ensure that the SQLServerAgent service is running.

- Ensure that the job, tasks, and schedules are enabled; this is especially true if you have made changes to an existing job.

- Ensure that the T-SQL or stored procedures in the job steps work.

- Ensure that the job owner has the appropriate permissions on all affected objects.

- Ensure that the steps operate as planned and fire in the correct order. For example, step two fires when step one completes successfully.

- If you are using e-mail or pager operators, ensure that SQL Mail is enabled and set up properly.

- Check the job history to see if the jobs are firing.

- Verify that the job is scheduled properly. SQL Server allows only one instance of a particular job to run at a time.

If you need to troubleshoot multiserver jobs, there are a few more areas to look at:

- Make certain that an operator named MSXOperator exists at the master server (MSX).

- The master server cannot be a Windows 95/98 system; it must be Windows NT.

- If the job will not download to the target server, check the download list at the master and the error log at the target for any problems that could block the download.

When you are troubleshooting alerts, many of the same cautions apply. In addition, you should verify the following items:

- Ensure that the alerts are being generated in the Windows NT application log. If the message is not sent to the application log, the alerts manager cannot see it.

- If you have alerts based on performance thresholds, ensure that the polling interval is set properly. SQL Server will poll the Performance Monitor every 20 seconds by default.

- If e-mail, pager, or net-send notifications are not timely, check that the delay between responses is not set too high.

Exam Essentials

In every section, there are certain topics to pay special attention to; this section is no different. Pay close attention to the following items.

Remember to write alerts to the Windows NT application log.
If your alerts are not written to the application log, the alerts manager will never see them and, therefore, they will never fire.

Know how to troubleshoot multiserver jobs. Multiserver jobs are a new feature designed to save time in SQL 7; once you configure them, you will rely on them quite heavily, so you need to keep them going at all times.

Key Terms and Concepts

Multiserver job: This is a job that is designed to run on a remote server.

Sample Questions

1. You have just made changes to a job that was designed to create a large database, then immediately back it up. The job worked fine last time, but now it does not run. What is the most likely cause?

   A. The job is not enabled.

   B. The task cannot be changed once it has run.

   C. The job has been deleted.

   D. There is no schedule associated with the task.

   Answer: A. When you change a job in some way, you need to be sure that all of the components of the job are enabled.

2. You have just created a new custom alert that does not seem to be firing. What is the most likely cause?

   A. The condition that causes the alert never occurred.

   B. The alert is not enabled.

   C. No operator is associated with the alert.

   D. The alert is not being written to the Windows NT application log.

   Answer: D. All errors must be written to the application log; if not, they will not fire.

Diagnose and resolve distributed query problems.

Many companies today have more than one SQL Server; in fact, some companies have large numbers of them. In such companies, users need to be able to access data that may be stored on more than one of those servers, which is what distributed queries are for. These queries will allow users to access remote tables just like they were local tables in a standard T-SQL statement.

If you are using distributed queries, it is most likely that the tables in question are not replicated; if they were, there would be no need to use the distributed query. This means that if your distributed query setup fails, your users will have no way of accessing their data. When users cannot access data, they become irritable and cranky, and they like to make lots of support calls.

To make sure that this does not happen to you, some of the more common problems regarding distributed queries and how to fix them will be examined.

Critical Information

The two biggest problems you will run into when working with distributed queries are connectivity and security.

If your distributed queries have never worked for any of your users, your problem is most likely that you did not properly link the servers involved in the query. You should ensure that you have properly set up and configured the linked servers. For more information on how to connect to a linked server, see Chapter 4, "Managing and Maintaining Data," or the SQL Server 7 Books Online.

If your distributed queries are working fine for some users and not for others, the problem is more than likely incorrect permissions. If you are using Windows NT account-delegation security for your distributed queries, you will need to configure the security appropriately on the linked server; that is, your users will need logins and user accounts on the linked system with the appropriate permissions assigned.

Exam Essentials

You will not be hit especially hard with the information in this section on the test; in fact, you may not get questioned at all. However, there is always the chance that you will get one question from the pool. For the exam, you should take the following concept with you.

Know how to configure linked servers.   Chapter 4 examined how to configure linked servers—the context and methods. Become familiar with those procedures, because, if you know how to configure linked servers, you'll know how to troubleshoot them.

Key Terms and Concepts

Distributed query: This is a query that returns data from tables stored on more than one server.

Linked server: This is the remote server in a distributed query. This server does not need to be a SQL Server; it only needs to understand ODBC.

Sample Questions

1. Your clients are trying to use a distributed query that one of your developers has recently created, and it does not seem to be working. What is the most likely cause?

   A. The servers are not properly linked.

   B. The developer entered the syntax of the query incorrectly.

    C. The users do not have permission on the local server to execute the query.

    D. The remote server is offline.

Answer: A. If this is a query that has just been written, it is possible that the servers were not properly linked before the query was created.

2. True or false. All of the servers in a distributed query must be SQL Servers version 6.*x* or higher.

    A. True

    B. False

Answer: B. Any ODBC database can be part of a distributed query.

Diagnose and resolve client connectivity problems.

If your clients could not connect to your SQL Server, what good would it do to have a SQL Server? The answer is *none*—your system would be the equivalent of a large, beige paperweight. That makes your ability to troubleshoot client connectivity a very important issue.

A few areas will be examined here, including network connectivity, Net-Libraries, and DB-Libraries. The knowledge of how to troubleshoot these problems will prove invaluable to you in the office and the test center.

Critical Information

The best method for troubleshooting any problem is to start at the bottom and work your way up. If your clients cannot connect, you should make certain that the server is online, since another administrator may have shut it off, that the client is plugged in to the network, and that the hardware components are working.

The next step would be to check that the protocol is configured properly. There are a number of settings for the various protocols, so if you have just installed this machine, it is possible that some of those settings were misconfigured. Just try to find the server in Network Neighborhood (on a Windows machine) or the equivalent; if you don't see it on the network, your problem is with your operating system, not SQL.

Next, you need to check your Net-Libraries. SQL Server listens for client calls over any protocol that you have installed on your system, but for the client and server to talk, they must be running a common Net-Library. While you could use TCP/IP Multi-Protocol (which supports data encryption) or a host of other Net-Libraries, the default Net-Library is Named Pipes.

To test Named Pipes, you should first go to the server and open one of the graphic administration tools, or run OSQL from the command prompt—this will verify that Named Pipes are working locally. The next step would be to test Named Pipes from the client to the server using the makepipe and readpipe tools, as discussed in the "Necessary Procedures" section.

If that completes successfully, you know Named Pipes are working; if not, you have other network problems that have nothing to do with SQL, such as a corrupt protocol stack.

If Named Pipes come up successfully, but you still cannot connect, you probably have a DB-Library problem. You should verify that you have the same Network-Library and DB-Library on both the server and the client computer. This can be done with the Setup program or the Client Network utility.

Necessary Procedures

For this section, it is a good idea to know how to use the makepipe and readpipe programs as well as the Client Network utility.

Using Makepipe and Readpipe

The following series of steps will guide you through the use of makepipe and readpipe for testing Named Pipes connectivity. These tools are important—you will probably get a test question on them.

1. To test Named Pipes, you will need a client and a server. On the server, go to a command prompt by selecting Start ➤ Programs ➤ MS-DOS.

2. At the command prompt, enter **makepipe**.

3. When the server starts waiting for a client to use the Named Pipe, you should see:

   ```
   Making PIPE:\\.\pipe\abc
   read to write delay <seconds>:0
   Waiting for Client to Connect. . .
   ```

4. From a client machine, enter the following:

   readpipe /S*server name* /D*string*

   For example, if your server's name is DBServ, and you want to send the message "testing123" to the Named Pipe, enter:

   readpipe /Sdbserv /Dtesting123

   You should get something like the following listing in response on the client machine:

   ```
   SvrName:\\DBServ
   PIPE: :\\DBServ\pipe\abc
   DATA: :Testing123
   Data Sent: 1 Testing123
   Data Read: 1 Testing123
   ```

5. On the server machine, you should see something similar to this:

```
Waiting for client to send . . . 1
Data Read:
Testing123
Waiting for client to send . . . 2
Pipe closed
Waiting for Client to Connect. . .
```

6. To close the Pipe, close the command-prompt window.

Using the Client Network Utility

You should also know how to check the DB-Library version and default Net-Library by using the Client Network utility:

1. Open the Client Network utility in the SQL Server 7 menu from the Start button.

2. Click the DB Library Options tab.

3. Notice the filename, version, date, and size of the library.

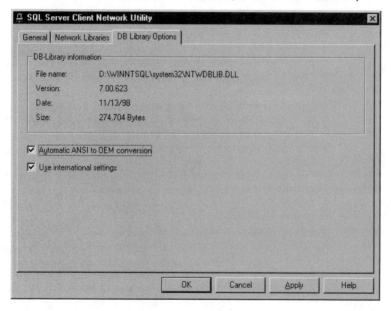

4. Click the General tab and notice that the default Net-Library can be changed.

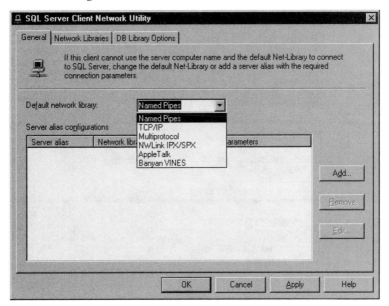

Exam Essentials

Since client connectivity is the reason you install a SQL Server in the first place, you can be certain to see several test questions regarding this topic. While you must know in general how to set up client connectivity and keep it running, here are some specifics that will help you through the exam.

Know the steps.   As the saying goes, "When you hear hoofbeats, look for horses, not zebras." Some administrators are so anxious to find and solve weird problems, they forget to look for simple solutions first. Start at the bottom and work your way up.

Know the Client Network utility.   This section could not cover every use of the Client Network tool, but you do need to be familiar with it and how it functions for the test.

Key Terms and Concepts

DB-Library: This is an Application Programming Interface (API) that developers can use to allow their applications to access data stored on SQL Server.

Named Pipes: This is an Interprocess Communications (IPC) mechanism that allows clients to talk to servers in a client/server scenario.

Net-Library: This is a Dynamic Link Library (DLL) that SQL uses to communicate with a network protocol.

Sample Questions

1. One of your users is complaining that they could access the SQL Server yesterday, but this morning, they can't seem to gain access to the databases. What should you do?

   A. Find out if the user can gain access to anything else on the network; if they can't, fix the connection.

   B. Check the DB-Library version and make sure it is the same as the server's.

   C. Make sure the client and server are running the same Net-Library.

   D. Have the user reboot the machine and try again.

   Answer: A. The very first step is to make sure the user can access the network; just because they logged on to the local machine, it does not mean they are on the network.

2. True or false. If you have Macintosh clients on your network that use the AppleTalk protocol, you must use the AppleTalk Net-Library on the SQL Server.

   A. True

   B. False

   Answer: A. The client and server must use a common Net-Library to communicate.

Diagnose and resolve problems in accessing SQL Server, databases, and database objects.

If your users can access the server and log in OK, but they cannot subsequently access the databases, your server is worthless to them. Your users must be able to access your data at all times without interruption; therefore, you must know how to keep this data online and accessible.

In this section, some time will be spent looking into the Database Consistency Checker (DBCC), which will allow you to fix database access problems. Then, you'll read about suspect databases and how to fix them. This will not be tested on extensively, but it is good to be familiar with this topic.

Critical Information

The first thing to check when your users cannot access a database or one of its objects is the permissions—wrong permissions can bar a user from accessing the object they need. If permissions are not the issue, you may be looking at a corrupt database. To check and repair a corrupt database, you need to become familiar with the Database Consistency Checker (DBCC). The DBCC acts as a collection of T-SQL statements that are used to check the physical and logical consistency of your database. Here are a few of the statements with which you should become familiar:

DBCC CHECKTABLE: You can run this command to verify that index and data pages are correctly linked and that your indexes are sorted properly. It will also verify that the data stored on each page are reasonable and that the page offsets are reasonable.

DBCC CHECKDB: This command does the same thing as the CHECKTABLE command, but it does it for every table in a database.

DBCC CHECKFILEGROUP: This command does the same thing as the CHECKTABLE command, except that it works on a single filegroup.

DBCC CHECKCATALOG: This command will check for consistency in and between system tables. For example, if there is an entry in the sysobjects table, there should be a matching entry in the syscolumns table.

DBCC CHECKALLOC: This command verifies that extents are being used properly and that there is no overlap between objects that should reside in their own separate extents. NEWALLOC performs the same function, but exists only for backward compatibility; use CHECKALLOC instead.

Since you should run these statements on a regular basis, it is best to schedule them. The easiest way to schedule them is to create a database maintenance plan and select all of the options for validating and repairing data.

Another particularly nasty problem is a database that is marked as suspect. This can happen to a database if one of the files becomes corrupted, deleted, or renamed. If the file is corrupted or deleted, you will need to restore from a backup. If it has been renamed, you only need to rename it to its original name and find the person who hacked in to your system and renamed it in the first place. Once you have restored the file to its original state, stop and restart the SQL Server—the automatic recovery process should unmark the suspect databases.

The only other thing that might cause a database to be suspect is a lack of permissions on an NTFS drive. You can fix this problem by logging on to Windows NT with an administrative account, taking ownership of the files in question, and granting the SQL service account read and write permissions to the file.

Necessary Procedures

For this section, it is a good idea to know what a suspect database looks like when it happens.

Finding a Suspect Database

In this section, you will mark the Northwind database as suspect to see what it looks like in Enterprise Manager:

1. Open the SQL Service Manager and stop the MSSQLServer service.

2. Open your C:\MSSQL7\Data (or whatever drive the file is on) folder and find the file named northwnd.mdf.

3. Rename northwnd.mdf to northwnd.old.

4. Restart the MSSQLServer service.

5. Open Enterprise Manager and notice that the Northwind database is grayed out and that the caption next to it says, "Suspect."

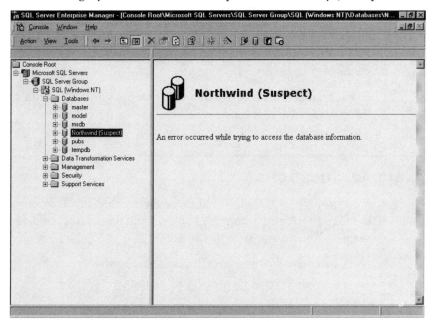

Exam Essentials

When you take the exam, you should be aware of the following topics.

Know how to use DBCC to repair problems.   DBCC will find and repair a number of small problems for you, so you should know how to use it. Remember, too, that not all DBCC commands that were supported in 6.5 are supported now. Good examples of commands that are no longer supported (even though they may return results) are MEMUSAGE and DBREPAIR.

Know how to bring back a suspect database.   If you know the procedures to restore a database, you know how to bring back a suspect database. Just make certain that it has the right NTFS file permissions and that it has not been renamed.

Key Terms and Concepts

DBCC: This is a collection of T-SQL statements that are used to find and repair minor database problems as well as check the status of your server.

Suspect database: This is a database that has gone offline due to being corrupted, deleted, or renamed.

Sample Questions

1. When your users complain that they cannot access the Accounting database, you open Enterprise Manager and find that it is marked suspect. What is the most likely cause?

   A. One of the database files has been renamed.

   B. One of the database files has been deleted.

C. One of the database files has been corrupted.

D. One of the database files has been moved to another directory.

Answer: C. Answer C is the only one that can happen without user intervention. The other three require deliberate action.

2. To repair minor errors in a database, which command should you use?

   A. DBCC DBREPAIR

   B. DBCC CHECKTABLE

   C. DBCC CHECKFILEGROUP

   D. DBCC CHECKDB

   Answer: D. Answer A would have been right in a previous version of SQL Server, but, since it is no longer supported, you now use DBCC CHECKDB.

Index

Note to the Reader: Throughout this index **boldfaced** page numbers indicate primary discussions of a topic. *Italicized* page numbers indicate illustrations.

MSX. *See* master server
MSX operator. *See* master server
 operator
MTS (Microsoft Transaction Server), 41
multilingual character set, 60
 and multiple language support with
  Unicode, 61
multiple data files
 for single database, 17, 19
 using, **135–136**
multiple servers, accessing data on,
 258–261
Multi-Protocol, 62
 installing, 70
 and Windows NT Authentication
  mode, **90**, 95
multiple Publishers/single Subscriber
 model, **43**, *43*
multiple Publishers/multiple Subscribers
 model, **44–45**, *45*
multiple sites, and replication, **39–40**
multiserver jobs, **240**, 256
 troubleshooting, **319**, 320
multitasking, 9
My Computer, monitoring size of catalogs with, 81

N

Named Pipes
 and client connectivity problems, 324
 defined, 328
 installing, 70
 support for, 62
 testing, **325–326**
 as upgrade requirement, 36
 and Windows NT Authentication
  mode, **90**, 95
.NDF extension, 17
nesting roles, 11
Net-Libraries
 and client connectivity problems, 324

installing, **62–63**, 70, *70*
IPX, 7
 required for authentication, **90–91**, 95
 testing, **326–327**
Net-Library, defined, 72, 328
net-send messages, 74, 243
NetBEUI, 62
NetWare clients
 authenticating, 7
 connecting with IPX/SPX, 62
NetWare servers, 62
network libraries. *See* Net-Libraries
New Alert Properties dialog
 for error-message alert, 248–249,
  248
 for performance alert, 249–250, *250*
New Job Properties dialog
 General tab, 245, *245*
 Schedules tab, 246–247
 Step tab, 245
New Job Schedule dialog, 247, *247*
New Job Step dialog, 245–246, *246*
New SQL Server Message dialog,
 250–251, *251*
No_Log switch, 188
No_Recovery switch, 32, 190
No_Truncate switch, 189
nonclustered index, and filegroups, 23
nonlogged operations
 planning backups for, **31**
 and Select Into/Bulk Copy database
  option, 133
non-Microsoft SQL Server databases,
 and replication, 45–46
nontrusted connections, 7, *7*
 defined, 95
 and Mixed mode authentication, **91**
Novell clients. *See* NetWare clients
n-tier
 defined, 15
 security for, **12–14**
ntext data type, 20

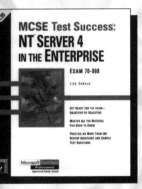

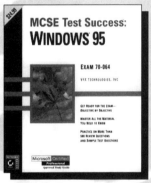

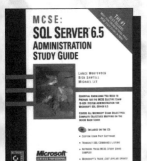

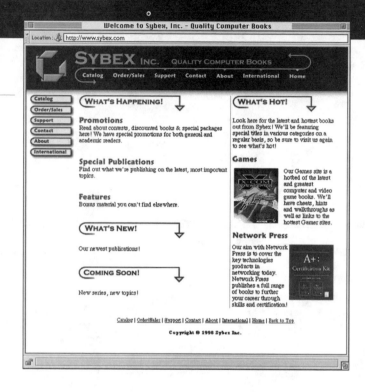